MW00942321

See The Light

LAURA MASON LOCKARD

SEE THE LIGHT Copyright © 2019 by Laura Mason Lockard.

All rights reserved. Printed in the United States of America. No part of this book may be used or reproduced in any manner whatsoever without written permission except in the case of brief quotations em- bodied in critical articles or reviews.

I have tried to recreate events, locales and conversations from my memories of them. In order to maintain their anonymity in some instances I have changed the names of individuals and places, I may have changed some identifying characteristics and details such as physical properties, occupations and places of residence.

For information contact author@lauramasonlockard.com

www.lauramasonlockard.com

Cover design by Damonza

ISBN: 9781796928198

First Edition : March 2019

10 9 8 7 6 5 4 3 2 1

This novel is based on a true story and is dedicated in loving memory to my son

Henry Sean Campbell

What would happen if one woman told the truth about her life?
The world would split open.

- Muriel Rukeyser, "Kathe Kollwitz"

Penny Candyland

Once upon a time there was a generation of people who would eventually become our parents. They grew up during The Great Depression and money was scarce. They wore second hand clothes and recycled feed sacks.

Then World War II happened and the boys went off to war while the girls mostly stayed home, except for the brave and adventurous ones who joined the WAC's and WAF's or became army nurses. Others got jobs in steel mills and other industries necessary to support the war and their icon was Rosie the Riveter.

Then, one day, the war ended. The survivors came home and the consuming desire to create normalcy drove everyone to build a new world. They tried to forget about all the things they had seen and done, and the efforts they had made to survive The War and The Depression and the world coming down around their ears.

So that is exactly what they did. They didn't want their children to suffer any of the hardships they had suffered. And they had lots of us. That's how we came to be called the baby boomers.

Our parents created Penny Candy Land: a land of make believe where we grew up. Historians now call it Mid Century America. Our mothers gave up their jobs to stay home and take care of us. Our fathers got work in the booming factories and industries and earned enough money for a nice house in the suburbs and a car with fins to take for a Sunday drive.

In many ways, it was a wonderful place and time to grow up, at least for some of us. There was a saying back then: the nail that sticks up gets pounded. If you didn't do what you were supposed to do and think what you were supposed to think, there was trouble. Social pressure kept most people in line, denying parts of themselves if necessary.

Beneath it all, the wounds of the past festered. The oldest baby boomers went away to college and came home dressed like hobos and bag ladies. They'd discovered the real world! They said they'd been lied to. They said everything our parents stood for and believed in was bullshit. It was into this crucible that I was born: the youngest of the siblings, the youngest of the cousins, the youngest of the baby boomers.

I loved the world I grew up in.

But I was born to destroy it.

CHAPTER 1

August 5, 1981

Most people can't pinpoint an exact moment in time when they knew their childhood was over. But I can. The sun shone golden on that summer evening; the jet trails in the sky glowed orange. The air was heavy with the scent of fresh cut grass. It was a completely normal summer evening.

I was eleven years old. I was fresh out of the sixth grade and due to start junior high school in a month. But I wasn't thinking about that. I couldn't even have told you what day of the week it was let alone what month. There was just the play that filled the days. Life wasn't perfect, but the summers seemed like they were.

I shifted my weight as I stood at the top of the driveway, my bicycle at my side, waiting on my eight-year-old niece to catch up. Noelle had a new bike that year and was still learning how to ride the thing. She wavered back and forth along the driveway, trying to pedal up the hill. I laughed to myself thinking about the day my father taught her how to ride it. He had her going really good, until she stopped and fell over sideways into the rose bush.

My mother sat on the edge of the porch, emptying the dirt out of her garden shoes. I cupped my hands around my mouth and yelled over at her, "We're riding up to the overhead bridge!"

"Oh no you're not!" my mother shouted. Her pants were covered with dirt and she had weeds in her brown hair. I doubted she'd chase me up the road in that condition. "You can just stay home this evening." She put her hands on her hips.

What the heck was this? I thought. We'd been riding up there all summer! Then suddenly, she's making a big fuss about it? It was irrational.

"Why? You never complained before!"

"Well, this time I am."

"But why?" I persisted. "Supper's over. It won't be dark for hours, and there's nothing wrong with the weather. What's your excuse?"

"I'm the parent, and I don't need an excuse!" she snapped.

I rolled my eyes. I was not the kind of child who accepted answers like that. I was spoiled! I figured I had just as much right to ride my bike in the neighborhood as anybody else. It wasn't curfew, so what did she care where I went? We roamed pretty much freely in those days, out in the sticks. As long as we showed up at dark to come in and get a bath, nobody ever worried where the heck we played. I only told her where we were going to be polite.

So I turned, climbed on my bike, and called, "Come on, Noelle."

My mother watched our figures grow smaller as we peddled up the driveway. "Fine, go ahead! But you just remember I told you not to!" I heard the screen door slam.

It was all kinds of fun to sit on the overhead bridge spanning the highway, which was like a river of concrete flowing under our feet. People we knew drove underneath and waved.

I also looked forward to the time alone with Noelle, because we always could have good talks. She lived in California with her mother, my sister Linda, and I only saw her for a few weeks each summer.

The road stretched out before us, wild raspberries and brambles growing along its gravel scattered banks. We rode along without much conversation as it was uphill most of the way and hard riding.

A few minutes later, we arrived at the bridge. It was as hot as Hades and I wished I'd brought a canteen of water. We parked our bikes on the bridge and sat talking about trivialities, telling jokes, and generally horsing around. Caught up in our own little world, we didn't notice the dark shadows under the bridge lengthening, their bony fingers reaching farther and farther. A strange man passed under the bridge driving a pickup truck.

"Ewww! Did you see the way that guy looked at you?" Noelle laughed.

Then, we promptly forgot all about it.

Sometime later a noise startled me. We both spun around to see a man emerge from the woods along the road. He smiled at us. We relaxed. Just some local guy, apparently.

"My brother and I were huntin' chipmunks in the woods back there," he said as he gestured behind him, "when he fell and hurt his ankle. I think it's broken. Will you girls come help me carry him out so I can get him to a hospital?"

"Sure we will!" I said. Noelle stood for a moment with her mouth open. Then she followed me over to the side of the road and into the woods. I've had people ask me, why would you go with him? The honest truth was, who doesn't want to be a hero? Back then, being told not to take candy from or get into cars with strangers was the extent of any warning we got. The help-your-neighbor ethic, while rarely taught openly, was still modeled every day. I might've been suspicious of a really weird looking person, or someone who acted strangely. But he was none of those things. It never even occurred to me to question his motives.

For a little way in the woods, the man walked alongside me, making small talk. I didn't know him, but he seemed friendly enough. Noelle tripped over some jaggers, and I heard her call out. The man looked at me in alarm, then went back a few steps and helped her up.

I stood at the crest of a hill, straining to see in the dim light of the woods. Doubts began to cloud my dreams of heroism. How far in there was his brother? Where was his brother? Shouldn't I be able to see him by now?

Before I had a chance to respond, I felt a hand clamp tightly across my mouth. I couldn't breathe, and my nostrils filled with the smell of car engine grease and gasoline.

"Don't scream," he said calmly. But his voice was totally different. Everything about him was totally different. He transformed completely in the split second between when he let go of Noelle's arm and walked three steps ahead to where I stood.

"Don't scream," he repeated. "I'm gonna let go now, and if you scream, I'm gonna kill you. You understand?"

Since I couldn't talk, I attempted to nod my head. He relaxed his hand, but kept his arm around my neck, turning me slightly so I was facing Noelle. I glanced down and saw what I thought I felt: a knife, pressed against my stomach. Noelle stood there, speechless in her pink shorts and halter top, looking back and forth from him to me.

She looked so small. Her leg was bleeding where the jaggers cut her.

"I don't wanna hurt you," he mumbled in my ear. Right. In one breath, he's gonna kill me, and in the next he doesn't wanna hurt me? Well thank God he's rational, I thought sarcastically.

"What are you gonna do?" Noelle squeaked.

"I'm just gonna fool around with your sister," he grunted. "Lay down on the ground. Now!" She startled, and dropped to her hands and knees. "No! Lay down the whole way. Facing away from us. Don't you look at me!"

Avoiding eye contact, he pulled off my shorts and underwear. So, he was gonna rape me, I thought. I knew what that was, sort of. Something like this happened at an amusement park nearby, that year. Or maybe the year before. But I heard the older kids talking about it, and pieced together what it meant. Or at least part of what it meant.

"Get down on the ground," he ordered, shoving me. "Don't look at me!"

Noelle started to cry. She'd rolled over and seen this man, standing there, for the most part disrobed from the waist down. She rubbed her face, smearing dirt and tears, and cried harder.

"Shut the hell up!" the guy yelled, waving the knife at her. She started to wail. "You," he ordered, pointing the knife at me again. "Make her shut up, right now! Or you're both gonna die. This is gonna happen, you understand me? There's nothin' either of you can do about it. So shut her the hell up!"

Not moving, because of the knife, I tried to get her to look at me. "Noelle," I called, trying to sound calm and reassuring. I was older. I was supposed to be in charge.

People ask me if I was terrified, but I wasn't. That came later, after it was all over. There was no flush of adrenaline, no pounding heartbeat, as I realized I was in what Dad called deep, dark, dire trouble. I was numb. I went into some sort of primal survival mode where the only thing I was thinking about was how to get Noelle away from this guy.

The first thing was to get her calmed down, so maybe he would calm down. "Noelle," I called again. This time, she looked at me. I swallowed hard, and said to her, just above a whisper, "Just be quiet, OK? You trust me, right? Everything's gonna be all right. Just do this for me. Just lay there and be quiet. Don't make a sound. OK?"

I didn't feel the physical pain either. I left my body and floated up into the canopy of tree branches and dappled sunlight.

CHAPTER 2

The Emergency Room

I was in shock. I was aware of the smooth feeling of a sheet against my face, waves of intermittent nausea, and cold sweat. I faded permanently back into reality on a hospital cart in the emergency room. My first sensation was that somehow, in some unimaginable way, I had become someone else. None of my memories were missing, but whatever internal compass we all possess, that tells us who we are, was gone.

Completely.

I was cold and in a great deal of pain. I don't think there was any part of me that didn't hurt. I lay there, in the grey tile room trying to be perfectly still so that no one would notice that I was awake. My mother sat on a metal chair in the corner of the room, silent. Outside the door were the sounds of people moving about. I could hear yelling, but I couldn't make out anything. Nobody paid any attention to me and I hoped it would stay that way. But then one tear escaped.

My mother noticed. She came over and started stroking my hair, repeating over and over, "It's going to be all right now. They're calling a doctor." She had that same tone of voice and expression that I remembered from infancy. The information about the doctor was supposed to make me feel better but it had the opposite effect. I hated going to the doctor's. I wanted to go home.

The wooden door opened a tiny crack. A short nurse squeezed through the door. She glared over her shoulder at the people in the hallway. When she saw me, she brightened, but in a way that seemed contrived.

"How are you doing? Better, I hope. We have a doctor on call and he'll be here shortly. His name is Dr. Lin. He's a very nice doctor so you don't need to be afraid of him. Your mother and I will be staying with you throughout the procedure." She pulled up a chair beside the cart. "Are you cold? I brought you a warm blanket."

I just nodded.

"When the doctor gets here," she explained as she tucked me in, "it's very important that we do this exam. We need to make sure you're OK. We also need to collect evidence for the police."

"You called the police?" I yelled.

"Well, of course we did," countered my mother, defensively.

The nurse held up her hand. "We're required by law to call the police in these cases. You may decide later to press charges."

"I most certainly will not!"

The two of them looked at each other.

"I have to ask you an important question. Who did this to you? Someone you know?" the nurse asked.

"No. I never saw him before."

"You're sure?"

"Of course I'm sure."

"What did he look like?"

"He was tall."

"How tall?"

"I don't know."

"Six feet?"

"I guess."

Having never actually guessed anybody's height before, I was caught totally off guard by this question. Let's face it, when you're a kid, adults are just plain big, and they're all pretty much the same.

"He had long, dark stringy hair and a beard, blue eyes, and a tattoo", I added.

"Where?"

"On his arm. This one." I pointed to my arm. "It may not have been a tattoo. It could have been paint or something. But it was some kind of a mark."

"How old was this man?"

"Twenty or thirty."

My mother rolled her eyes. They all thought I was being uncooperative, but the truth was I couldn't judge how old an adult was. They were all just ... old.

"Was he black or white?"

"White."

"What was he wearing?"

"Blue jeans, tennis shoes, and a dirty red and white tee shirt. Dirty. All of his clothes were dirty."

"Anything else?"

I thought hard for a moment. "His hands smelled like car engine grease."

The nurse looked shocked. "How do you know what car engine grease smells like?"

"My brother works on cars all the time," I shot back.

"And you never saw him before?"

"No," I spat, annoyed by this repetitive question.

"I'll be right back. I have to get the evidence kit. We just got them last month. This is the first time it's ever been used." The nurse said, as she arranged my bed linens.

Sure, I always wanted to be a pioneer, to chart out new territory and be the first at something. But being the first person they ever used the rape evidence kit on was not what I had in mind!

"Oh, and there's a nice policeman here who wants to talk to you," the nurse said on her way out.

"Excuse me," interrupted my mother. "Could we possibly call her pediatrician? I'd like him to be present for this. I'll call myself, if I can borrow your phone."

"Certainly."

I didn't know it at the time, but the ER went to hell in a hand basket. Nobody knew what to do but everybody wanted to be in on it. When we arrived, the place was empty. Within 20 minutes, it swarmed with police, EMT's, paramedics, reporters, curious hospital employees, and anyone else who could come up with some lame excuse to be there.

"Just lay still," said my mother. "I'm going to call Dr. Plotkins. Then I'll be right back." She headed out into the chaos.

"Are we in trouble? Are they gonna put you in jail?" Noelle asked. She'd been sitting on a chair in the corner the whole time, unnoticed, still covered with dirt and dry leaves.

"No." I reassured.

"What are they going to do to you?"

"I don't know."

The door opened and my father crept in. He picked up Noelle and carried her out. I didn't know it at the time, but from the moment we walked in he was suspect number one. Apparently they had some weird idea that the fathers always did it. So everyone was out there glaring at him as if he were the devil incarnate, until I started insisting it was a stranger. Then, they ignored him, too.

No sooner had my father left when the door opened again. In walked this muscular, tough-looking police officer. He removed his hat, dropped onto a chair, and looked at me in an expression of pity and discomfort.

"Are you OK?" he asked. He extended his hand for a moment, as if to smooth my hair, and then reconsidered. He was embarrassed, scandalized, and uncomfortable.

How do you think I am, I thought to myself? This interrogation was taking place while I was lying naked under a blanket, and I was afraid of him. I swallowed hard.

"Fine."

He looked at me as if he wasn't quite sure how to interpret that. Then, he flipped open his notepad and clicked the top of his ink pen. "I'm Officer Donaldson." He cleared his throat and pointed the pen at me. "Did someone you know do this?"

"No."

My mother entered the room like a clap of thunder. "I thought I made it clear I wanted to be present for this!"

"Whatever you say, Ma'am." Nonplussed, he looked down at me again. "Can you tell me what he looked like?"

"It was a tall man with long, scraggly brown hair and beard. The beard was thinner on the sides."

"How tall?"

"I dunno exactly how tall. But he was tall."

He shifted his weight impatiently. They were all so upset with me because I couldn't give them a number.

"Was he as tall as me?" he asked.

Lying flat on the table, I had no idea how tall the cop was either. "Probably," I evaded.

He sighed and went on. "What was he wearing?"

"Dirty jeans, dirty red and white tee shirt, sneakers, and he had some kind of mark on his arm."

"A tattoo?"

"Maybe. It was partially obscured by his shirt sleeve."

He regarded me uncertainly, not expecting my vocabulary to be what it was. I looked like a normal kid until I opened my mouth.

"She was raised primarily among adults," my mother defended.

He shot her a doubtful look. "Which arm?"

I hesitantly pulled my hand out from under the blanket and pointed. Then I pulled the blanket even more tightly up under my chin. I was also a little dyslexic, but didn't want to explain to him about how I didn't have a left and right like everybody else.

"Right," he muttered as he scribbled along. After he finished, he flipped his little scratch pad shut. "You're sure you don't know this person."

"Yes. I'm sure I don't know this person."

"I'll talk to you again a little later." He stuffed his hat back on his head and left.

"Dr. Plotkins is here for this exam," consoled my mother.

I sighed and rolled my eyes. Did I ask for that? Did we absolutely need yet another person involved in this humiliating ordeal? I didn't complain because I knew she'd chew me out for being ungrateful. Many years later, she told me he never even sent a bill for it. Which was extremely humane of him, but it irritated the hell out of me that nobody bothered to ask what I wanted.

There was a long period of uncomfortable silence.

"Where's Noelle?" I finally asked.

"She's sitting right outside the door with your father." She turned away from me and dug in her purse. "Did this man do anything to hurt Noelle?"

"No."

"I didn't think he did, but I had to make sure."

I swallowed hard and decided not to say more. At that point, I was expecting some sort of 'thank you' or any vague acknowledgment. I got her home, didn't I? Was it too much to ask for someone to say, 'Gee, thank you for keeping a cool head, for getting Noelle away from the criminal.' Apparently it was asking too much. But that fight was still a few years off. None of us had any idea then about how we would still be arguing over every little word uttered that night – or not uttered that night – for the next decade.

When the OB/GYN doctor was escorted in, he took one look at

me and almost fainted.

"He is just out of his residency. He's never seen this," the nurse apologized to my mother.

I was able to tolerate the exam, barely. It seemed to take forever. There was blood, which shocked me and made me kind of sick. I didn't remember bleeding. I closed my eyes, clenched my teeth and didn't move. My mother and Dr. Plotkins stood helplessly by, holding onto me in one way or another. I'm sure they felt they were being supportive, but I was oblivious.

The procedures were endless. They took samples of everything and then filled envelopes with it. During the finger nail scrapes, my mother scolded in frustration, "Couldn't you have at least scratched him or something?" I would have liked to scratch her. Any time the subject came up, it was always if-only-I'd-done-this, if-only-I'd-done-that. Maybe they should all have to go through it, I used to think, to see if they could pass with a more acceptable grade.

They took all the clothes I had worn, even the jacket my mother brought along so I wouldn't be cold. I wondered how the heck I was going to get home. If I was going home. I sure didn't want to stay in that hospital, no matter how sick I was. Please God, don't let them admit me. Don't admit me, I thought over and over.

"We can make a warm outfit for you to wear home out of a couple hospital gowns", suggested Dr. Plotkins. Did the rest of them expect me to go home naked?

As I was putting on my shoes, the young doctor came in again. He looked rather embarrassed. I didn't know this at the time, but a big debate raged outside the exam room between my mother and the police. The debate was about my ability to consent. Really, the entire conversation was not germane. The law said I was not capable of consent. But they had it anyway. Nobody wanted to believe this really happened, here, where they'd lived their entire lives. They found it easier to believe than an 11- year- old kid sought out sex with an adult. My mother was incensed, and told me years later that she didn't know how she managed to keep enough composure to avoid smacking the cop in the mouth.

They sent the young doctor to go fishing for evidence to back up this theory. So he hemmed and hawed around for several minutes, then finally spat it out. "I'm really sorry I have to ask you this, but do you have a boyfriend?"

"No", I said.

He turned and left. I knew, in a mechanical this-goes-there sort of way what sex was. And I knew that rape was when somebody forced you to do that. But I knew nothing about all the cultural stereotypes and myths surrounding both rape and sex. Thus, the hidden meaning behind the doctor's question was lost on me. I didn't know that sexual desire existed, or that because of it, adults thought sex was *fun*. I didn't know what a virgin was, and didn't know I should've been wondering if I still was one. The only difference between the rape and some other type of attack, if he'd run me over with his car, for instance, was that rape involved taking off your underpants, therefore it was embarrassing.

So I didn't understand why all the adults were acting so weird. They all assumed that I shared this secret knowledge. I decided I had to fake it, because admitting I didn't know would put me at a disadvantage.

As the car pulled away from the ER, I could hear a hushed conversation up in the front seat.

"I told those reporters that if they put her name in the paper we'll sue. She's a minor. It's *illegal* for them to print her name in the paper," whispered my father. "And they can damn well try and sue me for that busted camera."

"They wouldn't even dare," my mother agreed.

While they stewed over the various forms of public humiliation we were about to face, I looked out of the window and had a thought. The stars were out. The night was almost over. Then another day would pass, and then another, and then a week, and then a month, and then a year, and then a decade. Someday, this day would be twenty years in the past! What would life be like then? Surely the influence of this event couldn't extend that far in the future. And if it wouldn't matter in twenty years, why should it matter now? Maybe I didn't have to let it affect me at all.

But I was eleven years old, and had no idea what those days and weeks and months and years had in store for me.

CHAPTER 3

The Next Morning

Mom was like a bucket of ice cold water the next morning. "Hey, wake up! We're going to Gee Bee's to get your cowboy boots."

Huh? I snapped awake from the sleep of the dead. My mother had given me a pill the night before. She had a pill for every occasion. I felt awful, but it took me a few seconds to remember why. Was she serious? I looked around my bedroom. It felt like a different time and place.

"I'm not going! I don't care one iota about boots! How could you even think about it at a time like this?"

My mother was undeterred. "You've been nagging me all summer and they're on sale right now. At Gee Bee's. And the sale ends tomorrow. So let's go. Rise and shine!"

I cringed. I hate that saying and I heard it every morning. I wobbled into the bathroom to get ready and saw a bloody handprint on the wall. I wondered if it was mine or my mother's. Later that day, it was gone, not a word said.

On autopilot, I brushed my teeth and ran a comb through my hair. Then I went to my closet to wake up Noelle. About a half hour after we were put to bed the previous night, she came into my room because she was afraid to sleep alone. She slept on the floor of my closet each night, underneath the secure canopy of my dresses and shirts until she went home about three weeks later. I guess she thought that because I'd protected her from that man, I was the only one who could.

Her stuffed toys were piled on her blanket, my shoes and junk pushed to the front like a fortification. One stuffed toy was missing, Mr. Whiskers, the rat. He was her favorite and she kept him with her most of the time.

I went downstairs for breakfast in the kitchen. Dad built our red brick split level ranch house himself in the early 1950's. It had a long living room with a picture window that could be converted to a formal dining room at one end when my mother opened out her drop leaf table. Also on the main floor was the eat-in kitchen and an enclosed but unheated sunporch accessed by a door at the other end of the living room. A hallway lead to the front door and the stairs going up to the bedrooms and down to the basement. Upstairs were three bedrooms and a bathroom, a closet with stairs to the attic that my mother used as a sewing room. Under all that (the split level part) was the TV room / basement, garage, and another bathroom. As the house was built into a hill, the TV room was at ground level in the back and opened out onto a cement patio. Tucked underground in front, that room was always cool down there and the best place to be in the summer, as we did not have air conditioning until the mid-1980's. The cellar was under the main floor and the attic above all of it. The kitchen had an outside door that opened to a concrete slab. That feature was later replaced with a wooden deck, as everyone enjoyed sitting out there because it faced south. There was another porch outside of the front door but it was mostly decorative as it faced north and was always cold.

Bacon sizzled, toast browned in the toaster, and orange juice sat in small glasses on the table. An egg hissed as my mother flipped it over in a pan on the stove. Noelle sat in my father's chair, knees tucked under her chin. She had Mr. Whiskers under her arm and her long pink nightgown pulled taut under her. If you had ever had breakfast at my house, you would know this scene was contrived. We never had Norman Rockwell mornings. We fought, bickered, and couldn't decide what to eat.

I sat down in my mother's chair, which would normally be construed as an act of war. Instead, she approached me with a big smile plastered across her face.

"Would you like your eggs over easy? Or maybe scrambled?"

"I'm not hungry."

"Eat! We may not be back until lunch."

I rolled my eyes. Perhaps I was not blunt enough. "For the last time, I DO NOT WANT to go shopping!"

"We're going shopping!" she snapped. "There's a sale! You need school clothes!"

I looked at her like she had lobsters crawling out of her ears. "You're not seriously thinking of sending me to school? After yesterday?"

"Well what do you expect us to do? There are compulsory attendance laws! It's not like I can just keep you home because I feel like it!"

"You could get me a private tutor! Tell them I'm sick long term and find out what can be done. I've heard of other kids who can't go to school so obviously there's something."

"You're outta your mind! Do you have any idea what that would cost? Besides, I thought you were excited about junior high."

I shot her a look that could wither an oak tree. "Are you kidding me? Now? After yesterday? I hate school! I've always hated school! What happened yesterday proves it's never going to get any better. I don't even want to live here anymore." Then the perfect solution struck me. "I could go back to California with Noelle. I could live with Linda," I suggested.

"When we talked about that, it was about a visit, only. Those plans have changed. Noelle isn't going back for another three weeks. We've already changed the airline ticket. By then, school will be starting. And you're not living with Linda." She put her hands on her hips, scowling at me. "You've never lived with your sister, but I have. Let me tell you it's not like what you think it is!"

She was right about that – I really had never lived with my sister. I was an outlier, an anachronism, a disturbance of the natural order. My sister and I shared the same birthday 21 years and 12 hours apart. She was in her senior year of college when I was born. My brother, Bob was a year younger than her, and John was four years younger than Bob. The only sibling living at home when I was born was John, who was still in high school. More than a few of my school mates had parents who graduated with my brothers or sister. Heck, I even had a few teachers who graduated with them! This contributed a great deal more to my social problems at school than I understood at the time.

"So why does Noelle have to hang around this dump?"

"Because of the police."

"What the heck do they care?"

"Because if they catch this guy," she snapped as flecks of scrambled eggs flew from the spatula she was waving around, "they need both of you to identify him!" She slammed a plate of scrambled eggs down in front of me. "Now, eat your God forsaken breakfast and stop arguing with me!"

She slammed the frying pan into the sink. Noelle started to bawl. My mother rubbed her eyes like she had a headache.

"Look," I said, "let's just say this never happened. If we all agree it never happened, and we go on and never mention it again, then it never happened."

"Things don't work that way! That's just denial," my mother countered.

"If you think I'm gonna get up in front of a bunch of people and tell them about this, you really are out of your mind."

She leaned over me and wagged her finger. "Your problem is you don't listen! If you'd listened in the first place, none of this would have happened! Do you realize that if you don't testify, this could happen to someone else?"

"Oh, so you think this is my fault? Is that it? If this is all my fault, then how could it happen to someone else? Unless that was their fault? Or is my badness contagious? If it happens to someone else, then let them go testify! I'm not having anything to do with it."

She stamped her foot in frustration. "You completely misunderstood what I said! I didn't say it was your fault, I was just pointing out that..."

"That you think it's my fault! Why don't you just admit it? If you make me stay here and go to back to school, then you're ruining my life! And that's YOUR fault!"

"Ugh! You're such an aggravating child! I need an assburn!" She then fled the room. Really, she meant aspirin but she had her own unique dialect. Now, I know that I'll never hear that word any other way.

Betrayal! That's what it was. I'd had this California trip in mind all summer as a long term solution to all of my problems. It WAS true I'd been invited for a visit - which is not the same as moving in indefinitely - but I was full of childish confidence that I could get my way once I was out there. I thought that if I moved to the other side of the continent, I could put everything behind me. I could wipe the slate clean, so to speak. Become somebody else. And now I couldn't go because of what happened last night? All the more reason to go! As of last night, the slate started cracking under the weight of things to be wiped clean! I stabbed an egg with my fork and ate in grumpy silence.

Later that morning, we arrived in Gee Bee's parking lot in Natrona Heights, which is – not surprisingly – on a hill above the town of Natrona. Natrona was a mill town in those days full of heavy industry along the river and company housing. The main road in Natrona Heights was Freeport Road. Along Freeport Road were several shopping plazas, restaurants, churches, and other types of businesses. Behind the business corridor were larger, more expensive houses than those found in Natrona. Gee Bee Plaza was one of the places where we went shopping. Farther down the road was a number of other places we frequented: an Altmeyer's that sold fabric and housewares; a Howard Johnson's restaurant, a hobby shop that featured slot car racing and Heights Plaza with a Horne's department store that was actually one of the oldest strip malls in Pennsylvania, having opened in 1955. The large red letters of the store greeted us as I followed my mother into the crowded store, Noelle tagging behind with Mr. Whiskers hanging on for dear life. All I really wanted was to be left alone, but my mother persisted and brought me several pairs to try on, smiling hopefully. I picked out a pair just to satisfy her. As I sat on the metal bench in my socks and packed the boots back into their cardboard box, I noticed people looking at me, whispering. I pulled on my shoes without untying them.

"Get me out of here", I hissed. "Now!"

She picked up the box and threw me a worried glance. "I was hoping we could look at some clothes. You also need a couple pairs of dungarees."

"Oh my god, Mom! Don't say that! They're called JEANS! Anyway, I don't care! I need to get out of here NOW!"

"OK but I have to pay for these."

"Fine. I'll be waiting in the car." I turned and stomped out, arms crossed. The car doors were locked, so I couldn't get in, but at least there was nobody around.

A few minutes later, my mother came out with a bag dangling from one hand and Noelle hanging from the other. She unlocked the car.

The ride home was as silent as a tomb. I sat in my seat, arms folded across my chest, staring straight ahead. Noelle sat alone in the back seat, feeding chocolate covered raisins to Mr. Whiskers.

"I really like your new boots", said my mother. "They'll match everything you have." Her attempted optimism was met with a wall of ice. Nobody said anything after that.

After we got home, I went to bed. My head felt funny. It ached and I was a little dizzy. My mother appeared in the doorway a few minutes later. She sat down on my bed, still holding the bag.

"All those people were staring at me!" I screamed. As I looked past my mother into the mirror, I could see why. There were bruises on my face and arms. It was as if I was covered with purple finger prints. On seeing that, I did something I rarely did. I lost it, and ended up bawling in my mother's lap.

"I'm sorry I made you go shopping. I thought getting you up and out was the right thing to do. I guess it didn't turn out so well. I should have left you alone. I don't necessarily know how to handle this, either." Noelle bounded up onto the bed and the three of us clung together.

"He was the meanest man I've ever seen," cried Noelle. "The meanest man I've ever seen in my entire life!"

I don't remember how long I cried, lying on my mother's lap, but it wasn't long. It wasn't long because I remembered thinking there was something they weren't telling me. I remembered thinking that I didn't trust them. The police were coming in a few hours, and I was really afraid of them. I had to get a hold of myself. I had to be in control or they'd figure out I was clueless. And then what?

Something startled me awake late that night. I opened my eyes to stillness. The moon shone through my window, illuminating everything with a bluish silver light. Noelle lay asleep on the closet floor, her breathing slow and rhythmic. Downstairs, the refrigerator shuddered. I rolled over to look at my clock. 11:11. Weird!

The cat jumped on my bed and darn near scared me to death. Tam was my mother's cross-eyed, yowling Siamese cat. He plopped himself down on my bed, hoisted one leg high over his shoulder and began to groom his butt.

I got up for a while and tried to put makeup over my bruises, but

I wasn't as successful as I hoped. I sat pawing the contents of my dressing table looking for something that might work better.

After a while, I lay down in my ruffled canopy bed. Where was the girl who wanted that bed? It was a lifetime since I knew that girl and the one I was now. Thanks to my mother, I had a matched set of bedroom furniture back then. She bought it piecemeal from places like Goodwill: the bed, a tall dresser, a short dresser with a mirror above it, and a dressing table with a cheval mirror. The room also had a built in desk and bookcase that my father put in when he built the house, along with a normal closet with sliding doors. My room was originally my sister Linda's room. By my time, it had fashionable blue shag carpet. My mother made all this furniture match by painting it white and "antiquing" it, a fad from the 1960's and 70's. She also made the matching curtains, bedspread, dust ruffle, and canopy stretched over a brass frame, which did double duty as a cat hammock.

I turned out the light, snuggling against the warm cat. I felt so tired and emotionally drained but I still couldn't sleep. I rolled over again, and the Bible jabbed me in the back.

I suppose it's kind of weird to have a Bible in your bed. That was my brilliant idea for warding off evil, kind of like people you see in movies wearing garlic and flashing crucifixes at vampires. I sold Noelle on the idea that first night home. Now she slept with one, too. When my mother discovered it, she gave me a big, long lecture on how it's the ideas in the Bible that protect people, not the physical Bible. Yet, I didn't care.

Picking up the Bible after it jabbed me, I was consumed with rage. If it was the ideas, not the Bible itself, then where were the ideas when I needed them?

"How could you let this happen?" I fumed at God, shaking my fist at the ceiling. "What an idiot I was, for hoping that things would be different this year! "Why couldn't you just let me die?" I felt like I should've died. I wished I had.

"Pssst!" Noelle was poking me. I must have fallen asleep at some point as the sky was lightening outside.

"I have to go back in my room. Will you come with me?"

When I got out of bed, I got the chills. I wondered if I was catching something. I tucked Noelle in, then returned to my own bed. Pulling the covers tightly about me, I went to sleep for another couple of hours.

When I woke up, I didn't just think I was getting sick, I was sure of it. That distinctive sick feeling pressed like a bag of sand on my head. I shivered for a while, then got up to go to the bathroom and made a horrible discovery: I couldn't pee. Whenever I tried, it felt like my abdomen was on fire and I felt like I had to go all the time! Shaking with fear, I wet a washcloth with cold water and wiped my face, then had to bend down to keep from passing out. I crawled up the hallway on my hands and knees and knocked on my mother's bedroom door.

A newspaper rustled. "What?"

"I don't feel good." I murmured, as I dragged myself into the room

"What's the matter?"

I relayed my list of symptoms.

"You must have some sort of infection, my mother said, cautiously.

Then, sounding more alarmed, she gasped when she saw me. "You look like you're going into shock! Come and lie in bed while I get you a doctor's appointment. Don't worry, you'll be feeling better soon." she said as she tucked me into the covers.

Soon, I could hear my mother downstairs on the phone. "I need an emergency appointment right now and don't you dare tell me you don't have any!"

A few moments later she was back upstairs. "Can you get dressed?" I nodded. "Then go ahead, but don't put any of your dirty clothes in the bathroom hamper. I don't know what you have yet."

My anger flared. I may not have known much, but I knew what venereal diseases were. I understood the hidden implication that I was dirty, like some kind of common trash. When the adults lost their calm veneers and momentarily expressed their disgust and revulsion at what happened, I mistook it as a reaction to me personally and backed farther away from them, seething.

"Get dressed, Noelle, we have to go into town," my mother called from somewhere in the house. There were the sounds of dishes hurriedly being thrown in the sink.

Later, I endured the humiliation of another exam at the Miner's Clinic in the nearby town of New Kensington, where we went to see our doctors. It was a strange, atomic-age looking place with round sections, ramps, funky windows and open stairways with greenery growing under them. Originally intended for the area's numerous coal mining families (of which my father was one), it had become more of a community health center by my time.

The doctor explained that although I had no injuries that required surgery, I had lots smaller ones that enabled the infection.

Honeymoon cystitis, he said.

What? How could anyone say that? I glared at that doctor, and for a moment, I thought I'd lose all control and hit him. If I did that,

I could predict what would happen when my dad got home from work. "I've had the day from hell!" my mother would tell him. "She punched out the doctor!" No, I didn't want to face that scenario. So, I sat on my hands and bit my tongue.

It was in my previous life that I did things like that. How many times had I lay on my bed, after some misadventure, listening to them downstairs in the kitchen? My dad walking in from work, hardly having time to put his lunchbox down before my mother lit into him. She would say, "I've had the day from hell! She blew up her chemistry set! Or, she got the little girl down the road stuck in a tree! Perhaps, she caught a snake in woods and brought it home! Today, she took an entire bowl of dough from the refrigerator and sold it to the other kids as silly putty!"

Where was that kid now? Gone - a stranger in her place.

It took a day and a half for the antibiotics to start working. In the meantime, my mother fed me tea and had me sit in a hot tub.

"I had something like this once, and the trick is to get your kidneys started again. That way, you can flush your system out," she explained. After sitting in the tub for an hour, I was finally able to pee, although it was mostly blood, clots, and tissue. Exhausted and weak, I went to bed early.

***

I awoke in a hospital bed unable to move.

"She's awake," someone whispered. The smell of antiseptics and death hung in the air. My mother's face emerged from the grayness. Tears streamed down her face. Light gently flowed into a window somewhere nearby as monitors beeped. All my closest relatives walked past my bed, each hesitating for a moment, patting my hand, or kissing me on the forehead. I was dying! Oh thank God! Death had come to liberate me from what happened and I prepared to embrace it. Everything faded and blackness engulfed me like a warm bath. It was dark, but I wasn't afraid. It was perfectly peaceful. Almost blissful.

After an unknown lapse of time, I opened my eyes. A cluster of pink roses, suspended atop a delicate stem, hovered above my face. I blinked. The air was heavy with the fragrance of flowers. I lay in a coffin, wearing my favorite dress. There were fancy curtains... I recognized this place. It was the funeral home where my Grandmother's funeral had been. But it was my funeral! I wondered if I was dreaming. It seemed so real that I wasn't sure how to tell.

I sat up, pulling the pink satin blankets down until I could slide my legs out from under them. As I eased my way out of the coffin, I noticed that I was also wearing my first pair of high heeled shoes. They were black pumps and had a strap across the top. After the momentous tantrum I had to throw to get my parents to buy those shoes, I was really touched that they decided to bury me in them.

After I climbed down, I noticed something else that was odd. Instead of being on top of the typical gurney type thing with wheels, the coffin sat on top of something resembling the altar at church. It was wooden, and had that Greek version of Jesus' name that looks vaguely like the word *this*.

I wandered around my own wake, not sure what to do next. I was pretty sure nobody could see me or they would have all run away screaming when I sat up in my coffin. So, was I a ghost? People were talking, but I couldn't understand a word anyone said. I saw my maternal grandmother, Grammy, sitting in a chair, wearing her black crepe dress and antique mourning jewelry. Her funeral had been in the same room. So was she was a ghost too? Maybe she could see me. I sat down next to her.

"I thought I was dead."

She looked up at me. "You were. But you came back."

"Why? I don't wanna come back!"

"There's something you have to do. It's very important that you do it. I am here to remind you of that."

"What?"

"Triumph over this. Transcend it. It's a very old story that desperately needs a new ending. Your task is to provide that."

I stood there for a few seconds, my mind gone blank.

"But I don't know how! Things were bad enough before. Even then I wasn't normal. After this? Normal isn't even in the cards for me anymore. If I can't be normal, I think I'd rather die, all things considered."

She scoffed. "Is that really what you think you want? Normal?"

I swallowed. I thought about what I wanted but I was too ashamed to say it out loud, but she went on as if reading my mind was nothing out of the ordinary.

"You can be so much more than normal! Honestly, you set your standards far too low. You can be accepted and loved for who you really are. If you take this journey, you will win all that and more. More than you can even dream of now. Now, I'll give you a clue - you will find it in Pittsburgh. For right now, just survive. Everything that you need will be given to you when you need it."

I looked down at the thick red plush carpet. I felt like somebody in a *Godfather* movie being given an offer they couldn't refuse. They had me over the proverbial barrel, I had to admit.

"All right," I finally conceded.

Then she asked, "Do you want some spaghetti?"

I was so shocked that I woke up and nearly fell out of bed.

"WHAT?"

"I said, do you want some spaghetti?" My mother stood in the doorway. I stared at her like she was an alien invader. "For dinner," she clarified.

I was back in my bed at home. I rubbed my eyes but could not shake the feeling of disorientation.

"Yeah, I guess so."

She nodded and turned to leave.

"Wait a minute! Was I in a hospital?" My eyes were wide.

"No."

"But, I swear I was in the hospital and I died. I ..." the words froze.

"You must have been dreaming. You've been pretty sick. We're going to stay home for a few days. I called Grandma and told her we won't be there this Saturday; that you're not feeling well." My father's mother was still alive. She was the only grandparent left.

"Did you tell her what happened?"

She sat down on my bed and thoughtfully patted the covers. "No. Your father and I discussed it and we decided to tell her nothing. She's getting up in years and isn't well. It'll only worry her." She stared at me harder. "I don't want you telling anyone about this. Especially not that Krissy. It's nobody else's business and I don't want it spread all over the place. You understand me?"

I shrugged and turned on the small black and white TV set on top of my tall dresser. The conversation was making me extremely uncomfortable and I wanted to end it.

"I mean it! Do you understand what I'm telling you?"

"Fine!"

On her way out, she nearly ran into Noelle.

Noelle smiled innocently, then shut the door after she was gone.

"We're in trouble. I don't know what to do." Her purple striped bathing suit was still damp from a day of swimming in the neighbors' pool.

"What is it?" I asked, unable to think of any way things could possibly get worse.

"I went swimming at Tabitha's house today. Everybody was there, all the kids. They started asking me tons of questions about what happened up by the bridge," she whispered. "I didn't know what to say. Finally, I just I told them we were mugged. It was the only thing I could think of! Am I gonna get in big trouble? I didn't tell anybody anything, I swear! I don't know how they found out about it, but somehow they did!"

I could see where this was heading. It didn't matter how they found out. I would be blamed. I didn't see how my parents were going to keep up this illusion of secrecy. As I thought about it, I remembered that the ER was full of people that night. At least some of them knew my Dad; he knew everybody. There were police, paramedics, and hospital people who knew my mother. The police had been questioning everyone who lived up near the bridge, and they went all over the area with a police dog. Did they really think all these people would just pretend to know nothing, and never wonder who it was? Meanwhile, Noelle looked like she was ready to sob. I sat down on the bed next to her, and draped an arm around her shoulders.

"Don't worry. I know you didn't tell." I said, comforting her.

"But what about Grandma?"

I gestured in futility. "If she ever finds out, you know she'll blame me." Then, I said, "Did they buy it? Telling them we were mugged?"

"I don't think so."

"They're just a bunch of kids, for heaven's sake. They probably wouldn't understand you even if you did tell them."

"Not exactly. It was Tabitha's parents who asked."

I lay back on the bed and sighed. This was really, really bad. I got that feeling that Tabitha's parents did not like me a whole lot. They were nice to me, and even let me take home a snake that I'd caught on their patio. They thought I was a tomboy and probably didn't want Tabitha to turn out like that, let alone pick up my prodigious ability to get in trouble. Wasn't Tabitha's mother a nurse? I thought so, but I didn't know which hospital she worked at.

"Don't worry about it. There's nothing you can do."

"That man at the bridge knows my name, and he thinks we're sisters! And something happened when I was out with Tabitha and Grandpa. I'll bet that's why her parents were asking."

"What was it?"

"Well, we rode into Lower Burrell with Grandpa in the back of the truck. He went in to the hardware store and left us in the back. We were just sitting back there talking when a man opened the door on the back of the truck."

"Was it the same guy?"

"I don't think so. I don't really know if I remember – I'm not sure. This guy told us our father asked him to come and get us. We knew right away he didn't know us at all, since Grandpa is my grandfather and Tabitha's neighbor. We were sitting against the back of the cab so he couldn't reach us. We told him no – we were supposed to wait here, and after a few minutes he left. Then Grandpa came back."

"Did he follow Grandpa home?"

"No – we didn't see any other cars come down the road. And believe me, we were watching."

"Did you tell Grandpa about it?"

"No. Nothing really happened and .... I didn't want to make things any worse."

My thoughts turned themselves over more slowly than usual. Panic was the last thing we needed, so I had to calm her down. I remembered the dream. I wasn't sure if I totally believed it. If I could just keep a lid on this long enough for it to blow over, maybe I could do this. I could survive by ripping pages off the calendar, one day at a time.

"Noelle, don't freak out! That man only knows your first name. He still doesn't know where I live, and he's never going to find you in California with just your first name."

"Are you sure?"

"Yes I'm sure. Even if he did know your last name, what's he going to do, look it up in the phone book? Nobody around here even has a Los Angeles phone book! And he thinks we're sisters. He doesn't know you live on the other side of an entire continent."

"What about you?"

"I can take care of myself."

Truth be told, I was more than a little jealous of Noelle, being about to just go home and walk away from the entire thing. I wondered how I was going to manage all this. Was that man looking for us? Logic insisted not. It was just paranoia. Yet, there was something disturbing about this, something even more disturbing than worrying about what the neighbors were saying and it wasn't just affecting me. My parents insisted that everything was fine and back to normal. They told us over and over never to say anything to anyone; it was over and done with. In spite of their claims, deadbolts appeared on all the doors and a loaded shotgun leaned against the wall next to my father's side of the bed. We were under siege - both from the rest of the community and from an unidentified criminal who could be stalking us or lurking anywhere.

CHAPTER 4

One Month Later

Almost a month went by while I did little but lie around and watch TV. Noelle bounced back after being questioned at Tabitha's and was still playing with the neighbor kids. So far, no one else had confronted her about it in our close-knit neighborhood.

We lived in a place that was called Allegheny Township, located in Westmoreland County near the intersection of three counties: Westmoreland, Allegheny, and Armstrong. It was very rural in those days and we were surrounded by farms and woods. A few highways cut through it along with numerous back roads. We lived along a dead end dirt road called Phillips Lane. There were three small shopping plazas and a few housing plans. Our housing plan did not have a name that I know of, but back then we called it Friendly Acres because of a prank pulled off by my brother and his best friend, Tony. We had a couple of feuding neighbors who were getting on everyone's nerves so they painted a "Welcome to Friendly Acres" sign and nailed it up on a telephone poll up by the Township Maintenance Garage at the top of the road. For years, people would say, when we described where we lived, "Oh you live in Friendly Acres!"

One day, I woke up and heard locusts buzzing in the trees. Feeling nostalgic about the end of summer I thought I would play with Kris today. Kris and I'd been close companions since I was less than two. I met her back when our mothers used to push us both up the road every day in baby strollers to get the mail. Back then, the mailboxes were at the top of our road by the school bus stop. Like me, she was the youngest of four children. She was lucky. All of her family lived at home. Her house was like an endless pajama party. Maybe that's why she was so much more socially aware than I was. I felt like I was absent the day everyone else got a copy of a manual of *How to Be Normal*. No matter what I did or said at school, it seemed to be the wrong thing. Kris fell into the role of coaching me: what to wear, what not to wear, what to talk about at school, and when to absolutely keep my mouth shut. She saved me from an incalculable number of playground ass kickings.

I called her on the phone, put on my silver astronaut costume and headed out in the summer heat to the shed. Our clubhouse, known as my "laboratory", was in the loft of my father's storage shed. As clubhouses went, it was top of the line. The upper story had been recently built. It still smelled of fresh lumber, mingled with the oily smells from my father's machine shop underneath. It had electricity and we made good use of the unused furniture stored up there. We had a sofa, end tables, lamps, chairs, an old black and white TV, and even a bed for when we had a sleep out.

Off to one side of the building was my dad's carport. He built double doors opening onto the carport roof to make it easier to move furniture in and out. We thought of them as French doors opening out onto a deck. The bluish green carport roof was made from wavy fiberglass sheets. If you walked in the wrong place on the "deck" you would fall through. Naturally, we weren't allowed out there, but that never stopped us. We just did our best to tread carefully and not get caught.

I climbed up the steep ladder. The upstairs sweltered in the pent up heat like a car parked in the sun. I opened the French doors and the windows to cool the place off, then turned on the TV and sank into a chair. The lab was full of memories. Days of summers gone, when the place resounded with laughter and stank of my experiments. Summer used to last forever. This one seemed to pass so quickly. I wandered around the laboratory as I waited, wondering why the usual feelings of excitement and contentment that normally went with summer were missing. It was the same old place, so why did it seem so different? It was as if I was watching my life, instead of living it.

As I stood there, holding a rusting can of Raid in case a spider appeared, one of those stupid childhood songs rang in my ears. Only a month ago I sat in this very room, with the neighborhood kids as we sang that stupid song:

> Miss Lucy had a steamboat; the steamboat had a bell,
> Miss Lucy went to heaven, the steamboat went to
> Hello operator, give me number nine.
> And if you disconnect me, I'll kick you in the
> Behind the 'fridgerator, there was a piece of glass.
> Suzy sat upon it, and cut her little
> Ask me no more questions; tell me no more lies,
> The boys are in the girl's room, zipping up their
> Flies are in the meadow; Bees are in the barn ....

The song would not go out of my head. I was being haunted by a tune from Girl Scout camp, for God's sake. I threw the can in an old barrel and sat down. I thought I was about to be sick. Then the door downstairs slammed shut and I went cold with terror, speechless.

"Are you up there?" called Kris after a period of loud silence.

I knew it was Kris, but still words were slow to form. "Yes," I finally managed.

A few seconds later, her blonde head appeared through the trap door and I extended a hand to help her up. We stood and regarded each other as strangers. Not a word had passed between us but we both knew something was different.

"So, what have you been up to lately?" she asked to break the silence.

"Not much", I answered, watching myself from somewhere else in the room. "I haven't felt too well."

She looked through all of the peepholes to make sure no adults were around, then closed the French doors, flooding the place in darkness.

She turned around to face me, bellowing, "What the hell is going on? And don't tell me 'nothing'! I haven't seen you for weeks and you look 10 pounds thinner. Noelle has been running all over the neighborhood with Lisa and Tabitha and if anyone asks her a question about you, she runs away. Strange cars come in and out of your driveway at odd hours. Everyone's parents are acting weird. Now I repeat: What, the hell, happened?"

"Nothing happened; it's just been kind of a bad summer."

"Bad summer, my ass! I don't buy it. Something's majorly wrong and your mother told you not to tell me, didn't she?"

"Yeah, I guess so," I admitted. I wondered if she had way better

ESP than me.

She pounded a rickety old table in frustration. "I knew it! Your mother's had it in for me ever since that day I wouldn't let you ride my big red tricycle!"

I did remember that. It was true. We were preschoolers, and she wouldn't let me ride the thing. My mother went ballistic.

"You have to tell me. Please! I won't tell. I'm your best friend! Have I ever let you down?" she said, earnestly.

"Well, no", I conceded. "But you have to promise never to tell anyone. If my mother finds out I dunno what she'll do to me."

Kris promised, "Cross my heart, hope to die, stick a needle in my eye."

I sighed and went on, as now there was no backing out. Maybe there would be some relief in the telling. Or that perhaps, as in most other things, she would know what to do.

"Noelle and I rode our bikes up to the bridge a few weeks ago and ..."

"And ..." she gestured impatiently.

All the stern warnings rang in my ears, but I went on. "This man came out of the woods, and told us that he was hunting and his brother fell and broke his leg, and would we help him, and as soon as we crossed the road he... " I heard my voice say plainly.

"He what?"

"He," I groped for words. What to say? I couldn't bring myself to choke out the plain truth. Mugged? Sounded to inconsequential. "He abducted us." Yes. That sounded good.

"Did he do anything?" she interrogated, leaning forward.

"What do you mean?"

"You know exactly what I mean."

I turned away and looked out the window. "Well, yes, but please – I'm begging you - don't ask any more about it! I can't say anymore!" I spun around to face her again. "You promised you would never say anything. If my mother finds out I told you, my ass is grass!"

"Did your parents call the police?"

"Yes, or well, the ER – somebody did. I guess I wasn't in too good of shape when I got home."

"Don't worry, I won't say anything," she consoled. And we sat there, in the dark, because neither of us knew what to say.

The telltale crunching sound of a car in the driveway startled us. Pie-eyed, we stared at each other.

"There's a car in your driveway!" she whispered. We cracked the French doors and peeked out.

What I saw made me sick. "Oh God, no! It's the police in that unmarked car nobody's supposed to recognize. I forgot they were coming. We have to get outta here! If we go down in the woods, they'll never find us."

Kris stared at me. "Don't you want them to catch this guy?"

"No! I just want everything to be the way it was before. I know I always complained that I hated it, but it was way better than the ways things are now!"

"But you can't do that! It's the police! And, that guy is still out there somewhere! Please talk to them! He could do this to somebody else, like me! You wouldn't want this to happen to me? I don't think I could deal with it."

I sat for a moment, stunned at this ferocity.

"Well, just what makes you think I can deal with it?" I snapped.

"Because you can deal with anything."

"Since when?"

"Since always!" She put her hand on my arm. "Look – just ... please?"

It was advice, but not the kind I expected. I wanted her to take over, tell me what to do to keep it all quiet, and say something to make everything like it was before. Instead, I'd frightened her. She wanted me to cooperate with the authorities. In that case, I wished she could go with me, but I knew that was beyond impossible.

"Oh all right. My mother would kill me if I didn't show up, anyway."

"I'll see you tomorrow at the bus stop," Kris said, reassuringly. "You can tell me how it went."

Oh no! The summer was over? No luck convincing my parents to get me a home tutor, so it was pretty much certain that I was actually going to have to get up and go to school in less than 18 hours. But I didn't have time to panic about that with the cops all but knocking on the front door.

"Maybe I'll be sick tomorrow. Or even right now."

"Don't. You'll like junior high. It'll be different! You'll see!"

I had an ominous feeling. Kind of like how the people felt while they were being led to the gallows, I imagined. "I guess," I mumbled as we climbed down out of the lab.

Kris stood in the shadows next to the door, waiting until the coast was clear to go home. "If for no one else, do it for me," she whispered as I stepped out into the warm evening light.

The cops were still getting their stuff out of the car. I ran down behind the bushes and came in the back door. I had only gone a few steps before I ran smack into my mother.

"What do you have on?" she demanded, grabbing me by the elbow.

"Just my astronaut costume. Why? What's the matter with it?"

"What's the matter with it? I'll tell you what's the matter with it!" she hissed. "You're lucky the police are coming out here at all, and the only reason they are here is because you're ELEVEN years old! If you were fifteen or sixteen, no one would believe you or give a damn so you get upstairs and change into something normal RIGHT NOW!" She shoved me toward the stairs just as there was a loud knock at the front door.

She said she'd tell me what was the matter with it, but she didn't. I had no idea what she was talking about. My mother's agitation made me think there was so much more to this situation than I could ever dream of. I pulled on a pair of jeans and a T-shirt, trying to figure out what the heck was going on. What did being fifteen or sixteen have to do with anything? Why wouldn't they believe me? What reason could I possibly have for lying about something like that? If I wanted to lie I'd have said nothing and spared myself the humiliation. Whose side was my mother on? Was she helping me or them? I had nothing but my usual defenses to fall back on. Namely, trying to appear older and conceal ignorance. All the while hoping I could figure it out soon enough to beat the adults at this game. I was on my own, it certainly seemed.

Downstairs, I could hear my mother playing hostess. I seethed at what I took to be a display of shallowness and fakery.

"Thank you SO much for coming! Can I get you anything? Coffee?" she greeted.

"What's Grandma so mad about?" asked Noelle, appearing in my room.

"I don't know. We have to go downstairs. Don't say anything. Just let me do the talking." I took her by the hand and led her downstairs.

"There they are," announced my mother as we entered the living room. Noelle and I remained defensively near the exit.

"You remember Officer Donaldson, don't you? And Tom Warden?" my mother asked.

The first officer was the one from that night, in the ER. He looked even more tough and brawny every time I saw him. The second officer seemed more sympathetic and friendly. He wasn't in the ER that night but had been along on every visit since then. I didn't know at the time that this policeman was a friend of my father's. His friend wasn't satisfied with the way it was being handled and sort of attached himself to the case. With him being a part time officer, the police department wouldn't turn the case over to him. Yet, they couldn't just tell him to butt out. My father was a significant figure in the local township political scene and they couldn't afford to alienate him too much. So out of this delicate little dance, Tom Warden became my sole ally in the police department.

I sat on the edge of a chair as Officer Donaldson emptied his briefcase on the table. Tom Warden sat across from me, holding Noelle on his lap. She was giggling and thrusting Mr. Whiskers at him. It made me nervous; she was too quick to trust these people. Years later, Noelle told me that the main thing she remembers from the whole event was sitting on the policeman's lap.

"Noelle, don't put your stuffed animals in peoples' faces," my mother scolded before turning to Donaldson. "Do you want them both to look at the pictures?"

"Yeah. Might as well." He opened a folder and arranged 20 or so pictures on the coffee table. Noelle looked at them first, Tom Warden holding her up so she could see over the table. "Is the man you saw in any of these pictures?" Slowly she shook her head no.

"All right, how about you?" He gestured towards me. I got up and examined the pictures, carefully, one by one.

"This guy looks a lot like him."

"Does not!" yelled Noelle.

Suddenly I was mad enough to spit. Didn't I tell her to let me do the talking? "Does, too!" I snapped, pinning her to a chair with a sharp glance.

"Does not!"

"That's enough, you two," bellowed my father.

"Are you sure you remember?" asked Officer Donaldson, making an obvious effort to treat me with some tenderness, even if it was completely out of character for him. This entire assignment made him extremely uncomfortable. A month before this interview, the local drunks and people calling the cops on each other's dogs represented the worst incidents in that town. Years later, I was told I was the first person to report a crime like that in the area where we lived. He had no training in that type of stuff, and was almost as helpless as the rest of us.

"Yes. I'm sure. I don't think that's him, but it does bear a certain resemblance."

The two police exchanged a knowing glance with raised eyebrows, as my unusual vocabulary went under their scrutiny again.

"Do you hang around with older kids?" he asked.

They all gaped at me. They were fishing for a particular answer, obviously. What were they trying to get at? I decided that the only safe answer was a stupid answer.

"I don't know. Define 'older kids'. Kris is in 9th grade, so technically she's older."

The room let out a collective sigh of exasperation.

"I've told you before there aren't any older kids in this neighborhood! At least not anymore," said my mother, effectively rescuing me from the fire. "If there were, I'd know about it."

Officer Donaldson stooped down to my level and said with a smile, "Why don't you two go play while I talk to your parents alone." Anytime adults wanted to talk about something important, it was always time to go outside and play!

"What do you suppose they're going to talk about?" asked Noelle as we crept up the hallway.

I was so angry I was seeing stars. They certainly had a lot of gall. I said nothing, but led her down the stairs that ran behind the living room. I wasn't supposing anything. I was gonna spy on them.

Her eyes widened, then she looked disapproving at me. "Well, what gives them the right to talk about me behind my back like that?" I retorted in a whisper.

"The Crime Lab found evidence from the materials collected during the hospital exam. Some hair and a blood type. Found semen. Mixed with her blood," Donaldson told my parents.

What the hell is semen? I thought. Later that night, after everybody was in bed, I looked it up in the dictionary and was beyond repulsed. Could this possibly get any worse? I sat up half the night looking up various words associated with sex and reproduction in the dictionary. Nothing I read explained the adults' behavior.

I had Kris to thank that I even knew some words to look up.

Two summers ago, we were sleeping out in my tent in my front yard. Talking late into the night, she told me something shocking about what men used those things for, and where babies came from.

"Ugh! That's disgusting!" I said. "There's no way that's true! My parents would never do anything like that!"

"It is so true!" she retorted. "My sisters told me!"

Those thoughts sat on the shelf for a while but eventually, we had the when-you-get-your-period class in health class at school and I ended up asking my mother about it, and she embarrassingly admitted it was true. Then she handed me a book that outlined the basic mechanics of it. Being a nurse, she was far more direct about it than most mothers, who ended up giving a blundered speech about flowers, insects and womanhood leaving the listener even more confused than before.

The conversation in the living room snapped me back to the present. "And of course, the dogs found where it happened in the woods," continued Donaldson. "Well then, if she can identify him, I don't see why you can't arrest him," my mother said.

"Ma'am, it's not that simple. We knew of a couple men who fit the description, and we did check them out, but they have alibis. There was one guy from Apollo, has a record like that, but I have a statement from his shift supervisor at the steel mill that he was working at the time."

"People can lie!" my mother interjected.

"Let's face it, you can't swing a dead cat in this town without hitting someone who fits that description," he continued. "We did find an empty case of beer at the crime scene, which we collected and sent off for fingerprinting. I thought maybe he polished it off before he committed the crime. But she says he didn't smell like beer, and if he drank that much beer, she would've been able to smell it. We'll contact you if we find anything more." He lowered his voice and cleared his throat. "Do you know if she's pregnant?"

"I don't think so, but it's too early to be completely sure."

The room went silent.

"How is she, overall?" asked Tom Warden.

"I can't tell," my mother answered.

"Does she ever appear upset about it?" asked Officer Donaldson.

"She cried for a few seconds in the ER, then once the next morning, but that was it. She never cries now, just lays in bed and watches TV." The room went silent again. " She did go out and play with the girl down the street today, so I guess that's a positive sign."

Donaldson shifted his weight, the floor creaking under him. "So you really don't think there could be any possibility that she knows who this is, and isn't telling? That's she's protecting somebody?"

"No, I most certainly do not! She's eleven years old. She's never dated, or had any kind of involvement with boys. I consider the entire question to be beyond absurd."

"I'm not implying anything here," Donaldson soothed, "I just have to consider all the possibilities. It just seems strange to me, that she doesn't seem all the upset about it. Maybe I'm totally wrong, I dunno. But I have to ask the question."

"Are you sending her to school?" inquired Warden.

"Yes. I don't see any good reason not to, or any realistic alternatives."

Silence again.

By then, I'd heard quite enough. They had no right to send me out of the room and talk about me like some kind of non-entity.

Having them think I would lie to them was even worse. I took Noelle's hand and led her back into the living room, fully intending on giving them a piece of my mind. As soon as they saw us, they looked like we usually did when we got caught doing something bad. My bravado left me in the lurch, and stood there like a fool, saying nothing. The adults all looked at each other, then at Donaldson, as if to say," well, you're in charge, so say something!"

Donaldson shifted his weight, and thought hard for something to say. "You know," he finally began, "you don't have to be afraid of all men because of this."

"Yeah," agreed Tom Warden. "For instance, you don't have to be afraid of your father." He gestured towards my dad. I knit my eyebrows together and wondered if they took me for a complete idiot. Donaldson broke the tension by standing up to leave, and the atmosphere suddenly seemed as if they'd just been over for a friendly chat and some iced tea.

"Thanks for stopping out", said my father, pumping Tom Warden's hand.

"Yes, do come again. We'll be happy to co-operate with you in any way we can", added my mother.

"You take care," said Tom Warden to me as he walked past. "I hope you're doing OK."

"She's starting junior high tomorrow!" answered my father, as if that were something wondrous.

I cringed. "Don't talk about me in the third person when I'm standing right in front of you!" I snapped. My father scowled.

You bastards! I thought. Swelling with fury, I shot Donaldson a fiery glare. I was so angry that I temporarily lost control of my mouth.

"You know what I don't understand?" They gaped at me in awe.

"I don't understand why anybody would ever do something like that to another human being! My friends say that adults do that to each other, but you know, I think they're lying! It's disgusting! It's ..."

I stopped short, realizing that both of my parents were standing close enough to back hand me if I allowed the foul language now flowing freely in my mind to come out of my mouth.

Donaldson paled and gulped audibly. I could see it cross his face, although I didn't realize what his expression meant until years later.

Oh my God. This is real. This really happened.

He stopped pushing my parents to let them give me a lie detector test after that.

"We'd better get going," croaked Donaldson, although he wasn't out of the hot water yet. Just then, Noelle re-entered the hallway. None of us even realized she was gone. But now, there she stood, with an armful of stuffed toys.

"Guess what? Mr. Whiskers' wife is pregnant", she said in a singsong voice. The adults stood there horrified, speechless.

"Little pitchers have big ears," my father recovered, looking at my mother over the rims of his glasses.

"Who's Mr. Whiskers?" asked a bewildered Donaldson.

"Oh, he's my rat!" She held him in the air and waved him about. "Do you want to see her? Her stomach is getting big and everything!"

"Uh, that's OK. Maybe some other time. We have to go." He was out the door before anyone could say another word.

"You two, go to your rooms!" ordered my mother.

"Noelle, I believe you committed a faux pas," I giggled as we crept up the stairs.

"What's that?"

"Never mind. You gave them exactly what they deserved. I'm really gonna miss you when you go home this weekend."

CHAPTER 5

The First Day of Seventh Grade

It seemed like I'd been asleep a few minutes when Dad stuck his head in my bedroom door and called out, "Better get up! You don't wanna be late for school!"

Ha! You wanna bet?

I had been awake most of the night and I felt terrible. It was hard to tell what produced the most insomnia: having to go to school the next day or having told Kris about what happened up at the bridge, after being specifically told not to. Why did it seem that every time I tried to turn over a new leaf and live my life right, I ended up on my face in the dirt? Parental obedience: one of the childhood cardinal virtues I received lectures on regularly. Yet I still couldn't pull it off. There was nothing left to do but try for some degree of damage control.

I crawled out of bed and stood staring at the closet. Same problem every year. There you are in front of a closet full of nice brand new school clothes, and the weather is still too hot to wear any of them. So I put on the nicest summer outfit I could find and sat down to try and remember how to apply the new makeup my mother bought me. In junior high, you are supposed to wear makeup and carry a purse. If you didn't you were a traitor to your gender; unless everyone carried a purse every day, the boys would know who had their period. Then, we'd all have to crawl down a hole and die.

My hair was absolutely awful. I'd decided to grow it out and now, I was really regretting that. It was at one of those terrible in between stages. I tried to pin back my awkward bangs with barrettes, and almost cried but didn't out of fear of ruining my makeup.

Once upon a time in my other life, I would have looked forward to this day. It was a new school full of new faces. Our school, Weinels Elementary School stood along Shearsburg Road near Shearsburg Crossroads. At Shearsburg Crossroads stood an ancient wooden fruit stand. We used to go on field trips there. You know you live in the sticks when you go on field trips to a fruit stand! Weinels was an old red brick building with huge single pane, six over six windows covered with peeling white paint. Inside, the quaint classrooms had huge slate blackboards. In the summer it was hotter than hell and in the winter you froze to death. Down in the basement, it had one of those ancient boilers with a zillion arms snaking off in all directions. Kris used to joke that it had been a fort in the War of 1812.

Allegheny Hyde Park Junior High, on the other hand, was a much newer building with a unique circular architectural feature that was probably built in the 1950's or 60's. Three different elementary schools fed into Allegheny Hyde Park: Weinels, Washington Township, and Hyde Park. Two thirds of the school population would be new. A fresh start, almost. On the other hand, the kids from my elementary school could still ruin it by telling everybody I was weird. That was my official school label: weird. I was weird because I told elaborate little yarns on the playground to entertain and impress, only to have my appreciative audience rat on me for making up stories. Kids who "made up stories" were not considered creative in that time and place, they were weird. Kids who taught themselves algebra and chemistry were not intelligent. They were weird. Kids who had a strong stubborn and independent streak did not have potential. They were weird! I had no pride in any of my academic accomplishments, nor did I think of them as accomplishments. They were simply a way to escape an environment with which I was constantly at odds.

So, as a result, that morning I wondered if they were right. Did what happened to me over the summer prove I was weird? I found myself wondering about innate destiny. Was the weirdness caused by something within me, some deep irreparable flaw? After all, I didn't think things like this happened to the nice little girls who didn't talk back and did what they were told. My mother's constant attempts to make it into an object lesson on parental obedience only reinforced this idea. Yet ironically, it happened on one of the few occasions where I did listen to an adult: the wrong adult. I was trying to be a Good Samaritan and look what happened! Was self-improvement just plain futile? I stared at the made-up face in the mirror and a stranger stared back. Would the other kids be able to tell, just to look at me?

It was with this cynical and irate attitude that I hauled my sleep-deprived ass to the end of the driveway to wait for Kris and begin our daily sojourns to the bus stop. Damage control. My mother said over and over again, don't tell anybody, especially *that Krissy*. So, what was the first thing I did on the first day out of the house? I wondered if Kris would stop being my friend over it. If only I was on a plane bound for my sister's house in Los Angeles!

As I walked down the driveway, I wondered how exactly to do this. If only I could take back what I said. Or, maybe I could convince

Kris that I made it up. But what's a believable story? That I invented the whole thing? Saw it on TV? Or that it was really about someone else? Bingo!

As I wandered up to Kris, she gave me a long, calculated look. "You look nice! Great purse. New?"

"Yeah."

We picked our way carefully through the gravel in our new shoes. I hesitated, not sure how my revelation had changed things between us.

"I have a confession to make."

"What's that?"

"Well, you know what I told you about yesterday? I sort of, well, wasn't totally honest about it."

She stopped walking. "What do you mean?"

"It didn't really happen to me. You see, it happened to a friend of mine and I was trying to, well, spare her any embarrassment caused by it. I'm sorry I lied."

She looked at me as if I took her for a complete dork. "Now why would you lie about a thing like that?"

"I don't know; I guess I'm just an asshole."

"I think you're lying now. What? Did your mother get a hold of you or something? And I didn't tell anybody, so she can't know you told me. Why do you want me to think you made it up?"

"Look, I made it up. It has nothing to do with my mother, OK? Can we just not talk about this anymore? I said I was sorry."

A long moment passed.

"If that's what you want."

To prevent any further interrogation, I changed the subject. "So who do you think will be at our bus stop?"

The bus stop was at the top of our road by the Township Maintenance Garage. They had a yard full of interesting stuff – piles of various sized gravel, ashes, salt, pipes that run under roads, snow plows, tractors – in other words, multi-use playground equipment. In elementary school, we always climbed on the piles. Now that we were sophisticated women, we would not be joining the boys in the ash pile. Instead we talked about girl stuff on the other side of the road and put our books and purses inside the mailboxes when it rained.

I stuck close to Kris on the bus. My first surprise was a new bus route! Instead of going down Shearsburg Road towards the Elementary school, it went up the hill and across the bridge. I stole a glance at the crime scene where the vegetation was still trampled down by invading police and dogs. My heart began to pound in my chest. I tried to swallow and looked over at Kris, who was talking to someone else and didn't catch the significance of the moment.

The new bus route was long and the bus wound endlessly around the curvy roads in the lush green foliage. In the new few stops some friends of Kris's got on and sat with us. They formed an insulating barrier between me and the rowdy kids in the back of the bus.

"Cow Patty!"

The back-of-the-bus ring leader called this out every morning as a tough looking girl boarded the bus alone at a stop at the end of her driveway. If it bothered her, she didn't let on. In fact, the two of them traded insults for the entire trip while the rest of the bus laughed after each comeback, sitcom style. Looking back, I cannot think of a less dignified mode of transportation.

An eternity later, the bus rattled into the circular driveway in front of the school.

"Come on," said Kris, pulling on my sleeve. "Earth to Laura. It's time to get off."

"I can't."

"You have to! What are you gonna do? Spend all day locked in the bus garage?"

Maybe that doesn't sound too bad, I thought. Then it happened for the first time. I smelled roses. Stunned, I looked around. Yet, as suddenly as the smell was there, it was gone. Every other kid in the township my age spilled into the junior high like a tide going out. I remembered what I had to do. Keep a lid on it. Act normal. Time was passing, each minute carrying me farther and farther away from that transformative day. I followed Kris into the school. We stopped in front of several rooms, checking to see which one had my name on the list.

"This is your homeroom. I'll see you later in band. For God's sake, stop looking like you're going before a firing squad! It will be a lot better than elementary school. You've got to believe me!"

I went into my homeroom, and not finding any sort of seating chart, sat down behind a group of kids that I knew from last year to be non-hostile.

The room was plain, with drab green walls, that same old institutional school color. The bulletin board in the front of the room held a construction paper tree with each of our first names printed in block letters on a leaf. So, junior high wasn't that far removed from the 6th grade. I couldn't imagine showing up for your first day of college, or even high school, and seeing your name on a paper tree.

Movement drew my attention to the window. A police car sailed smoothly into the parking lot alongside the new community building and police station next door. Seeing it was another reminder, and it made me uneasy. Why did everything remind me of it? Would I ever go a whole day in my entire life when I wouldn't think about it? I had to do something. I opened my purse and took out a notebook and a pen, and started writing. Anything.

"Hey, guess what I heard!" said the kid in front of me, turning partially towards me. I looked up from my notebook and listened, trying not to appear overly interested.

"What?" asked another kid.

"My brother is a paramedic. He said an eleven- year- old girl was raped by that overhead bridge up on Route 56."

"No way! When?"

"About a month ago." He looked straight at me. "That's not too far from where you live, isn't it?"

The kids all turned and looked at me expectantly. I swallowed, and mustered up as much composure as I could. Failure at this juncture could be fatal.

"That's at least a mile from my house. I never heard anything about it. We were on vacation most of the summer." I shrugged, hoping to appear nonchalant. "I don't think it's true. Sounds pretty farfetched to me."

"It is so true!" he insisted. "We drove past there the same night, and there were police cars parked all over and dogs searching the woods."

"I heard something about it, too," said another girl. "My parents said it was people making a big deal out of nothing, just a couple of teenagers fooling around in the woods. The girl's parents just reported it to the police just to save face."

I gulped. "Do you know who it was?"

It seemed like an eternity until he answered. "No. They didn't say the name over the radio. I asked my brother and he didn't know."

After that, I was never directly confronted about it at school. How many kids knew about it, or knew that it was me, or had heard some perverted version of the truth, I never found out. So school settled itself into a dreary and lonely routine. I went, I did the things that were asked of me, and I went home, where I lay on my bed and listened endlessly to Simon and Garfunkel's *Sounds of Silence*.

✱✱✱

Indian summer still held Allegheny Township in a warm, humid embrace when my birthday came around in early October. I sat in the car beside my mother, the sun as bright as butter that Saturday morning. We were on our way into Leechburg to pick up my birthday cake from the bakery.

The borough of Leechburg was a few miles away from our neighborhood down Route 56, on the opposite side of the Kiskiminetas River. Leechburg started out as a Pennsylvania Main Line canal town and then became an industrial town like all the others near us. We didn't go there as often as it was smaller than Lower Burrell or New Kensington, but it did have a few unique things like an awesome independently owned bakery, a public library, and my mother's hairdresser, Pauline. The shops were in old Victorian buildings with octagonal tiles and tin ceilings.

My birthday dinner was that evening, one of those aunt and grandmother type deals. Quiet, simple, and non-controversial. Nevertheless, the bakery in Leechburg was not a chain back then and sold cakes that were noticeably better than everyone else's. The Princess Pastries chain, my mother complained, was taking over. We didn't like their cakes as well as Leechburg's. I was all but drooling in anticipation of this cake.

We pulled into a parking space along Market Street in front of the pet store window. I climbed out of the car and pressed my nose against the glass. A litter of blonde cocker spaniel puppies tumbled about in a pen full of newspaper shavings, their little yips and growls barely audible through the window.

"Come on. I don't wanna be here all day. You can look in the pet store another day. I have a roast in the oven."

"Look how cute! Can I have a puppy for my birthday?"

"No! I've already got enough things to take care of."

We crossed the street, and continued on to the bakery. "But I'd take care of it!" I protested.

"Who would be stuck with it while you're at school? Puppies are too much work. They have to be taken outside all the time. They wake you up at night and chew things up."

Totally engrossed in this argument, we were about to pass the old Post Office. I turned my head and there he was, sitting on the steps, casually smoking a cigarette, right in front of me! He looked up, our eyes locked, and the world stopped. I stood perfectly still, waiting. I couldn't move and I couldn't look away. Finally, he stood up and started towards me, then suddenly turned and crossed the street without even looking at the traffic. Cars honked, tires screeched, and fists popped out of open windows. There was a black, two door sedan parked across the street. He climbed into it and started the engine with a load roar, then took off.

As soon as he was gone, we started walking again. That's when I realized that I was still holding my mother's hand and that she'd seen everything. Neither of us said a word about it. We continued down the street and picked up the cake. When we came back past the post office, there was nobody there.

On the way home in the car the silence was leaden. I decided I was not going to let this bother me. I wasn't gonna think about it, I wasn't gonna talk about it. Forget it.

I had almost forgotten about it when we arrived home and I opened the cake box, which I put on the shelf like ledge that ran along the top of the built in cabinet in the living room. I sniffed the icing; it smelled so good! The cake had white icing as its base, with yellow roses winding their way around the words, 'Happy 12th Birthday '. The baker left a big glob of icing on the bottom of the box. My mouth watered as I stuck my finger in to retrieve it.

"Hey! I better not find any finger marks on that cake!"

"Can I have the big yellow rose, since it's my birthday?" I asked, subtly popping the icing glob in my mouth.

"Yes, but not until this evening when we cut the cake." She moved toward the telephone desk in between the kitchen and the living room and picked up the phone.

"What are you doing?" No answer. Then I knew exactly what she was doing. "Wait! Don't!"

Too late! I stood there dumbfounded as she rattled off the details of our little encounter to an unknown police officer. She grew angrier at each turn of the conversation.

Slamming down the receiver, she said to me, "You, stay around where I can find you. If they pick him up and call back, you'll have to go identify him."

I shot back, "I'm not doing this and you can't make me!"

"You'd better learn to be a little more grateful! I have to call them and nag them and put up with their bullshit and I'm not putting up with yours too! So for once in your life, do what you're told!"

"This is exactly why I told you to call the State Police when this first happened," interjected my father from the doorway. "And you didn't listen. You insisted on calling those local cops, and they don't know what the hell they're doing."

"Maybe you're right, but it's too late now. If I didn't know better, I'd think those guys are protecting somebody. I mean, I told them about three or four families around here that have men like that hanging around their garages. They acted like I was nuts! I nag them and pester them and all they do is make excuses."

"They may be or they may not be. Either way, you'll never know. All I can say is this," he looked over the top of his glasses at me and gestured in my general direction, "She obviously doesn't want to be dragged into court over this and you're not gonna make those cops do anything they don't want to." Having said his peace, he stomped off towards the shed.

"You can't make me do this!" I continued. "I'm not getting up in front of a bunch of people and talking about that! It doesn't matter! Why can't everything just go back to the way it was!"

"Because it can't! Do you want this man running loose doing God knows what to God knows who? If you'd just listened to me in the first place! I told you not to go up to that damned bridge!"

"I'm not going to sit here and listen to this! It's not my fault! What, was I the one with the knife? Was I the adult?"

"No, but you were older than Noelle and you lead her into danger..."

"I saved her damned life!" Oops! I slapped my hand across my mouth too late. My mother's eyes bulged.

"You watch your language, you little asshole!"

"If I'm a little asshole, and you're my mother, what's that make you?"

I knew that was my cue to run, and I did! I ran as fast as I could, bawling all the while, across the yard. My mother was gaining on me, so I headed for the big maple tree in the front yard. Grabbing the lowest branch, I flipped up into it and scurried to the highest place I was sure would hold me. As I suspected, my mother was not willing to chase me up the tree. She stood on the ground and shook her fist at me.

"Sooner or later, you'll have to come down, you can't stay up there forever!" she screamed. "And when you do, you're gonna get it!"

The neighbors were no doubt just loving this.

Well, I knew I couldn't stay up there forever, too. I also knew if I avoided her long enough she'd cool down. She gave up and went back in the house. I sat in the tree shivering and wiping boogers on my sleeve.

After a while, I heard my dad's tractor start up. He spent the morning mowing and was now raking leaves. I climbed down the tree, making sure that Mom didn't see me from the kitchen window, though I could hear pots and pans banging. I ran over to the shed.

"What's the matter with you? Fighting with your mother again?"

"Yeah, sort of..." My mother had the unfortunate job of always being the bad guy. Dad, on the other hand, was all fun and games, AKA The Fun Parent. One of my older cousins told me that before he was sent away to the Korean War he was more of a typical 1950's father. When he came back 18 months later, he found himself on the outside looking into a tight unit consisting of my mother and my three older siblings, apparently a common situation for deployed soldiers. To reconnect with his family, he became the parent that was easier to approach.

When I was in elementary school, I had a strict bedtime of 9:00PM. Being a late person by nature, I was never tired when 9:00 came around. Unfortunately, my mother fought with me every night and forced me to go to bed. Then, after she'd gone to bed herself and become engrossed in some book, I'd sneak downstairs to the raid the kitchen. Inevitably, I met Dad, who had the same intentions. He made popcorn and all sorts of other wonderful treats. Then he would take me down in the basement with him to watch TV, and put me in bed when I fell asleep on my own. Since this clandestine activity was given some legitimacy by my father's participation, I never got in trouble. But sometimes when I wouldn't get up in the morning, my mother would yell in frustration, "If you ever went to bed on time, you'd be able to get up!"

"Want to help rake leaves?" he offered. "I'm going to rake them up, put them in the trailer, and drive them down to the compost pile. If you help rake, I'll give you a hay ride!"

I snorted in the last of the boogers. "OK. Can I use a big rake?"

"Sure. I'll get another one out of the shed."

I spent the rest of the afternoon with my dad. He even let me drive the tractor a few times. After the leaves were done, he was ready to burn garbage. Funny how back in those days you were allowed to do that. There was no recycling back then but we did separate the trash. Paper and cardboard went to the "waste paper baskets" and was burned weekly at the burn pit down by the woods. Regular garbage went in the trash can.

Dad lit the pile and we sat on a couple of logs, watching the cinders rise and dance with the smoke. I'd spent a lot of time sitting with my dad back by the burn pile. You couldn't leave it until it was ready to be put out for fear of setting the woods on fire. Sometimes we talked about things and sometimes we just sat and stared into the flames. My dad was an amazing man. He worked at ALCOA for his entire adult life. He was a machinist, and his job was more or less to fix theoretical machines. When the engineers designed things that didn't work right, they called him in to troubleshoot, which would probably require an engineering degree to do this job now. He started out as an apprentice, right after being discharged from the Army in World War II, at the plant in New Kensington next to the New Ken bridge. In the early 1970's, his department moved out to the new ALCOA Research Lab outside of town. Kris's father also worked at ALCOA in the same department and they used to carpool together.

Given his background, most activities with Dad revolved around planes, trains, or automobiles. Which is why I decided to ask him about an idea that occurred to me in the library shortly after Noelle went back home. My parents refused to send me to California, but that didn't necessarily preclude my going on my own. To run away properly, a kid needs an airline ticket. I wasn't having any of that sort of running away you did in elementary school, where you'd get to the top of the hill lugging your suitcase and realize there was nowhere to go, and have no choice but to turn around, go back home, and get laughed at. No, this was serious adult type running away, with a plan and a destination! Couldn't I save up the money and buy an airline ticket? Then, I could take a cab to the airport some morning while my parents were at work. Once I landed at the LA airport I could just call my sister and ask her to pick me up. If I was already out there, and on my own dime no less, they might not make me come back. They'd have to buy another ticket and this wouldn't happen because they were notorious tight wads.

First, there was the money problem. So I took advantage of this nice little interlude to do some research.

"Dad, how much does a plane ticket cost?" I asked, trying to sound innocent.

"Oh, it depends on when you go. Weekdays are cheaper. I would say around five hundred dollars, unless you are flying out of the country and then I'm sure it's a lot more."

Ouch! That was way more than I was expecting! "And how much would it cost to take a taxi from here to the airport?"

My father laughed aloud. "At least fifty bucks! Do you have any idea how far that is?"

I did a few quick mental calculations ... with my allowance of 5 dollars per week, to come up with $550 dollars would take me ... about 2.1 years! That was assuming that I didn't eat lunch, go to a movie, or buy anything.

"You can't save that much up," he observed. "Besides, no airline is going to sell you a ticket."

I gaped at him in astonishment. How did he know what I was thinking?

"Why not?"

"Because you're twelve and you don't have an ID or a credit card."

"What does that matter? They get their money and I get my ticket. What's the problem?"

"You know that when Noelle flies, we have to go sign papers because she's an unaccompanied minor. They just don't fly minors without paperwork and parental consent."

"Yeah, but, she's younger than me. And how are they going to know how old I am?"

"You have to have an ID. Like a driver's license."

"Well, that's not fair!"

He shrugged and patted me on the back. "Maybe not, but that's the way it is. I don't make the rules. I know you could get yourself from here to there on your own. You're plenty smart enough to ask questions and figure it out. But it just isn't done that way."

✱✱✱

The following Monday, I sat on one of the wooden benches after everybody else had gone into the gym, picking lint off my gym shorts. It was still hot and steamy from the last class taking showers. I only had a few minutes before roll call. I always tried to split the difference and go out as late as possible as there were several bullies in my gym class to avoid. They became so problematic early in the year that my mother complained to the school principal.

Since then things had quieted down, although it was still dreadfully lonely. I could stay calm and sleep walk through my day to day life but I couldn't connect with people. I was rudderless, and in such a state I had little to contribute to any conversation, and no reason to approach another person in friendship. The friendships I had before that summer evaporated in the mixture of indifference and new routines. Only Kris remained. Oddly, at that time I didn't recognize the reason: she knew what was going on. She had a reason to invite me to her house, time after time, and not take my refusals personally or be overly upset when I did come and do nothing but stare listlessly at the TV. She also honored my request to never bring that subject up again.

Startled by the late bell, I got up and hot footed it into the gym for roll call.

"Today the boys' and girls' gym classes will be together," announced the teacher. "You've been learning volleyball techniques for most of this grading period. From this point on, we will be playing tournaments. Here's the list. Check and see what team you are on. There are four teams, but only two teams will play at a time, alternating every other week. Those of you who are not playing will be practicing with a partner on the other side of the gym."

Luckily my team was not playing this week. I picked up a ball and wondered what to do next. A partner?

"Hey, what did you think of that movie they showed in History?" It was Tim, a boy I knew from Sunday school. He also sat in front of me in history class.

"I didn't realize you were in the boys' gym class this period."

"That's because I had a medical excuse. Unfortunately for me, I ran out of them. So here I am." He tossed a volleyball at me. "Wanna be volleyball partners?"

"I guess. But I have to warn you. I'm not any good at this."

"Neither am I. I just wanted to tell you, I think it's really disgusting the way Mary Jane and Denise pick on you. I hope somebody comes along and gives them a dose of their own medicine."

I smiled weakly.

"You're so different at school. Why I remember you were the only girl in Sunday school with enough kahunas to beat the snot out of the preacher's son." He put his head back and howled. "Gosh, that was the main entertainment at all the picnics and pot luck suppers, watching you and the preacher's son fight."

I had to laugh too, at that remembrance. How many church events had we been to together, over the years? Tim's grandfather and my father were both elders, so it was a lot. We belonged to Puckety United Presbyterian Church in Lower Burrell, known locally as "Puckety UP", thanks to the sign along Route 56.

Church was different. Nobody picked on me there. Well, except the preacher's son, but I picked on him just as badly. Maybe it was different at church because my father was an elder and close friends with the pastor, Rev. Fisher, or maybe it was just different because it was different. At church, I felt safe. Now, I had a little bit of church in gym class.

The following Sunday morning, Tim and I formed a little nucleus of junior high kids who declared our independence by sitting in a little herd in the last pew. It was good that we were in the back as we passed notes and giggled during the doxology. My parents let out a collective sigh of relief that I was actually acting somewhat normal again.

Since my father had a session meeting after church, my mother and I took her car and left after the service. We were about half way home when the black two door car appeared, seemingly out of nowhere, and pulled alongside us. I looked over. There he was! Sitting in the back seat! I froze, unable to look away. He stared back at me, then leaned forward and said something to the two men in front. They both looked over at us. The car swerved toward us.

My mother reacted, slamming on the brakes and skidding to a stop in the gravel along the shoulder. The car sped off ahead of us.

"Buddy, if you think I'm gonna race ya, you've got another think coming!" she yelled with a raised fist. "The nerve of some people!"

I said nothing. That didn't just happen. Just forget about it, I told myself.

She pulled back onto the road and drove slowly the rest of the way home. Once or twice, she looked over at me. I sat still as a stone.

"That was that guy again, wasn't it?" she finally asked. "Tell me the truth!"

"If I said yes, what would you do?"

"Call the police again! You did see him, didn't you? In that car!"

"No, I didn't! And I'll deny it till my dying day!"

She pounded her fist on the steering wheel. "Why do you have to be so darned uncooperative?"

"Because it's over! I don't wanna talk about it anymore. I don't wanna think about it anymore. I went back to school and lived to tell about it and life goes on. It doesn't have any effect on me anymore. So just drop it!"

"It is not over! Do you realize that you could still be pregnant?"

I rolled my eyes in disgust. Even I knew how that worked. If you had your period, then you didn't have anything to worry about. Or at least, that's what Kris said.

"Oh pah-leeze! It's been almost two months!" I said.

"That doesn't matter. You still might be."

"No, I couldn't!"

"Yes you could!"

"And so what if I was!"

"We'd have to take you for an abortion!"

"And if I refused?" I parried.

"I'd hold you down by the neck and make you! Why do you always make my life so impossible?"

At home, no sound except for two doors slamming.

I'd never heard of abortion before. I would never have admitted it, but the possibility of being pregnant had worried me for a while. Although it never occurred to me until the day I overhead the police ask. After that, I thought about it a lot. What the heck would happen then? I asked an acquaintance at school, someone I didn't know that well. If I asked Kris, she'd know why I was asking.

"If somebody was pregnant, is there any way to do something about it? To make them, like, not pregnant?" I asked.

Horrified stare. "Yeah, they could get an abortion."

Hearing that brought up a memory. I was over at the neighbors, playing one day. That very same summer, in fact. As we sat there that day, pounding shapes out of playdough, the girl next door looked at me and said, "I don't believe in abortion." She was three years younger than me, and I thought she was trying to be a know-it-all.

"What are you talking about?" I'd asked.

"It's when someone has a baby, and they don't want it, so they kill it."

I was aghast. "That's a lie. Nobody would ever do that."

So that's what abortion was. My whole situation never ceased to amaze me with new horrors. From then on, it took a crowbar to pry me out of that house. Of course, I refused to acknowledge that, and when asked about why would only reply, "school." For a little while, things were quiet within the shrunken boundaries that now defined my life. But as I was soon to learn, some things have a way of refusing to stay in the tight little boxes we put them in.

CHAPTER 6

At The Aunt Farm

My mother sat at the massive oak dining room table of the Aunt Farm that fall, sipping coffee and carrying on some deep conversation with the three aunts. That house, known within the family as "The Aunt Farm", was a manifestation of Pap's quirky personality. Built around 1910 in a small field at the end of a country road, it was full of odd features like hidey holes under the eaves, secret compartments inside closets, and a hole in the foundation for the cats to go in and out. The front porch had thick turned banisters which were covered with peeling paint just begging to be picked at. And whenever one of us did, someone would yell, "Don't eat that! It might have lead in it!" On the porch was the old porch swing, painted the same color green as the banisters but peeling much less.

When my grandparents grew too old to live alone, three of my mother's sisters moved back home to take care of them. Two had never married and one was widowed young. After Grammy and Pap died, they kept up the living arrangement. Thus: The Aunt Farm.

Rule: everyone in my mother's family had to have a weird nickname.

Aunt Gerk (Gertrude) was more or less, the leader. A retired nurse who never married, she had a boyfriend by the time I knew her that the older cousins nicknamed The Aardvark. His real name was Carl Percy but the kids all called him "The Aardvark" because he hung around at the Aunt Farm all the time. Many years later when we were cleaning out the Aunt Farm after their deaths, we found a pristine white 1930's peignoir set in the attic, which prompted Mom to tell the story of her planned dirty weekend with the Navy guy she almost married during World War II. However, when he was on shore leave, he got some other girl pregnant and had to marry her instead! So she swore off men and put her energy into her career. She was an expert listener and was very kind and thoughtful, sort of the unofficial family psychologist.

Aunt Biggie (Thelma) was the oldest sister and had the fastest comebacks of anyone I ever met. Nobody ever had the last word with Aunt Biggie! She went to college in the roaring 20's and used to tell hysterical stories about bootleg liquor. She became a school teacher but discovered that she hated it. She married Uncle Steve, long dead by my time, but never had any children.

Aunt Margie had a somewhat rare neurological condition called Sturge-Weber Syndrome that involved a port wine stain on the right side of her face. She had some developmental delays as a young child and was very quiet, and very sweet. Grammy used to take her to a hospital in Pittsburgh every week, riding on a street car, for whatever treatment was available at the time. She became a nurse's aide at the Shriner's hospital for Crippled Children in Pittsburgh, where she also lived until she retired and moved back to The Aunt Farm to help care for her parents. The children there absolutely loved her.

Other non-resident aunts included Aunt Mainie (Marion) who lived on the shores of The Lake of Egypt in Southern Illinois with her husband, Uncle Stacey and Aunt Lo-Lo (Lois), a retired nurse anesthetist who lived a few miles away in New Kensington, but often hung out at the Aunt Farm. Aunt Marion and Uncle Stacey's home was the location of some major fun times. My mother's nickname was Snooks.

I lay on the porch swing on a warm fall day in 1982, almost asleep. Life was miserable, school was a bore, and I was too tired to even try and keep up with the conversation inside. It was a dark, nondescript type of day; not raining and not sunny, not cold and not hot.

A shadow fell across my face, as if someone had stepped between me and the sky at the end of the porch.

I opened my eyes, but there was nothing there.

Then I smelled it again: the roses. I stood up and walked around the house to the back yard where the old kitchen garden used to be. Grammy's quince tree stood there bare and scratching at the sky. Beside it, was the rose bush. Due to the mild weather, it still had a few stunted blooms. Usually a blush pink, the leftover blooms were curled and tinged with brown. Yet, the fragrance of roses filled the air.

Off in the distance somewhere, a church bell began to ring. I heard it many times before. I always wondered if it was ringing for a funeral. It seemed to grow louder and then fade as the wind gusted and fell. Out of the corner of my eye, I saw something move towards the kitchen door but when I turned to look, there was nothing there. I walked back around the house and went inside.

Why was it that time seemed to have forgotten that house? Places can remember people – it wasn't the first time I'd sensed that. My grandmother's belongings were still there even though she'd been dead for 10 years. Her presence seemed to saturate the rooms. I half expected to look up from the kitchen table and see her walk in.

Aunt Gerk was in the little lean to of a kitchen, reaching for a fresh can of coffee on the top shelf of the pantry. All the cousins hung out at the Aunt Farm. They went through coffee faster than the local diner. I poured myself a cup from the carafe and opened the fridge to get some milk. Inside the refrigerator, right next to the butter drawer, sat Grammy's prescriptions in dark amber bottles. They'd always been there, as long as I could remember, but I never had much cause to notice them before.

"What was Grammy like?" I asked. "I mean, what was she really like? I remember her, but she was so old then."

"I'm surprised you remember her at all," said Aunt Gerk. "How old were you when she died? Two maybe?"

Aunt Gerk wiped her hands on a damp dish towel, and sat down at the dining room table with a cup of coffee for herself. I followed. "What exactly do you remember?"

"Well, I remember her lying in a hospital bed over in the corner of the living room. And I remember her funeral, or at least at the funeral home. It was in the evening. Dwight, Ronnie - all those guys - were there, standing in a circle, talking, wearing suits and ties. I remember her lying in her coffin, too. It had a pink satin lining. She had on a pink nightgown with a spray of violets on her wrist. I wanted to touch her. Mom held me up so I could. I touched her hand. It was cold."

"It amazes me that you remember so much. And you are absolutely right. When you were born she was bedridden and had Alzheimer's. I don't even think she could talk."

"So what was she really like? When she was herself?"

"She was a proper Victorian lady. She never went out without her hat and kid leather gloves. But she liked to go out, and liked to travel. She went to New York City once when she won the grand prize in a sewing contest."

She smiled at that remembrance, and took a cigarette out of her gold mesh cigarette holder. Taping it gently on the table, before lighting it, she went on. "But she usually traveled nearby. Anytime somebody was sick or needed help, she would go hop on a street car and be knocking on the door with a pot full of chicken soup under her arm. She was always involved with the church, the same little church she went to all during her childhood, that little Pine Creek Presbyterian. She was close to her sisters and to her mother, even though she spent a good bit of her childhood away from them. They used to meet at the old Jenkins Arcade in downtown Pittsburgh."

"Why didn't she live with her family?"

"Oh, don't you remember hearing about her father? He was killed in an accident when she was ten."

I nodded. I did remember that story. I'd just never really thought about its implications on her life.

"They lost their home after that. Her mother couldn't support the kids working as a schoolmistress, so the kids all went to live with aunts and uncles. I guess after that, she wasn't afraid of much, except maybe that Pap would die. Maybe that's why she reached out to people who were alone or in trouble for some reason."

I sat there and listened, filled with something like grief, and watched the cigarette smoke drift around the round chandelier and curl up towards the little gold flecks embedded in the ceiling tiles.

"And you know," Aunt Gerk went on, as if in her own reverie, "even when she was senile, for the longest time up until she had that stroke, she was still herself. She was never at a loss for something to say, kind of like Aunt Biggie. I guess Biggie gets that from her. I remember once, Pap walked into the room and she told him that she and Aunt Lean - that was her sister - were meetin' so-and-so and going ice skating down at the mill pond, and asked him if he wanted to go along. Now his mind was still clear, so he kind of looked at her suspicious like, and said no thanks. All the people she was talking about were long dead. Later that day, to tease her, he asked her if she had a good time skating. She put her hands on her hips, looked over at him and said 'Yes! We had a very good time, so aren't you sorry you didn't come?'"

And that, I realized, was it. It was the essence of her. There was something in her. Something that in spite of all the death, the heartbreak, my grandfather's failures, and people starving all around her during the Great Depression, caused her to rise like a phoenix from the ashes. And that's what I wanted to be, instead of an awkward, homely looking 12- year- old kid with a bad past and an unpromising future, lost and browsing through time like an old lady at death's doorstep who goes ice skating with long dead childhood companions.

A thought began like a little itch. Did all these little weird things, unexplainable emotions, mean I was going crazy?

"I have dreams about her sometimes, that are so real," I admitted. "I swear if we drove by the house, she'd be sitting on the porch. It's almost as if I can't believe she's gone. Sometimes that feeling lasts for days." I pulled a dimpled paper napkin out of the holder on the lazy Susan in the middle of the table and daubed my eyes with it. "Is that weird? To miss somebody you never really knew?"

Aunt Gerk turned her coffee cup around on the little plastic coaster, and ran her fingernail over a spot on the tablecloth. "Not really. Dreams can seem pretty real sometimes. But I'll tell you what.

Come on upstairs. I have something to give you that I think you'll like."

I followed her upstairs to the master bedroom, and sat on the massive Empire Revival bed. It was once my grandparents' bed. The furniture had been in the family for eons. We all had warm memories of climbing up on the big scrolls at either end and jumping off.

Aunt Gerk opened one of the hidden closets under the eaves, and pulled out a wooden box. Dust swirled in the air.

"I have some old jewelry," she explained. "There's this necklace. It was Grammy's. It's made from different kinds of seeds, see?" She held it up under the light. "It came from Florida. Uncle Lawrence brought it back for her when he went on a trip down there. It was one of her favorite pieces of jewelry. You can have it because I know you'll appreciate it."

I put it on and looked in the mirror of the antique dresser. There was something comforting about it. And again, I smelled the roses.

"Do you smell something like ...roses?" I asked.

"No. But if you do, it's probably this." She handed me an old bottle of rose water was sitting on the dresser. I squirted some out and rubbed my hands together. Yes! That was it. That was the smell. But where did it come from all those other times? I looked down at the dresser and noticed a clean circle in a layer of dust. Had the rosewater been hers? Like the prescription bottles, had it been sitting there for ten years?

Little did I know until many years later, but the seed in the center of the necklace had an uncanny connection to everything I was experiencing. It is an African Dream Bean – an herb used by indigenous shamans in Africa to contact ancestral spirits. Also called Sea Beans, they can travel far and wide by floating in the ocean and often wash up on beaches in Florida.

✳✳✳

Not long after that I was lying on my bed, feeling half awake, wearing the necklace and holding the dream bean out in front of me, examining it. Grammy walked into my room, just as normal and natural as you please. I should have been terrified but I wasn't, just surprised. Before I could say anything she put her finger to her lips, and motioned *shhhh*. She gestured for me to follow her. I did and she led me into my parents' bedroom. She pushed open the closet door and I saw a white coffin shaped box, with a baby lying in it, apparently sleeping – or dead. Seeing this, I startled awake. It was a dream after all but it seemed very real! All of the details of my bedroom, the hallway, and my parents' bedroom were spot on, unlike regular dreams where things don't look exactly like they do in real life.

It was late morning on a Saturday. Still feeling rather spacy, I went into my parents' room and looked in the closet, my heart pounding in my chest. There was no white coffin and no dead baby of course, and that made me feel a little saner.

I went downstairs and found my parents sitting around the kitchen table reading the newspaper.

"Boy, I just had a weird dream," I said.

My mother put the paper down. "What was it?"

"Grammy showed up at the foot of my bed, took me into your room, and showed me a dead baby in a white coffin inside of your closet! How weird is that?"

My dad coughed and got up to get a napkin to wipe up his spilled coffee. My mother blanched. I'd just hit a nerve, but how?

"Yeah, that's weird, all right," she said.

"But what does it mean?"

"What am I, a dream interpreter? Damned if I know. Dreams are pretty strange sometimes. What did you watch on TV last night?"

"Nothing with a dead baby in it if that's what you're implying. You really have no idea what it means?"

"No – sorry I don't. It's your dream, so only you know what it really means."

No matter how I approached it, they were totally evasive. It seemed like since that day up at the bridge, we made a permanent home in the land of 'there's-something-you're-not-telling-me'. I was tired of feeling like I was the only one who didn't get the joke, and the jokes were not funny either.

***

Our English class had been in the library for several weeks that fall, and during that time, I found a ton of interesting books. One of them I never expected to find in the library of the junior high school – it was a book on how to fly an airplane. I don't remember exactly how I came across it, but I checked it out immediately. Another idea! I read it in one or two sittings and learned that there was no age requirement to fly an airplane. What an amazing loophole! This might yet turn into a way to get to California!

I took the book home and showed it to my dad, hinting around that maybe this was something do-able? One evening that fall, before it got cold but after most of the leaves had come down, my dad was full of surprises.

"I called the Leechburg airport," he explained, "and they do give flying lessons. Twenty bucks per pop."

I sat breathless, waiting for him to continue.

"You have one scheduled for this Saturday." As I hopped up and down, he added cautiously, "We'll see after that. But I'm willing to let you try it. Consider it a belated birthday present."

"So where is this Leechburg airport?" Every time we went to the airport, we went to the one outside of Pittsburgh where The Red Winds restaurant was. I loved that place! We only ever ate in there once but it was the best restaurant experience of my life that far, and I tried to talk them into going back every single time we went to the airport. I had no idea there was an airport near home.

"It's not IN Leechburg obviously," he explained. "It's up above Leechburg. Closer to Vandergrift, out in Parks Township. It's only for small private planes. It's too small for commercial jets so they don't land there. That's why you've never heard of it."

The warm spell persisted but the day of my flying lesson was hazy. My blue windbreaker pressing against me in the breeze, I stood between a two seater Cessna aircraft and the flying instructor- a younger thin guy wearing a wool plaid shirt - as he completed the pre-flight check. He explained each step as we went along. I had no trouble at all following this, as I'd read and re-read the book from the library. I was beyond prepared.

The airport had a gravel driveway and parking area, with a large hanger with a checkerboard roof and a house on one side, and another hanger on the other side. The runways were grass. A group of men my dad's age – most likely WW II veterans like him – hung out outside of the offices by the hanger and watched us with mild amusement. I am sure they thought the idea of a woman – much less a girl – getting a flight lesson was equal parts of funny and ridiculous.

Next thing I knew I was headed down the grass runway going 70 mph and steering with my feet! I made a successful takeoff (with assistance). and then the instructor asked me, "where would you like to go?"

California? Probably not the first time up, but I did have a reasonable idea.

"Do you know where Harwick is?" I asked.

"Sure. That isn't far. We can fly over Harwick if you like. The easiest way to navigate is to find a road and follow it," he explained. "So head southwest and we'll look for Route 28."

It was disorienting to try to navigate looking down on everything. Up that high, the sunlight seemed stronger and the landscape appeared much more flat. We flew over my own neighborhood, and soon after the double lines of Route 28 appeared in the distance.

There were a lot of things about the Aunt Farm that didn't seem to make sense as I got older and thought about things more. For as long as I can remember we'd gone for walks in the woods to this place everyone called "The Big Creek." Or I should say "crick" because in Western Pennsylvania we don't have creeks, we have "cricks", even if it is spelled exactly the same way.

The Little Creek ran around the property at the bottom of the hilly front yard, then over to the neighbor Stella's house where it fed a small pond in her back yard. The Big Creek was a bit of a walk. The driveway continued past the Aunt Farm and down the hill, where the ruins of an old mine building sat off to one side. I could remember this building when it was still standing, with its windows full of spider webs. During our walks, we went down this road and across the little creek at the bottom, then followed a dirt path through the woods that was used by dirt bikes during nice weather. Aunt Gerk said that Duquesne Light – the company that owned both the mine and power plant – maintained the dirt road. Every spring, the huge puddles in this road were filled to overflowing with tadpoles. Eventually, that dirt road met up with another dirt road at a T in the woods. We would turn and walk to the left and this dirt road went all the way around The Big Creek. There was also a giant electrical tower next to it. We were forbidden to succumb to its siren call as the world's ultimate set of monkey bars. "You'll get electrocuted!" they said. Since that didn't sound like fun at all, we stayed away from it. A tall chain link fence surrounded the entire complex but was usually open at one or more gates. If it was not, the fence was pretty easy to climb over.

The next hill over from that one, separating the Aunt Farm from the river and New Kensington on the other bank, was Bouquet Hill. We were afraid to cross the power line run and climb up Bouquet Hill because the old people said that Henry Bouquet's army, during the French and Indian War, had a skirmish there with the Indians and now the hill was haunted by the British and Native American soldiers who were buried on it.

The Big Creek was scary in a fun way. Sometimes it was full of water and looked like a huge lake. Sometimes the water was black with scum on top, and sometimes there were only puddles on the bottom. Other times it was dry and the bottom was covered with a black sand like substance called fly ash. The dirt bikes drove all over it and up and down its banks when it was empty, but we were forbidden from going down in there. My mother said the fly ash was unstable and swallowed a steam shovel a long time ago – the implication being it could also swallow you. Dad said the fly ash came from the power plant, that they used to just put it out the smoke stack and it would rain down on everything like black snow. The EPA banned that practice so now it was pumped up to The Big Creek in the giant pipes which snaked around all over. At one end of the Big Creek was an earthen dam that you could walk across. On the other side of the dam was a series of concrete troughs that the water flowed out through, and there was a really cool 1950's bicycle rusting away at the bottom of one of them.

I recognized the New Kensington Bridge from the air. The bridge crossed the Allegheny River right next to the old ALCOA plant where Dad originally used to work. Many years abandoned even then, it still sits there with its broken windows and deteriorating brickwork. When I was little, New Kensington was a really nice town and we often went shopping there. The New Ken mafia controlled it in those days and they didn't suffer street crimes of any sort. There was a story about a guy who dared to rob a gas station and was found the next day floating face down in the river. When the mills closed down, people no longer had money to gamble and party. Between that and increased attention from the FBI, the mob faded away and New Ken became overrun with drug dealers.

Back in the day though, there were many great places to shop. There was Hart's Department Store that still had a Victorian era brass pneumatic tube system for sending change and receipts around to different checkout counters in the store. I remember it from being in the shoe department in the basement. They would put the receipt and your money in the tube and fire it off to the main register, and a few minutes later it would come back with your change. Hart's also had a bridal department that I loved to look through. Dad bought most of his shoes at Miller's, and there were several jewelry stores and a very fancy, old, art deco style movie theatre with balconies. There were also nightclubs run by the mafia, but I was never inside any of those. I remember looking in the doorway of one once, fascinated, until my mother grabbed my arm and whisked me away scolding,

"That's a bar! You can't go in there! There are men in there!" But I could totally picture the Aunt Farm Aunts in there during their younger days, drinking highballs, smoking long skinny cigarettes and dancing The Charleston.

Next to New Ken along the river was Arnold. There used to be a soda pop place in Arnold where we went to buy pop in dark green glass bottles. You returned the bottles when you bought more pop and got a few cents credit for them. The black cherry was my favorite. Next to it was the old Chambers Glass Works. An old abandoned relic even in the 1970's, it sat eerily along the river with its crumbling brick walls and old smoke stacks forebodingly dark against the sky.

"There's something I want to see," I said. The Duquesne Light power plant's white banded smoke stack appeared on the horizon. "It's near that plant. It's always been called The Big Creek but I don't know what it really is. I thought maybe we could tell from the air." A few minutes later I spotted it. Usually so foreboding, it looked like a big mud puddle. "There it is!"

"Wow, that is interesting," said the flight instructor. "I don't know what it is either, but I can tell you what those two smaller orange ponds nearby are. They're mine drainage treatment ponds. There must be an abandoned coal mine here. The water that runs out of them is polluted and acidic, and kills all the fish in the river. So they have been building treatment ponds like those to clean up the water before it goes in the river. Usually they are on top of the deepest part of the mine."

"That would be the Harwick Mine," I said. My mother sometimes talks about it. I remember driving through the buildings when I was little, I guess because my Dad wanted to check them out.

The concrete waterways let to the creek at the bottom of the valley and the two smaller orange ponds. A couple fly ash foothills lay in front of them which I assumed is why I never noticed them from the road. Directly across the street from the orange ponds was the Duquesne Light plant itself. Usually hidden behind its tall solid fence, I could see it was actually surrounded by many black piles of coal and probably more ash, chutes, and heavy equipment.

"It must be the Harwick mine," I said. "I knew it was around here somewhere. There used to be a railroad that belonged to it, that crossed the road down the hill from my aunts' house. We used to see trains there occasionally when I was really little, and they always told me the railroad was part of the Harwick mine."

Having seen all that, I followed the dirt road quite easily to the Aunt Farm and circled the house several times. I saw the aunts and several people in the yard. I waved and they waved back.

On the way back, he explained to me more about how the private pilot license process worked. The unfortunate part was that in order to get the license, you had to fly solo first. You could not fly solo until you were sixteen. So, once again my plan for running away from home flopped.

***

"We aren't buying anything else but a coat!" warned my mother. We were on our way to JC Penney in Lower Burrell. I sat in the passenger seat staring out the window at the fading twilight. It was nearly Thanksgiving, hence the need for a new coat. I was shocked to discover how much I'd grown when I tried to put on my old winter coat and couldn't even button it. The clouds near the horizon were still slightly pinkish orange, but the stars were beginning to come out.

JC Penney was part of a large two store strip mall, the other store being Montgomery Ward. Across the street, catty corner from the first intersection was the Hillcrest Plaza, the closest shopping to the rural area we lived in those days. It had more stores and was L-shaped. At one time JC Penney's had been in that strip mall where Hill's was by that time. Grant's occupied JC Penney's current location next to Montgomery Ward. We bought my first bicycle at Grant's. They had an old fashioned lunch counter in the back with a soda fountain, were you could get a real cherry Coke made with Coke and cherry syrup.

Also in Hillcrest was an Isaly's where we got iced cream and chipped ham, Thrift Drug, Endicott Johnson shoes, Radio Shack, Klingensmith's Hardware, Kroger's Grocery Store, and that mecca of teeny bopper clothes that Kris and I loved – Fashion Factory.

That was the year the stars became my new friends. I had a lot of nightmares in those days. Most of them were not worth writing down and many forgotten almost upon awakening. All that usually remained was the fear and panic. I'd lie in bed, hypervigilant, and listen for any sound that might mean that man had come back to get me. A car door slamming outside. A footstep on the stairs. The rattling of a doorknob. Regular night sounds at home took on a sinister meaning and I found a creative way to deal with it, thanks to a popular song. That song was "Up on A Roof" by James Taylor. Humm. We have a roof, right?

I checked it carefully from every angle of the yard and from the road. The place where the two halves of the split level house met, right below the chimney, was completely invisible from the ground. I could climb up the front porch railing and onto the roof quite easily. I would often go up there at night when I woke up terrified, sleeping bag in tow as the nights cooled off. Lying up there, knowing I was completely hidden, I could finally relax.

That is when I noticed the stars! There were far fewer shopping centers and lights in those days, and no streetlights, so they were very bright and clear. I could see the Milky Way and make out The Big Dipper. I'd looked up constellations in the encyclopedia but the illustrations of them were not very helpful, mostly being mythical figures drawn over groups of stars that were nearly impossible to find once outside. Even so, there were plenty of interesting articles on stars and astronomy that I read during those dark fall evenings. I made a mental note to hunt for more astronomy books at the library.

My reverie was interrupted by our arrival at JC Penney's. I followed my parents into the racks of coats.

"What kind of coat do you want?" Mom asked.

"I don't know. Something mature."

They exchanged a tired look. "Well, that depends on what your definition of 'mature' is. When I buy a coat, I worry about whether or not it will keep me warm."

That reminded me of a story about my mom that I'd heard at the Aunt Farm once, about how her mother gave her five dollars, which was then a lot of money and told her to go buy herself a party dress for her school dance. She came home with a new winter coat instead, having decided the party dress would only be worn once but she could wear the coat all winter. That was so Mom! I, on the other hand, would have been happy to freeze all winter - if that's what it took - to have the party dress.

"What kind of coat is *that*!" I gushed, pointing to a mannequin behind her. It reminded me of the coats from the 1940's I'd seen on TV.

"It's a princess coat." She picked up the price tag. "Wool. It's that burgundy rust color that looks so good on you. I bet it would match that hat you nagged me into buying. But it's not cheap, and not very practical for school. Let's look around and make sure there isn't something else you like that costs less money."

But I wasn't interested – I'd chosen! I had an aptitude for walking into a store and going directly to what I wanted. My mother claimed it was also always the most expensive thing in the store. It didn't matter that it was the first coat I tried on, come hell or high water I was going home with it regardless of how many others she made me try on.

"How about this one?"

"Too boxy."

"But it would be really warm." I shook my head.

"What about this?"

"That is the ugliest color I have ever seen." She sighed and hung it back up.

"She's picked out a coat, so let's go," said Dad, looking extremely bored.

"Just hold on a minute! We should at least look through the rest of them!"

I turned and picked up the princess coat, admiring its softness. Smiling, I slipped it on again, buttoning it up and admiring it in the mirror, turning from side to side. Then a thought occurred to me and I spun around.

"Hey Mom, don't you have a scarf that will match this?" But my mother was gone! And so was my dad! Confused, I looked around and saw nothing but rows and rows of coats. I had been coming to this store since I was born, but now it looked unfamiliar and threatening. Where could they have gone in such a short length of time? Why would they leave me here? I couldn't even remember where the exit was. I glanced around, frantic. But all I saw was other people, people who were not my parents, people I did not know!

"MOM!" I screamed, the shrill sound of my voice piercing the hushed atmosphere of the store. People turned and stared. "WHERE ARE YOU?!" I was about to panic and run in any direction when she appeared out of nowhere.

"SHHHH! Settle down! I was just on the other side of the coat rack, for Pete's sake! Stop yelling! You know how it embarrasses your father when you make a scene!"

"Why did you leave me here?"

"I didn't leave you anywhere! I was only 10 feet away! You can't seriously believe that we would leave you in a store!"

"Look," said Dad. "Just buy the goddamn coat!"

"Let me handle this!"

"This is a crock of shit," he observed.

She turned to me. "Come on. We'll just buy that one if you insist. Ugh! I'm never going shopping with you again!"

I sobbed as my father turned deep red and did his best to look like he didn't know us while we went through the check- out line. The argument continued in the car.

"You have a bad attitude. I don't know why you act like that every time we take you anywhere!"

"Act like what?"

"Infantile!"

"How dare you call me infantile? You abandoned me in the store!"

He glared at me in the rear view mirror. "If you don't settle down, I'm gonna pull over!"

"Oh for God's sake, just shut up and drive!" said my mother. "I thought I told you to let me handle it? You're making her worse!" She crossed her arms across her chest and addressed me in a defeated tone. "I've had it with you. I'm sick of being screamed at, sick of you always having to have your own way, sick of listening to how mature you are and then putting up with ... this! You were acting like a two- year- old in there! Why can't you just act like an adult?"

By the time we got home, the icy silence was so thick you could cut it with a knife. I took my coat and slunk away to my room. She was putting the dishes away. I could hear pots and pans banging in the kitchen, as I lay on my bed in the dark. After a while, I decided to go down to the kitchen to see if things had blown over. My mother got mad at me fairly often, but this somehow seemed different.

As I approached the kitchen doorway I noticed the jar sitting empty on the counter. That year in seventh grade I had Earth and Space science. This dovetailed nicely with my newfound interest in astronomy. We had been studying crystals that nine week grading period, so my mother and I went to the Carnegie Museum's Hall of Geology, got all interested in the subject, and grew a huge boric acid crystal as a special project for science class.

"Where's the crystal?"

She turned to me, calm, malevolent. "I broke it up into a million pieces and washed it down the drain."

I stared in horror at the empty jar. It seemed that the fate of the crystal had become the fate of whatever intimacy had been built between us over the last month and a half of geology immersion.

"But, that was my science project ...," I finally stammered. She turned her back to me and continued cleaning. "I'm going to lose 50 extra credit points!" I wailed.

Like a tidal wave, the madness swept all clear thought from my mind. I turned and ran out the front door. It started snowing at some point after we arrived home from JC Penney and the grass had a light dusting. Behind me I heard the lock click. It dawned on me that I was standing in snow in my bare feet. The world was crystal clear, like ice, but I was not. I pounded on the door with both fists.

"You let me in! I don't have any shoes on! OPEN UP!"

The door sprang open and she stood there, one hand on the door, the other on her hip, her eyes snapping. I stumbled in, screaming, and gasping for breath. Knickknacks on the shelf by the door smashed on the floor as she tried to restrain me.

"Just ... hold ... still ... you're hyperventilating! If you lie still ... I'll get a paper bag .. for you to breathe into!"

Having her try to put a paper back in front of my face only served to heighten the sensation of being unable to breathe, but I was too weak to get away from her. I felt prickly sensations all over my face and passed out.

I awakened later in my darkened bedroom, a cool wash cloth across my forehead. The door was open and a few rays of light from the bathroom penetrated the darkness. My temples throbbed and I was too weak to get up. Downstairs, my parents were arguing in hushed tones.

"This is getting ridiculous!" Dad observed.

"I'm sure you remember what it was like with teenagers."

"This is more than just a teenager problem! We need to do something."

"Like what?" she spat.

"I don't know! But *something* has to be done! Life is getting pretty unbearable around here and I'm sick of all the screaming and fighting going on between you two."

✳✳✳

Thankfully, we did do more than just screaming and fighting that year. I had fallen in the habit of playing around on an old upright grand piano in the church basement. In truth, I'd been noodling around on pianos for a long time, or at least since the first time I'd seen a grand piano up close. During his graduate student years at Ohio State University, my brother Bob rented a room from a guy who inherited a Victorian house full of furniture from his grandmother. I remember walking into that house on the first visit and thinking I want a house exactly like this when I grow up! It was a brick Queen Anne with a turret. The grand piano was nestled into the turret with its long lace curtained windows. I spent a lot of time practicing on that piano.

In this case, it came to the attention of someone at church at the right time as they were planning to remodel the basement and needed to get rid of a lot of junk, including this piano. So not long after on a decently warm day, the piano arrived on our back patio strapped to somebody's truck, and was wheeled into the TV Room. Mom complained that this big ugly piano ruined her TV room – she had to move the furniture around to fit it in. Nevertheless, she presented me with a big box of old piano music a day or so later.

"Wow, where did you get all this?" I asked. She had it with her when she came home from work that day.

"The Aunt Farm."

"Really? Why would they have piano music at the Aunt Farm?"

"Because we used to have a piano. It's long gone – Pap chopped it up and made it into a table many years ago."

"What? Why?"

"Because it was taking up half the living room, they were tired of it, and nobody else wanted it. It was really old, probably from the Civil War. It was a Victorian square piano. My mother inherited it from Aunt Mary Arthur who lived down in the North Side. She was very wealthy. I think Mom got the entire music room. There were huge jardinières and big fancy oil lamps. Those went to the Goodwill years ago."

I cringed. I would have loved to have had that stuff!

"Who played?"

"All of us, at least a little bit. My Dad was pretty good. I could play a little as could most of my sisters. There wasn't any TV back then so you had to provide your own entertainment. I preferred the player pianos but we didn't have one; instead we had that old thing. The player pianos were much more fun. It seemed like everyone had a player piano back then, just not us!"

Interestingly, our freebie piano was once a player piano, but someone had removed the player mechanism from it. Still, it was huge and carved all over, went almost to the ceiling. While admittedly it was somewhat ugly, it did have an amazing sound. The TV room had good acoustics, so between the two factors people in the living room would ask, "What the hell do you have down there, a concert grand or something?"

After she went upstairs, I sat down with the box on the brown plaid 1970's sofa and went through it. Most of it was from the 1890's through 1910's, with a couple books of cool 1920's jazz and big band era favorites. There were also a couple of handwritten notebooks that had apparently belonged to my grandfather, full of songs that he apparently liked, his shaped note singing cheat sheet, and detailed plans for making your own violin. In the back were his cheater music theory notes, which came in handy as I didn't know the bass clef.

Yet, what I was most drawn to was the old book of Beethoven piano sonatas. I worked my way through Book One of the piano method book and then got bored, so I moved on to them. It took some time to learn them but a strange thing happened. As I figured out each measure it seemed familiar, and I knew right away how it should sound. Or at least – how I thought it should sound. Zero to playing "Moonlight Sonata" from memory took a total of three months. I remember this because my father's sister – my Aunt Mary and her husband, Uncle Harold – visited shortly after the piano took up residence. They heard me playing *Chopsticks*. They returned for another visit three months later and I was playing songs written by Beethoven, which I played repeatedly, along with a couple of ragtime favorites, until my parents were ready to shoot themselves.

Uncle Harold told them they should send me to Julliard. My mother, horrified, informed him they would do no such thing. She felt people who studied music in college ended up working at McDonald's. They wanted me to be able to support myself!

Funny thing was, I could play these pieces like that as long as I kept my mind completely blank. I had to memorize them first. If I let any thoughts, words, or self-reflection enter my mind I would mess up, lose my place, and have to start over. This was very limiting as far as playing piano for anything other than my own edification was concerned – any opportunities at school or in the community required the ability to sight read, which I could not do.

CHAPTER 7

May of 1982

Downstairs in the demi basement that went by the moniker of The TV Room (whether there was actually a TV in it or not), I searched the dusty bookshelves. It was the bookshelf of cast off books, old books - stuff my mother didn't read but didn't want to throw out. The upper shelves were full of old college textbooks my brothers and sister didn't want to haul all over the continent. I was the only one who read the hand me down textbooks, because the TV room was my space, and they were in my space. I liked being a smarty- pants. Reading college textbooks was one way to do that. But that night I was looking for something particular: a textbook entitled *Abnormal Psychology*.

I barricaded myself in my room and shook the dust bunnies off it. Was I going crazy? If I was then there had to be something I could do about it. There were psychologists and psychiatrists who dealt with that sort of thing, right? Problem was, I didn't think my parents would believe me. So first, I had to prove I was crazy.

Reading that book was one of life's "eureka!" experiences. I found terms that described exactly the things I was experiencing. Like anxiety. And a name for the big meltdowns: panic attacks. I dug a highlighter pen from my desk drawer, and drew a bright yellow line over all the things I experienced. Armed with my text book and enlightenment, I went to confront my mother.

I found her propped up in bed reading. My confidence bolstered by evidence, I stood next to the bed and announced, "I just came to tell you that I am mentally ill, and I need a psychologist."

Dropping her book to her lap, she looked at me with that oh-you've-got-to-be-me-kidding look.

"See?" I held out the book. "I have all of the symptoms indicated in yellow."

She took the book from me skeptically.

"And there's a name in there for those episodes I have: panic attacks."

A panic attack is a strange thing. I had one whenever I had a big fight with my mother. They felt a lot like being drowned only without the water.

"The only thing I can't figure out is whether I'm neurotic or psychotic, but the weight of evidence seems to favor neurotic."

Her face contorted into a look of amazement. "Oh for Pete's sake, you are NOT psychotic! When you're psychotic, you don't think you need help; you think everybody else needs help. As far as neurotic, that may be, but I doubt it. And I know that you've been having panic attacks."

"What? You knew what they were all along, and you never TOLD me?"

"Well, no. I didn't see what good it would do. I thought it would make it worse. When people start to study psychology," she handed the book back to me, "they read about these symptoms, and start to think they have them all. Same thing when you study medicine. A little bit of knowledge can be a dangerous thing."

"So what exactly were you planning to do? Just let this go on forever?"

"No, I thought it might resolve itself. I was just waiting to see."

"Well it's not resolving itself, it's getting worse! You're legally obligated to obtain treatment for me when I'm ill. I need to see a psychologist!"

"I'll call the clinic in the morning and see, if that's what you want, but you're still not mentally ill."

"If that's what you think, then you're in denial!" I yelled, waiving the book at her. "I had a hallucination!"

She rolled her eyes. "You had an IM-agination."

"We'll just see about that."

"You're not mentally ill! You have these symptoms because of what happened to you last summer."

"How dare you!" I snapped. "It has nothing to do with that!"

"Well, I'm sorry if you don't like the truth."

"IF that were true, then how do you explain the panic attack I had in the summer before fifth grade?" She looked surprised, as if she hadn't thought of that before. "It's because of school!"

"I'll grant you that, I do remember it now. I still think that what happened last summer has something to do with it, and no matter how much you stamp your foot, you won't convince me otherwise. I will, however, try to get you an appointment with somebody if that's what you want."

Late that night, I woke up and went across the hall to the bathroom. Downstairs, I heard my parents having an intense conversation in hushed tones.

"I saw that guy when I was coming home from work today," my mother said to my father. "Don't forget – I know what he looks like. I saw him myself that day we picked up her birthday cake down in Leechburg! He was parked right by the bridge, standing outside of the car, talking to another guy. I drove past by the time it dawned on me. So I thought to myself, I have a pair of surgical scissors in my pocket. I'll kill the son of a bitch! I slammed on my brakes and I threw the car in reverse, started backing up. But by the time I got turned around he sped off across that bridge and there was no way I was gonna catch him."

***

That year on Memorial Day weekend, Aunt Gerk promised to take me around to some of the cemeteries where our ancestors were buried. We turned off the main road and eased through a small gate and wound around the fields of graves and up a small hill.

"This is the Covenanter Cemetery," she explained as she got the buckets, spades, and flowers out of the trunk. She handed me a bucket. "Here. Go over to the pump and get some water. We'll be right over there." She pointed to the old Covenanter section, off in a far corner. It was bordered on two sides by a dark forest of gnarled and twisted trees.

I took the bucket and started up over the hill, swinging it from side to side and humming some old tune suddenly come into my head, *there's a hole in the bucket, dear Liza dear Liza. There's a hole in the bucket, dear Liza a hole.* And there it was: the old pump. So this was where the Covenanter church was. I remembered this spigot. I drank water from it once, a long time ago, on one of these missions. It made me sicker than hell. Cemetery water. Ugh!

I filled the bucket and started back.

"Hey! Where's the water?" called my mother.

By the time I got down there, they already had flowers planted. "Who's that? Susan Grant Black?" I asked.

"Your great-grandmother. What I remember most about her is that she was a strong woman. She had 13 children, including a set of triplets. Raising children was her vocation, she used to say. We all called her Mammy. She was a midwife. She had an unbelievable green thumb. Boy, did she have a steel rod in her back; even her adult sons deferred to her. She lived on top of The Hill in that little white house."

I remembered her now. I had dreams about her when I was really little. The dreams were always in a cemetery, but not a normal one like we were in just then. The stones were arranged in concentric circles. I remembered a National Geographic magazine arriving one day, during elementary school, with a picture of Stonehenge on the front. It looked a lot like Susan Grant Black's cemetery!

"She was what was sometimes called an Appalachian Magic Granny," Aunt Gerk continued.

"Oh yeah," said Aunt Biggie. "She had the biggest green thumb of anyone I ever knew! She could grow anything and knew what herbs to take to cure diseases."

"Oh and, you know the rose bush in the back yard – the pink one?" asked Aunt Gerk. "That came from her garden. The hill used to be full of them. She had a huge hedge of them running along the road. They're a well-known old fashioned rose called Seven Sisters. There's still some out there – the big one back by the quince tree is a Seven Sisters rose. Our mother loved them too. Maybe because she had seven daughters?" So that was the rose bush I remembered from last fall, that was blooming at the wrong time!

"Odd symbolism, that," said my mother. "It always made me think of The Pleiades. It's a constellation – or more of as star cluster inside of a constellation. It comes up in the evening now since its spring – I can show it to you. In Greek mythology the Pleiades were The Seven Sisters – daughters of Atlas and Pleione. They were pursued for seven years by Orion the Hunter – who you can also see as a constellation nearby - until Zeus rescued them and put them in the sky as constellations. Eventually, Orion was put there too, and he's still chasing after them."

"We owned the entire hill back then, have since shortly after the Civil War. Our aunts and uncles all lived on The Hill too," said Aunt Gerk. That was how the older generation knew the Aunt Farm: The Hill.

Aunt Margie knelt beside the grave of her sister Emily who died in 1938, patting a petunia firmly into place. The well-kept grass of the cemetery shuddered around her in the spring breeze. Mar never really said much, but she was always there.

We did Grammy and Pap's graves last. As I sat there looking at the weather worn granite, it seemed that everything that ever mattered in my family happened before I was born. It seemed that instead of real memories my childhood was made up of stories. I missed them, these people I never met when they were alive. For some reason the sight of Emily's lonely gravestone made me cry and I could not stop. I sat there and bawled and hyperventilated and nothing anyone could say even made a dent.

"Oh, there's nothing to cry about," said Aunt Gerk, patting me on the back. "We always have such fun when we do this. Don't think about them being gone, think about how nice it is that they are remembered."

While my mother and the aunts were in the kitchen getting dinner ready, I went upstairs for a few moments of quiet to think. The window of the master bedroom was open. The sheer curtains fluttered in the evening breeze and I could smell fresh cut grass. I sat down on the Empire bed, remembering how, as kids, my cousins and I would hang out on this bed, and how we would hide inside the giant armoire which sat next to the attic door. It had been a long time since I was in the attic. Maybe there was a clue up there!

I crept up the steep and curving attic stairs, hesitating each time an old board squeaked in protest. The attic window was open to let out heat. Dust and cobwebs covered piles of articles pushed back under the eaves and old clothes in plastic covers hung from poles. Glimpses of the carved arms and legs of more old furniture peeped out from under boxes and paper. It had always been my fantasy to find old wedding gowns up here, with hoop skirts or bustles, dripping with faded lace. But dig as I might, all I could find were clothes from the 1940's – 1960's. Truly some of the worst polyester I've ever seen hung up there. But every row of clothes I penetrated revealed yet another, and so I kept looking.

In the corner by the stairs, on top of a pile of books, lay an antique baby doll. His white eyelet gown was smudged with dust and his baby bonnet drooped carelessly from the ribbons around his neck. His eyes were closed. It reminded me of the baby in my dream, the tiny dead baby I saw lying in a coffin. I picked him up, and his eyes slowly opened, their blue brilliance obscured by neglect. I hadn't realized how much time had passed until I was startled to hear my named being called from downstairs.

"I'm coming," I answered from the upstairs hall. "I'll be down as soon as I wash my hands!"

As I stood at the sink, I thought I heard something move and out of the corner of my eye saw a flash of grey. Drying my hands on a towel, I went back into the bedroom. There was nothing there. The smell of rose water hung in the air but it was cold – even though it was warm a few minutes earlier and hotter than hell in the attic. Then I noticed the portrait on the wall. It had always hung there but for some reason I never noticed it much until that day. It was of a young woman from Edwardian times, who looked kind of sad. I stood absorbed in the experience until the sound of my name being impatiently called from downstairs broke the spell.

Dinner sat steaming upon the table, a platter of fried chicken, a bowl of mashed potatoes, a gravy boat full of golden gravy. Aunt Gerk emerged from the kitchen carrying a bowl of cooked carrots in one mitted hand and a dish of homemade jam in the other, her sprigged apron damp and clinging to her blouse.

"What do you want to drink? We have homemade lemonade."

"Sounds great."

Soon everyone was gathered around the great paw footed table. They laughed and talked and told jokes, passing platters of food all around.

"Here, try some of these canned plums, they're delicious." The plums bubbled up from a china bowl in their rich purple juice. I took several out with the large serving spoon and dumped them in my dessert dish. Then I speared a whole one and popped it into my mouth.

"My mother made those", said Aunt Biggie. I froze in mid-chew. A chorus of laughter rang out.

"Well, she didn't make these ones! Do you really think I would serve 15 year old plums? "

"I didn't mean it that way! You always were such a brat!" said Aunt Biggie, somewhat insulted.

After dinner the sky was still light, so the majority of the party retired to the front porch. Through the dining room window I could see my mother and The Aardvark swinging on the porch swing, sipping lemonade and exchanging gossip with the rest of the crowd. Aunt Gerk was removing dishes from the table for Margie to wash.

"Who is that in the portrait in the bedroom upstairs?" I asked.

"Oh that is your Grammy's sister, Aunt Lean. She died before you were born."

Who didn't?

"Why did Emily die?" All I'd ever heard about her was that she died a long time ago.

Having removed the last dish, she sat down at the table with me. "Well, she got married, and not long after that she was going to have a baby. But it made her really sick – she couldn't eat anything and kept throwing up. Eventually she got pneumonia, and in those days there were no antibiotics, so she died. She was the first person in those new plots in Deer Creek, you know, and that is why they put your mother's baby there."

"WHAAT?" I demanded.

She looked surprised. "You don't know? I assumed that's what you were crying about."

"No! What baby?" I felt all the blood drain out of my head and thought I might faint.

"It happened long before you were born - I think it was in 1956." She sighed and lit her cigarette. "It was a still born baby – a girl – about three months premature. You mother went into labor too early. They went to the hospital but there was no heartbeat. The baby was born dead."

I swallowed hard and tried to remember to breathe. "What did she look like?"

"Like a normal baby, only a lot smaller. She didn't even have any fingernails yet."

"Did she have a name?"

"Well, not officially. The birth certificate just said 'Baby girl Mason'. But before she died your dad wanted to call her Rebecca." She took another drag on the cigarette. "There was no funeral. Your mother was still in the hospital, so your father and I went down to the funeral home and bought a little white coffin, and buried her with Emily."

"How does THAT work?"

"Well coffins are buried in concrete vaults underground. So they just open up the vault and the second coffin is laid on top of the first.

For the remainder of the evening, until the card game started, the adults sat outside on the porch. In the back of my mind I could not shake the feeling of unreality that hung over me. I had to check this out somehow. I had to confront my mother. To settle my mind, I walked down to the creek and sat on the hidden foundation of the old mine building. The creek murmured to itself while crickets sang, a large garden spider had spun her web among the overgrown weeds. I thought, and thought hard.

Not long after it first happened – and I had to admit to myself that the rape had been the beginning of it all – I'd had the dream where I died and was sent back. Which apparently never happened, but I was sick. While I was sick, my dead grandmother sat by my bed the whole time. I'd had a fever. I couldn't think straight and it was all very warm and comforting until I recovered enough to remember that she was dead. From that time on, I didn't see her, but often felt her presence. And I smelled rosewater when she was around. Why was this all happening? Did she tell me about the baby to prove she was real, so I couldn't go on thinking I was just imagining it?

It was almost dark when I returned to the porch. Lightening bugs winked from the deep shadows of overgrowth near the creek while a lone streetlight shone its meager light upon the driveway. It was the oldest street light I ever saw, with an exposed round bulb pointing down that was screwed into a little metal plate with edges like a pie crust. Bugs darted about, circling the little bulb. A gust of wind blew across the porch, slightly colder than before.

"Gonna rain tonight," someone predicted.

I was not dreaming and did not know what caused me to wake up that night, but I opened my eyes to see 11:11 on my old Radio Shack flip radio/alarm clock. Bright moonlight streamed into my room and the fragrance of rose water was heavy in the air. The window was open. Outside the wind sighed, and my lace curtains moved forward and then were sucked back against the screen. I heard some distant thunder.

"Are you there?" I whispered.

The curtains flew straight out from their rods as a powerful, chilly gust of wind whistled sharply through the window. As sudden as it came, the gust died down the curtains returned to their vertical position. I got out of bed and closed the window.

"I don't understand what you want," I told her. I couldn't see her but I knew she was there. "I believe you're real. Just don't scare the crap out of me, OK?" I was sitting in the dark talking to a ghost. I should have been scared out of my wits, but I wasn't.

***

The night was like molasses, thick and dark. I found myself standing on the road by the Aunt Farm. It was windy and cold, the clouds moving very fast across a bright moon. I could still see lots of stars, including the Pleiades, which seemed unusually bright. Everything was wet; a storm must have just passed through and it felt like another was not far behind. There were no lights on in any of the houses, apparently the storm knocked the power out. I hurried down the road to the Aunt Farm hoping my mother was there. In any case it was shelter.

I was stunned by what I saw when I came up the driveway. Discarded furniture and junk littered the yard. The steps to the front porch were gone. The house was dark and abandoned, its broken windows yawning in the blackness. I saw a flicker of light in the upstairs bedroom window. I watched, shivering, as the light moved towards the window. It was Grammy's ghost! Did she ever look ghostly with such pale skin and hollow eyes! Framed by the dark window, she was dressed entirely in flowing white and carried a single candle in her outstretched hands. She seemed to be pleading. I stood transfixed, terrorized and consumed. Then a sharp jerk on my arm startled me. I spun around and my mother was standing there.

"Come on! We have to get out of here now! We can stay at Stella's until the lights come back on."

We ran across the road as flashes of lightening cut through the darkness. The moon retreated into thick folds of clouds and faint, ominous rumbles came from the distance. Another storm was definitely on its way.

Stella's house all was dark except for two oil lamps that flickered and cast bizarre shadows on the walls. She set us up in an unused back bedroom with two sleeping bags for the night. One of the oil lamps stayed with us. The bridge down by the train tracks had been washed out by the storm, Stella told us. The phone was out, too. Before that happened, she'd called the electric company to report the power outage and was told that no repair trucks could make it into the area until the creek went down, hopefully sometime tomorrow. So ghost or no ghost, we were trapped.

"Did you see her in the window, back at the Aunt Farm?"

"No."

Somehow that answer was not convincing. "Really? Are you sure?"

"Don't worry", said my mother, "I'm sure we'll be able to get home tomorrow morning, somehow. Just try to get some sleep." She blew out the lamp as we lay down. I fell asleep but the storm kept waking me up. Several times I thought I heard crying outside. Then I was jolted awake.

"We have to get out of here!" my mother hissed. I looked out the window and there she was - the ghost, headed straight for Stella's house. The storm was gone but the wind was howling, and her white robes swooped out behind her, the candle in her hands piercing the darkness. My mother grabbed my hand and we were running again, out the other side of the house to another neighbor farther down the road. Off in the distance, I heard the whistle of a steam locomotive. We were about half way across the yard before the craziness of this situation dawned on me.

"Wait! Don't you see? We're in a dream! Nothing can happen to us here. Maybe we should just find out what she wants?"

"No!" cried my mother, pulling on my arm. A loud crash of thunder boomed directly overhead.

My eyes opened into pitch dark. I wasn't sure where I was! I rolled over and looked at the clock: 2:22AM. The room filled with the scent of rose water again.

The next morning, I shocked my mother by turning up for breakfast on time.

"I had a weird dream last night," I said.

"What was it? Not another nightmare, I hope."

"Well sorta ... I dunno."

She put a plate of scrambled eggs down in front of me and sat opposite. I stirred my tea.

"We were at the Aunt Farm."

"Who was?"

"Just you and me. It was all dark and stormy. Then Grammy's ghost showed up and started chasing us, and she was carrying this candle. Even though it was windy, it didn't blow out. You kept moving me, trying to escape her."

"Well that sounds like a nightmare to me. What do you suppose brought THAT on? It's not like the ones you usually have. Have you been reading that genealogy book or something?"

"No. But I think she's haunting me."

"Who?"

"Grammy."

"Why on Earth would she haunt you?"

"I don't know!

At that point we were interrupted by Dad. He hurried in and grabbed his aluminum lunch box from the counter. Mr. Ray had already picked up Kris's dad for work and was waiting out by the mailbox.

"See you tonight," he said as he gave my mother a quick peck goodbye. He seemed to know he was missing some weird conversation.

After he was gone, she took my empty plate and put it in the sink. "What makes you think anyone's haunting you?"

"Dreams like that one, and I keep smelling rose water at weird times, and I swear sometimes I can sense her. I can't see her though."

She turned from the sink and put her hand on her hip. "Are you sure you aren't just imagining this?" She had that I-don't-believe-you look. Then doubt spread across her face. "Well I'll tell you the same thing I told your cousin, Karen. A long time ago one Easter, we were at your Aunt Ruth's for Easter dinner. It was 1956 – before you were born. Your Uncle Grant and I were sitting in front of the fireplace and for some reason I can't remember, we all started talking about the worst way to die. Grant said he was most afraid of being burned to death. Not long after that we went home and Grant went off to the airport. He was leaving for a business trip. Anyway, on the way home I had this terrible feeling and I couldn't explain why. I was so nauseous I thought your dad was gonna have to pull over. When we got home, he turned on the TV and there it was, all over the news. An airplane crashed off the end of the runway at the Pittsburgh Airport. It was his plane. That's how he died – he burned to death."

"The next night, I was down at Aunt Ruth's watching Kenny and Karen because they'd given her a sedative. I'd put both of them to bed and I was sitting at the kitchen table with your Aunt Mary when Karen came out of the bedroom. She told us she was afraid to go to sleep because her father was in her room. So I told her, "you weren't afraid of him when he was alive, so why would you be afraid of him just because he's dead?""

It never occurred to me that she was psychic, as well. Sure, I knew about my grandmothers, so why did I just assume it skipped my parents? Or even, why did I find all those helpful books by Edgar Cayce, Robert Monroe and the like in her bookcases?

So if my mother wasn't afraid of ghosts, then why was she running away from this one?

I knew I had to get to the bottom of all this somehow. If you wanted information about the family, straight up with no filters, you asked my sister. Not that I knew her very well. I knew her daughter – my niece, Noelle, much better than I did her. She was 21 years older than me so we'd never lived under the same roof. She was a senior in college when I was born. She was also a hippy and became a Buddhist in college. She had a mildly adversarial relationship with our parents and had no qualms whatsoever about spilling their secrets.

Contacting her was easier said than done in my case, since she lived on the other side of the country. If I called her on the phone at home it would show up on the long distance bill, and my parents would be all over me wanting to know why I called out there. However, there was a pay phone at school just outside the cafeteria where the hallway went down to the locker rooms. It was at the end of a row of lockers, so it wasn't too obvious, and the hallway was usually empty when there we no class changes going on. It took me a few weeks to save up enough lunch money. I wasn't even sure how much it would cost to call California, but I figured five dollars should cover it. I copied my sister's work phone number from my parents' address book and when the planned day arrived, I slipped out of lunch as quietly as I could with a sack of quarters.

My hand shook as I dialed the number. It took a couple of tries –

I'd never called long distance on a pay phone before – but finally I did get an operator who told me how much money to put in, and I feed the phone its required sacrifice of quarters. And then I heard ringing.

"Hello?"

"Linda – it's me, your sister," I whispered.

"What? Wow – aren't you in school? And why are we whispering?"

"Because I AM in school. I'm on a pay phone in the hallway. I need to ask you about something and I don't want Mom and Dad to know."

"Um, OK, go for it."

"Did Mom have a baby that died?"

"Yes, she did."

"Why didn't anyone ever tell me about it?"

"Because they don't talk about it. They didn't intentionally not tell you, I don't think. They just never talk about it at all. Like, ever! They wouldn't even have told the three of us about it except that we knew about the pregnancy. So they had to tell us something or we would've been asking questions when the baby sibling we'd been promised never showed up. I remember it very vividly – all three of us were out playing in the front yard. Dad came out and said, 'The baby died', and went back in the house. And they never uttered another word about it again. But I'm not really surprised you know about it, since that was you – you know that, don't you?"

"What? What do you mean?"

"You were the baby. It happens more than people think. I guess it isn't easy to get born. Sometimes it takes more than one try. You're lucky though, cuz Dad was gonna name you Rebecca. Ha! You avoided that! How did you figure it out, if you don't mind my asking?"

"Grammy told me in a dream."

She laughed. "Sometimes I actually feel bad for them. Their own parents are undermining them from beyond the grave!"

"When Grammy is around, I smell rose water. Does that make any sense?"

"Yes it does – I've sensed her and smelled the same thing. So I guess it's a kind of clairvoyance? My roommate and I used to jokingly call it smell-voyance."

"Back to the baby - that would explain a lot of things then, like why I've always felt like I'm the wrong age and should be in college now, and why I was so freaked out about three out of four grandparents having died before I was out of diapers."

"Maybe you missed out on having a drink from the river Lethe?"

"The river *what*?

"Ah well it was kind of a joke – Greek mythology. The river Lethe is one of the five rivers of Hades – the underworld? Anyway drinking from it makes you forget everything. So according to the poet Virgil, you get a drink before you are sent back for your next incarnation, so you didn't remember anything from your past lives. Having past lives isn't unusual – everybody has them. But not everybody remembers them."

"So why do some people remember them?"

"If it's important to what you are supposed to do in this life, you'll remember the relevant ones. Otherwise they just get in the way."

The bell rang.

"Sounds like you have to go. But before you do, you might as well know the rest of it – you were Emily too. In fact, you're the only person I've ever met who got buried twice in the same grave."

"How do you know that?"

"Mom told me! She knew the day you were born! She's written about it in letters since then, freaking out letters about stuff you say that nobody but her sister could ever know."

"Like what?"

"Well, hard to remember off the top of my head, but she said you had a dream about tons of flowers all around the living room in the Aunt Farm."

"Yeah, I did have a dream like that."

"Well she says it was an exact description of Emily's funeral. Really freaked her out."

"If I was dead, what was I doing at my own funeral?"

"Most dead people go to their own funerals, from what I've been told. According to Mom, you've also described Emily's kitchen in detail, and I can't remember what else. I still have the letters if you ever want to see them. In the meantime, I have some books I can send. Basic books about reincarnation, that explain how it works and stuff."

"Does Mom know I was the baby?"

"I don't think so. If I were you, I wouldn't tell her that – it will probably really piss her off. Is that it? I don't want to cut you short, but, I think you are missing class. Better go to the nurse's office and tell them you're sick so you don't get detention."

She was right, the hallway was silent again. I wasn't even sure how long the next class period had been going on. So I took her advice. I wasn't lying either – by this point I was feeling rather sick. The nurse let me lie down for a while, and when I said I still felt bad by the next bell, she called my mother and sent me home.

On the way home in the car my mother seemed in an okay and sympathetic mood, so I decided I might as well go for it. Looking out the window, causally asked, "Aunt Gerk told me that you had a baby who died. Is it true?"

Her face clouded over and her knuckles grew white on the steering wheel. "Yes. It's true."

"Is there some reason why you kept this from me? Especially after I had a dream about it? I mean, I told you about the dream the next morning and you just sat there and looked at me like I was nuts."

"No reason... it's just...something we don't have any reason to talk about. There isn't much to say. It died very prematurely and we buried it. There wasn't a funeral or anything. It would have been a little girl. I didn't say anything when you had the dream because I didn't want to get you any more upset. Now you know, and I really don't want to talk about it ever again."

The validation was enough – I decided to respect that and leave her alone on the topic of the baby, at least. But that still left Emily.

We got home and she made me some tea and toast. I ate it in the kitchen and it did make me feel a lot better – I'd been so nervous about my long distance phone call that I couldn't eat my lunch. Afterwards, I went upstairs and found my mother propped up in bed reading. I lay down on my dad's side of the bed and for a while we just existed in quiet companionship.

"I'm reincarnated from Emily, aren't I?" I finally just asked.

She dropped her book onto her lap. "Well I knew this was going to come up some time, I just didn't think it would be this soon," she said. "I suspect that you are, but there is really no way to prove these things."

"What made you think so?"

"Well, it's kind of a long story. But I might as well tell you. Emily was pregnant. She had a condition called hyperemesis gravidarium – it means that you constantly throw up during the pregnancy. Lots of women throw up in early pregnancy, but what she had was a far more extreme version of it, where it becomes dangerous. I had it and so did your Aunt Marion, but not as bad as Emily did. Nowadays they put you on IV's and even feed you intravenously if they have to. Back then, they didn't have any of that. So she more or less starved to death. Near the end, she got so weak that she came down with pneumonia. There were no antibiotics – they really weren't available to the general public until after the war."

She took a swallow of coffee and set the cup back down on the nightstand.

"They knew she was gonna die. Your Aunt Gerk was a nurse in the hospital where she was admitted. In those days, they had these weird ideas about a good death. They brought everybody in to see you before you died. They took me as well, even though I was only eight years old. Of course, as soon as they started bringing all these people into her room, she knew what it meant but I didn't know anything. When I saw her, she was on a feeding tube and couldn't talk, but I could tell from the look in her eyes that she was absolutely terrified. I was only there for a few minutes and Gerk was standing with her. Before they took me back out, I turned around and looked at her and she looked back at me and I remember exactly the way she looked at me. Later that night, she died."

"When you were born, I was awake for the whole thing. They

didn't put me under like they did with the older kids. As soon as you were born, the doctor held you up so I could see you. You looked at me the exact same way Emily did that last time I saw her. So that's when I knew – the dreams you had later on just confirmed it."

"If I ever have a baby someday, will that happen to me again?"

"Not very likely. And even if it did, they can treat that now."

"What happened to the baby?"

"The baby died when she died. It wasn't old enough to survive on its own. They were trying to keep her alive long enough to give her a C-section, but she would have had to have lived another month for that plan to work. They had no way of keeping tiny preemie babies alive back then either."

"Do you know if it was a girl or boy?"

"No. They didn't do autopsies unless you were murdered or something like that, certainly not to find out a baby's gender. If you died pregnant, you got buried pregnant."

This confirmation seemed to create more and more questions! I'd managed to get married in that life. Now I was back at the beginning again, like in the game *Chutes and Ladders*.

"Before getting sick and all that, was I happy?"

She looked at me for a minute, trying to decide how to answer. "No, not really. I think you have a far better chance at happiness now, and while this is all interesting to talk about, it doesn't really matter very much. What matters is what you do with your life now."

"Now? Now sucks! Do you really think I'm better off now, with all this craziness going on? With school and everything else?"

"This is a short period of your life – this business with school and all. In six years, you'll be done with it. That may seem like a lifetime to you, but it doesn't to people who are older. Once you are out of school, you can do whatever you want! Live wherever you want, spend time with whomever you want. You've got lots more opportunities now than you ever would've dreamed of if you'd remained a housewife in 1938! We were in the middle of a huge depression! Nobody had any money – we were lucky if we had food. Women had so much fewer rights – I don't even think you can begin to understand how much harder it was for women back then."

She sighed. "It was really hard on my mother. She walked over to that cemetery every day for months and sat and cried over that grave. But being her, she made a lifelong friend in the process. There was a lady who lived in Harwick and had a little girl. Around the same time that Emily died, this little girl fell on the road one day and came down with blood poisoning. Which really isn't poisoning – it happens when bacteria get into your bloodstream, usually staph. They call it septicemia now. She scraped her knee on the road and she died really fast from the infection. So her mother was also walking the same road every day going back and forth from the cemetery, and they got to know each other, and became friends."

"This lady was from Eastern Europe and I think she lived in company housing at the mine. She'd bought a piece of property over by the cemetery and every morning she took her goat over there to graze, and at the end of the day she'd bring the goat back home again. Her biggest aspiration in life was to have a house of her own. So my mother nagged my father until he finally gave in and built this lady a house on her lot, and carried her mortgage. He was angry because he thought she would never pay him, and the depression was going on and I don't know where he even got the money to build it. But she did pay him back – every last cent."

She got up, went over to her dresser and removed a small box from her jewelry box. "I have a few things that belonged to Emily, and under the circumstances, I think you should have them. This locket was hers. It's pretty worn out as you can see, as it was the only piece of jewelry she had and she wore it a lot. So you can't wear it now because the clasp is broken, but there is a lock of her hair inside. This is her autograph book from high school. And a picture of her with her husband, shortly after they were married."

She handed them to me. I thanked her and took them into my room. I put the necklace away in my jewelry box, and sat for a while looking at the autograph book at my desk. My mother signed it, and all the aunts. Lots of other people I no longer remembered. All these cheerful high school farewells looking forward to bright futures – it was hard to imagine that Emily was dead a little more than a year after these things were written. I had the overwhelming feeling that I hadn't learned much or figured anything out. Born, lived, and died all within 18 years and didn't have a damn thing to show for it except for a few objects.

I also realized it explained how I felt about Grammy. She used to be my mother!

CHAPTER 8

June of 1982

I was grinning like a chipmunk walking into of the main office at school that morning, because I had an early dismissal slip in my hand. Right after band I was out of there! Woo hoo! My appointment with a mental health professional had come at long last! Mrs. Fine was a social worker, my mother explained. When I asked her why she didn't get a psychologist, she said there were none available outside of Pittsburgh, and that my pediatrician had recommended her.

"Give it a try! I don't wanna have to cart you all the way to Pittsburgh every week if I can avoid it," she said.

It is interesting that I ended up with Mrs. Fine as she was a rather amazing person in her own right. She was a founding member of the Pittsburgh Chapter of the National Organization for Women in 1967. Her husband was the medical director of the Miner's Clinic and together, they coached the miner's wives on how to join the picket line when the mines limited the number of miners who were allowed to picket during a strike. She also trained women to become steel workers and taught them how to deal with the harassment they would inevitably get on the job!

That afternoon I sat in the car next to my mother, filled with anticipation.

"There is something that you should know," she began. This undoubtedly signaled trouble. "I have already spoken with Mrs. Fine on the phone, and I told her about what happened to you this past summer."

A bubble of rage erupted inside me. "You had no right to do that!"

"I'm sorry if you don't like it. I felt she had a right to know and couldn't treat you unless she knew. And I knew YOU would not tell her!"

I crossed my arms over my chest and stared maliciously at the dashboard. "I wanna go home."

"You nagged and nagged me for this appointment, and by God, you're going if I have to drag you the entire way!"

I seethed with anger for the rest of the ride, and all the time waiting in the reception area. In the end, it didn't matter because Mrs. Fine didn't make me talk about it. Before she saw me for the first time, she contacted a college in Pittsburgh and asked for advice. Back then, the only people who were researching or knew anything about the effects of sexual assault on people were in large urban centers. They told her not to force me to talk about it.

Minutes seemed like hours and I was too angry to read magazines. And I was in public so I couldn't even fight with her about it. Finally, a woman about the same age as my mother with a bobbed haircut emerged from a back hallway and called my name.

I looked up. "Yes, that's me."

She introduced herself and smiled warmly, offering her hand. My anger forgotten, I shook hands with her and followed her back into her office. I sat there, nervousness creeping in. What had I got myself into? What exactly did they do? Funny it had not occurred to me to wonder about these things until I was actually there. Did she have a sofa in here somewhere, where I should lie down and she would ask me about my childhood? Which was still going on? She jotted down a few notes on her notepad and began.

"Your mother told me about what happened to you this past summer."

"I don't wanna talk about that!"

"OK. That's fine. I just wanted you to know that I knew."

"I really don't think that's what's causing my problems."

"What problems?"

"Well, to start with, there are these symptoms..."

"Can you tell me about the symptoms?"

"Well, I am neurotic, I have panic attacks, generalized anxiety disorder..."

"Woe, plain English will do", she said laughing. "Where did you learn those terms?"

"An abnormal psychology text book."

"Well, how about you just describe it to me, and that way I can double check your diagnosis?"

"OK. Sounds reasonable. Where to start? Oh, I get anxiety during the day at school a lot."

"What is it like?"

"It's more than nervousness, a little bit like having butterflies in your stomach, except that it makes me feel as if I can't hold still, and some terrible disaster is about to happen. You know how you feel if you have to stand up in front of a group and give a speech? Kind of like that. It's a feeling in the pit of your stomach. Of course, I'm in school, so some terrible disaster probably is about to happen. School is kind of one big terrible disaster all by itself."

"And when do you have this feeling? All the time? Or only at certain times of the day, or is it triggered by something specific?"

"Odd times, when there isn't any apparent reason, like right before the bell rings. Why then, and why not when it should be there like when someone's fist is rapidly approaching my face? Then I feel absolutely nothing."

"And how often does someone's fist rapidly approach your face?"

"Not that often. It's pretty much stopped since my mother went to the principal about it."

"OK then, back to the anxiety. Are there any other times you experience that?"

"Yes, but they are all more or less things that happen every day like the bell ringing. Sometimes I get it and I don't even know why."

She scribbled in her notebook some more.

"How about the panic attacks?" Seeing the look on my face she added, "This is just to get an overall picture. You can talk as much as you want about whatever you want, but first I need to get a general idea of what's going on."

"They go in cycles. First, I'll be really depressed, and then okay for a few days. Then something happens, like a fight with my mother or something else bad, and I have the attack. It starts out with an irrational fear, like I'm going to die. The first time I had one I really thought I was going to die! Anyway, after that I can't breathe, I lose control, my fingers and my face tingle, and eventually I pass out. Then the whole cycle begins again."

"What do you think causes this?"

"I hate school! I've always hated school! The other kids are mean. They pick on me and tell me I'm ugly. They hate me."

"Do you have any friends?"

"Yes, but I don't see them much in school. Lisa is younger and still at the elementary school. Kris is older, and not in any of my classes or my lunch period, except for band. They both live on the same road and I've been friends with them forever. And Kelly, she is in my grade and all, but I hardly ever see her because she isn't in any of my classes."

"So most of your friends are either older or younger?"

"Yes. I get along with older kids, younger kids, and adults. But I've never been able to get along with kids my own age."

"Do you have any friends your own age?"

"Yes – Kelly, who I mentioned before. We became friends in second grade. We were in the same class in elementary school, but now at Junior High we don't have any classes together. And Tim, who I knew from church – he's in my gym class and I sit with him at lunch. And Jenny. I don't know what happened with Jenny. She was my friend since kindergarten, but starting this year it's like she's mad at me or something. I have no idea why." My eyes watered.

"OK. We are going to start with these panic attacks. What's happening is called hyperventilating. All of the other physical symptoms are caused by the hyperventilating. If you can stop hyperventilating, you can stop the attack. You may still feel pretty awful, but at least you will be able to remain calm."

"How do I do that?"

"You have to pay very close attention to your breathing. At first, it may help you to breathe into a paper bag. That will lower the amount of oxygen you are taking in, which will decrease your symptoms. The most important thing is slow, deep breathing. The same is true with the anxiety. When you are having it, if you pay attention to your breathing, you'll discover that it is very shallow and rapid. If you use slow, deep breathing, the anxiety will lessen."

"You can have too much oxygen?"

"Oh yes. It sets off certain chemical reactions in your body. The same is true of having too much carbon dioxide. You can get them back to normal anytime you want, and I am going to teach you how."

After that, she asked me what else I wanted out of these sessions.

"Help getting along with people at school."

"Think back over the last couple of days and describe an event to me that illustrates your problem."

An event immediately sprung to mind. "I was getting my books out of my locker, and Mary Jane approached me and asked me who I like. I knew she was just looking for an opening to tease me!"

"What did you say to her?"

"I got mad and told her it was none of her goddamn business."

"And how did she respond."

"With a deluge of names, which was embarrassing because you never know what people will hear. Someone could hear her say a name and by the end of next period, it would be all over the school that I liked that person!"

"By getting angry you gave her what she wanted. Do you see that?"

"Yes, but what else can I do? If I ignore her, she will just hound me until I finally bite her head off!"

"You need to disarm her."

"Huh?"

"Say something that stops the conversation dead. I'll show you. In this case, you could have said something like: I don't really like anybody today, but if I think of someone I'll be sure to let you know."

I had to admit it would be hard for her to tell if I was being serious or putting her down, but I was still not sure this would change anything in the long run.

"Try it. Make sure you remain your happy-go-lucky self when you say it. They just want to get a rise out of you. When it stops being fun, they'll find someone else to bother."

"How am I going to think of things like that on the fly?"

"It will come with practice. What other things do they say?"

"How about when someone comes up to me and says "You're ugly!"

"Can you think of anything? ... How about just saying I'm sorry you feel that way."

"Or ... so what else is new?"

"Good! You've got the idea. I want to point out that kids joke like this all the time. I think that sometimes you misinterpret a joke as malicious teasing."

"I don't know about that."

"You might be surprised. There are more pressing issues in their lives besides making you miserable. Did you ever consider that when two people are whispering on the other side of the room and laughing that they might be talking about someone else? Or about something they saw on TV? It isn't always you. Try to remember that this week."

After my appointment, my mother stood talking to Mrs. Fine for several minutes. I could not hear what they were talking about, but from the serious expressions on their faces, it was no doubt about me. On the way home, she filled me in.

"Mrs. Fine told me that she spoke with someone in Pittsburgh, someone who has experience treating women who were ..." even she couldn't say it. "They said not to force you to cooperate with the police. So I just want you know, from now on I will stop pushing you to do that."

"Well that's a relief!"

I was correct in that I was diagnosed with Generalized Anxiety Disorder. That long ago, victims of violent crimes were not yet diagnosed as Post Traumatic Stress Disorder, which was documented in Vietnam Veterans but had not progressed much beyond that limited population. The other issue I had, un-diagnosable at the time, would now be classified as a mild high functioning Asperger's. Decades later, I learned that my son had it. I was shocked at how much of my own childhood experiences it explained, like not being able to get along with kids my own age and feeling like everyone else knew what was normal but I didn't, my odd savant like piano playing, and the ability to remember being an infant.

Throughout the rest of the week, I tried the breathing exercises every time I was plagued by anxiety, and enjoyed some success. I was having about five spikes of anxiety per day, I discovered, and I could get rid of them with the breathing exercises in about 15 minutes.

***

I sat at the table eating Co-Co Wheats, a few days before the end of seventh grade. It was dusk outside but everything smelled fresh and spring-like. Over the course of the winter of 1982, my diet became almost as constricted as the rest of my life. I was more or less living on Co-Co- Wheats and Campbell's Chunky Chicken soup. I got up to make a cup of tea when my mother came into the room.

"I saw an ad in the newspaper today," she opened. "It's for an astronomy club around here, called the Kiski Astronomers. They're having a demonstration this Saturday night at Gee Bee mall. Do you want to go?"

I inhaled some steam from my tea. "Why?"

"I thought it would be good for you to get out. You seem really interested in astronomy, so I thought I'd mention it. You can have friends other places besides school, you know."

"It's not part of the school?"

"No, apparently it isn't. Its community based. So, I doubt there would be anyone from school there. The high school maybe, but you don't know anyone there other than Kris's sisters."

My first impulse was to tell her no way. But I'd learned to think things through better thanks to Mrs. Fine. I realized life was pretty boring. Who knew what could come of this? It was easy enough to leave if I saw anyone from school or it was awkward. "Well, all right, I guess. But don't expect me to talk to anyone. If there's anyone from school there, we turn around and leave, no questions asked."

"Deal. I think you'll be fine once you get there and you might actually have fun," replied my mother hopefully.

At the moment, I was mesmerized by the clinking sound the spoon made inside the glass tea mug as I stirred it lethargically. I became aware that she was looking at me. I shrugged. "Whatever."

To be perfectly honest, I really did like astronomy. It all started with my little forays onto the roof. I'd borrowed some astronomy books from the library but finding constellations was hard! They either showed them in some random shape or with elaborate Greek mythological figures superimposed on them. I'd asked Mom for help a couple times. She could find more obvious things like the Big Dipper and The Pleiades. That past Christmas, my brother Bob got me a great astronomy book: The Stars. It made constellations easy to find! It was fun slipping outside at night to find patterns in the stars. They were like cold, sparkling diamonds in the blackness. Out there in the unknown - somewhere - could be happiness.

Most evenings, in those early days, I used to climb all the way to the top of the big maple tree in the front yard, where the branches are small and if you climbed any higher, they wouldn't hold you. From there, I had a sweeping view of everything. We lived on the highest hill for many miles. Rolling hills spread out like permanent waves in a sea of trees, the lights from houses winking below them. Each hill wore a crown of red lights attached to some sort of radio tower. The ruby lights flashed in succession, one hill followed by the one behind, like a ripple on a pond, until the last ruby blinked weakly at the horizon. I knew that Pittsburgh was under that final ruby, like some far off promise. That kept me alive. Someday, I would end up there and everything would be OK. Maybe the people I would meet there were waiting for me just like I was waiting for them. Maybe they were watching the same sunset and looking up at the same stars.

***

Not caring much and having very low expectations, I put on my favorite shirt and went to the astronomy event at Gee Bee's parking lot. There were a lot of street lights around so it was not a great place to do astronomy, but it was more of a recruiting event for the club than a true indulgence in the hobby.

I was relieved to see there was nobody from my school there! I met the astronomy teacher from the high school – Mr. Jack and several younger guys. Chuck and Jeff were obviously best friends and told me they graduated from the high school in 1980 (two years before). Bruce was married with a baby, and Keith was going into his senior year at a neighboring school district, Franklin Regional. They were all quite friendly and before long, I was chatting away with them, trying to come up with a way to explain how I became interested in astronomy without having to explain about sleeping on the roof of the house because I was afraid of being murdered.

"My brother bought me this great book for Christmas," I said. "Called *The Stars*? Well, he was into the subject a bit himself – and my sister too – back when he was an undergrad at Pitt he worked at this shop in Shadyside that sold crystals, and ..."

"Hey, come here a minute", interrupted my mother. Annoyed, I let her lead me towards one of the telescopes. She leaned in close.

"I just wanted to warn you, don't tell those guys about Linda and Bob! They were studying Astrology. Not the same thing! And that place that Bob worked? It was a metaphysical shop! These guys are into science, they will not understand, and they will think you're an idiot. I hope you don't think I'm overstepping, but I don't want anything to ruin this as it seems to be getting off on the right foot."

Geez, she was in full Kris mode. My irritation faded. I hadn't thought of that, and I realized she was right. "Thanks. I won't say anything about it."

From there everything went fine. We left an hour or so later with promises to see them again in a couple weeks at George Bailey's star party.

My first star party, as they were called, was on a fantastic day in June not long after school let out. The usual format for a summer meeting was to have them at member's homes. First, there was an informal picnic in the evening, then after dark everyone got their telescopes out and did their thing. They were scheduled ahead for the entire summer each spring, but were sometimes cancelled at the last minute due to clouds. Nothing to see with clouds!

I was beside myself with nerves and couldn't decide what to wear! I tended to manifest anxiety through clothing. I had no emotional investment prior to Gee Bee's, but now that I'd met them and liked them, I was very worried about their not liking me in return.

"Oh good heavens, you're not wearing THAT?" my mother said when she came up to check on me.

"What? Why?" I had a brand new pair of dress shorts which I'd paired with a lacy short sleeved blouse. I also wore one of Grammy's old brooches in the hopes that she would follow me and boost my confidence with a few blasts of rose water ghost smell. True, if I couldn't tell these guys about my siblings' forays into astrology, I sure as hell couldn't say anything about my ghost, but I'd know she was there and that was enough for me.

"It's a picnic for Pete's sake! You're a little overdressed. How about a t-shirt?"

I stared at her. "But, all my t-shirts are old!" I started to cry. "I don't have anything to wear! I'll just stay home! You go." My t-shirts would look pretty darn silly with a 100 year-old haunted brooch.

"All right, all right! Forget I said anything! It's fine really. It's more important that you feel confident."

"But look at my hair! And now, look at my face!"

"Relax! I'll go get a cold washcloth. It'll fix your face as long as you stop crying! Your hair is fine! You're just nervous! Stop looking in that mirror and lay down! I'll be right back."

I sniffled and lay down on the bed. Dad honked the car outside –

he was ready to leave and losing his patience.

"Here. Hold this over your face for a few minutes and take a few deep breaths. All right. Come on, let's get in the car. It will be fine. Really!"

It was not an easy place to find. We drove really far away and then wandered around unmarked roads for what seemed like a long time. Then Dad spotted a gas station and pulled in, and there was Mr. Jack, the high school astronomy teacher, sitting in his fancy red sports car.

"Hey, hey!" said Dad. "What luck!"

He rolled down his window. "Do you know where it is?"

"Sure! Just follow me. I picked up Rodger wandering around – he was lost, too. It's kind of hard to find."

I hadn't noticed him before, but behind Mr. Jack was a young guy in aviator sunglasses driving a blue VW bug.

A few minutes later, I found myself standing in George Bailey's driveway, leaning against the car and feeling dorky. My parents were chatting away with Mr. Jack. I'll be in his class in a few years, I thought. I wonder if he can tell I was bawling? Several other people pulled into the driveway and there was a lot of slamming trunks and car doors. It was a gorgeous evening! Warm and not humid, not a cloud in the sky. The sun warmed my back through my lacy blouse.

Then I had a queer feeling of being watched. Grammy? I looked around and to my utter shock the aviator sunglasses guy was smiling at me. Not just smiling, but smiling in an obviously admiring way. Wait – this can't be real. It can't be me. There must be someone else. I took in a deep breath, bit my lip, and looked around to see who he was smiling at. I broke out in goose bumps and my cheeks flamed. There was nobody else!

Oh God, where was Kris when I needed her most? I must look like a deer caught in the headlights! What should I do? I couldn't think of anything, so I smiled back. He looked young but he had to be at least 16 since he was driving. He had an intelligent, I'm-going-somewhere-in-life look about him, dark hair and brown eyes. A veritable Prince Charming, except instead of a white horse, he had a blue Volkswagen.

The idea that something like this could happen had never occurred to me before. This was no eighth grader! Oh heavens, if only the kids in school could see me now!

Dare I look up again? The cute guy was gone, but I saw Chuck and Jeff – two of the guys I'd met at Gee Bee's, were hanging out near the back door.

Chuck waved. Not knowing what else to do, I went over.

"Look behind you, it's yur-anus," he said with an Eddy Haskell-like grin. I wasn't sure what to say. It was becoming obvious that Chuck liked to tease people, and I was still pretty unclear about how to tell the difference between mean teasing and joking teasing.

Mr. Jack came to the rescue. "You can also pronounce that planet as urine'-us. I suppose neither one's better than the other."

"I always thought it was ur-on'-us," I added.

"Well," said Chuck, "Looks like we're all heading in. Grab yourself some food."

The buffet table was set up just inside the doorway. My parents were already there fixing plates. I poured myself a cup of coffee and picked up a few pretzels and chocolate chip cookies. My parents were already seated on one of two sofas in the room, chowing down on their burgers. Cute guy was sitting on the other sofa by himself. So I had a choice to make. OMG, what would Kris do? Kris would have the guts to go sit next to him and introduce herself, but I was a coward. Also, if I did something that brazen, I wasn't sure what my mother's response would be. Nothing like this had ever happened before so I had no way to guess. She might stand up and say: What do you think you're doing? Get over here!

While I was still mentally debating all this, Chuck and Jeff pushed past me and huffed down on either side of him.

"Rodger! Haven't seen you in a coon's age!" said Chuck. So that was his name. Rodger just smiled and nodded. "So, I hear you're going to Grove City this fall for Electrical Engineering."

I sat down next to my mother. Rodger looked over at me and smiled again, I blushed. Chuck smirked, then leaned over to Jeff and whispered something in his ear. Jeff giggled.

The meeting was starting. I had a bad feeling about Chuck. He saw us looking at each other. What was he going to do? Something to humiliate me, I suspected. This was my life, I remembered, so there was not going to be a happy ending. My anxiety levels rose through the roof and I swallowed coffee hard to quell a surge of nausea.

The meeting ended and everyone just sort of sat around talking, waiting for it to get dark.

"Can you hold this?" I thrust my plate and empty coffee cup towards my mother.

"Gee, you didn't eat much of anything," observed Dad. "What's the matter?"

My mother lowered her voice and leaned towards his ear. "That boy over there was making eyes at her and she's lost her appetite."

"I have to go the bathroom!" I bolted for the powder room next to the buffet table and locked the door, sat down on the toilet, and practiced my Mrs. Fine breathing techniques for a while. What to do?

Kris would know how to save this. I was clueless. Maybe I was just being paranoid. I should go back out and act like nothing was happening.

I stood up and looked in the mirror. Wait a minute, what's going on? I was pretty! Sure I'd seen my reflection in the mirror all fall and all winter but I'd never really paid attention to it, I guess. I had boobs! Even though my crying jag had washed off most of my makeup, I still could have passed for sixteen. When did this happen exactly? It wasn't half a year ago I stood ankle deep in slush outside of Allegheny Hyde Park Junior High School and thought, nothing good will ever happen to me again. And now ...?

"Let's do this!" I told my older looking self.

The living room was empty – they'd all left! I ran for the back door and then remembered what Kris always said – act dignified! I suppressed the urge to run, wiped my sweaty palms on my shorts, and exited the house calm, dignified.

They were still in the back yard, slowly making their way towards the field where George's observatory was. His wife's evening primroses perfumed the air.

Cute guy walked toward me. "Hi", he said, "I'm Rodger." He held out his hand.

"Laura", I said, and shook his hand. I liked the sound of that. These people were the first group of friends I ever had who only knew me by my new name. Not that it was that different from my old one. Kris still called me "Lori" and probably will until the day she dies. During the winter of that first year, Kris and I met some kids while out shopping at the Plaza in Lower Burrell and they had mistakenly picked up my name as Laura. I liked the sound of it so much better. So I adopted the name and just started writing it on all my papers at school. For this, I endured a good bit of torment, but I didn't care. When the other kids teased me I thought of it as the cost of assuming a new name.

He winked. "So, you come here often?"

"Not really." I laughed. Of course, I didn't know anything about pick-up lines or jokes about pick-up lines, but he laughed, so I laughed. "Tonight is my first star party," I admitted.

"Hey, Rodger!" We both turned to see Chuck and Jeff sniggering over by the cars. "Com'mere a minute!"

"Excuse me. I'll be right back. I have to get my telescope out of my car. I'll meet you up there."

I was feeling uneasy again. I threw Chuck a stern glance, but he pretended not to notice. The three of them stood by Rodger's car, Chuck and Jeff still giggling. Then Rodger turned beet red.

The faint odor of his aftershave still hung in the air like magic. My eyes burned and a lump rose in my throat. My parents caught up with me and for the first time, I felt embarrassed. My mother was wearing polyester pants and Dad had his clip on sunglass flipped up. There was NO chance of appearing cool to these guys. I'm here with my parents, for God's sake! Well, if you can't be cool, at least be nonchalant, Kris always said. Part of me wanted to go home, lock myself in my room, and cry really hard. But that was the cowardly way. Instead, I took a deep breath. Nonchalant.

"This is George, who we told you about", said Bruce, introducing the old man. And what a character old George proved to be, for even at 80 something he could go into a room and remember the names of everyone in it. He used to be a professional magician, my mother told me later. He always seemed to be hosting the Emmy Awards and was extremely fun to listen to.

George spent that entire winter building himself an observatory and this was its debut star party. About the size of a shed, it had a dome top that slid off on rails so you could use the telescope. Pictures taken from astronomy magazines adorned the walls. We all had observatory tours and then a group photo. After that people dispersed to their own telescopes.

I wasn't sure what to do. Then I saw Chuck and a few other guys over at Rodger's telescope. He pointed his finger at me and made that little "come here" signal. I decided my best bet was to act as if nothing happened. After all, I didn't know what they actually said. So I went over to where Rodger was setting up his telescope.

"So," said Chuck sarcastically. "Your first star party. You met Jeff already."

Jeff blushed and said hello. He was Chuck's sidekick. You pretty much never saw one without the other, and they were pretty much opposites. Jeff was quiet and reserved with a blonde bowl cut, while Chuck had dark brown hair with an 80's poodle perm, glasses, and a sarcastic teasing attitude.

"I'm sure you remember Keith." Keith nodded. He was tall and thin with black hair. "He goes to Franklin Regional. You're going to be a senior this year, right?" Keith nodded.

"Of course, you've already met Rodger here." Chuck and Jeff exchanged an amused look. He turned to the other guys. "This is the one I was telling you guys about, who we met at Gee Bee a few weeks ago." We all stood around awkwardly for a few minutes and tried not to look at each other.

"Hey, I have an idea!" said Chuck, holding up his camera and pointing towards the highway just visible below the horizon. "I bet if we set this flash off down Rodger's telescope we can aim it at those cars!"

That broke the ice! Giggling and laughing, we set the contraption up. Chuck would flash the strobe light into the eyepiece and a beam of light, created by the telescope's mirrors, would flash from the other end. I'm sure the light was bright enough for the cars to see flashing from the hilltop. I don't doubt there were some UFO sightings reported that night.

"What are you guys doing?" asked Mr. Jack, the astronomy teacher. "Oh", he laughed when he saw what we were up to. "Strobing those cars? Just don't cause any wrecks."

Then, we all just started to talk. We talked about so many things that I enjoyed but had never had anyone else to talk with about, like stupid things we did as kids, chemistry experiments gone awry, and model airplanes. All things Kris would tell me never to talk about in social situations. With my fellow geeks, I soon forgot all about the long list of social rules and just had fun, for once.

"What are you looking at, Rodger?" asked Chuck.

"Um ... Mars."

"That's not very exciting! Find a nebula or something. There's Hercules! There's a star cluster in that."

"All right! Hold on! ... There. Take a look."

"Your telescope is very nice; how long have you had it?" I asked.

"I bought it a couple of years ago. I may sell it and get a bigger one, but it's not bad."

One by one, they all stepped up to the telescope, and I crossed to the other side to make room, ducking low to avoid blocking their view with my head. On my way, my foot caught one of the telescope legs, sending the star cluster bounding from view.

"Aaww!" they exclaimed in unison.

I drifted away from the group and sat down in a lawn chair. How could I do something like that? Everything was going just fine and now I'd blown it! It was all I could do to avoid crying.

A few minutes later Rodger drifted away from the other boys, who were still horsing around. The telescope was re-adjusted.

"Anything wrong?" he asked.

"No, I just thought I'd sit down for a minute." I was afraid to look up at him.

"Are you sure?"

"Yes, I'll be back in a minute." He looked over his shoulder. The guys were starting to throw him sly looks.

I watched him walk away. For a little while, I was not me. I was almost a normal girl. I wondered what he'd think if he knew the truth. The whole, nasty, ugly truth, including what happened last summer. Would he still like me? Would any guy?

He turned back towards me. He was smiling. "Last chance if you want to see the star cluster," he called.

So, war is war. I picked myself up and went back over. The star cluster was so low in the sky, I had to stand on tip toes to reach the eyepiece of the telescope. As I stood there, trying to steady myself enough to see, I felt his hand under my elbow, steadying me. He was talking to Chuck and didn't notice me look over at him. Did he think I was a klutz who would damage his property? Or did he sense, somehow, how fragile I really was?

Like all pleasant evenings, this one ended. I walked back down the hill with my new friends. Somewhere along the way I slid on the damp grass. Rodger reached out and caught me. We both laughed it off, but something happened: I came back to life. For a year, I'd been falling, until he caught me. I woke up from some sort of coma and everything was alive! The air smelled like fresh cut grass, there were crickets chirping, the dew was cool. The world was alive and so was I!

I'm sure he never knew how much that evening changed me, although I am pretty sure Chuck teased him about it unmercifully. I never saw him again. Yet, he was the first tangible shred of evidence that the future might hold something worth living for. That I might not be flawed for the rest of my life.

***

I stood in my room, in front of the big full length mirror, bent over at the waist blow drying my hair. I was too excited to sleep the night after the star party. As I tossed and turned, an idea I'd been thinking about for some time became clear in my mind. I should dye my hair red! My hair was always a little bit red, but I wanted it really red. If I had to start from scratch and re-create myself, I wanted to be vivacious. I needed red hair to proclaim it.

My mother groaned and warned me I'd regret it. I fought back and insisted I'd just ride my bike down and buy it myself if she didn't take me, and I had enough saved up from my allowance to buy it. So she gave up and drove me down to Ben Franklin. She did talk me into starting with the temporary stuff. I rushed home and did it. Now, in a few minutes, I would see the results.

Hair mostly dry, I switched off the hair dryer, finger combed it a little and stood up. Over the past year it had finally grown out. I now had this big mane of relatively brilliant auburn hair. As I stood there looking at it, I was amazed. The awkward, homely ugly duckling of a kid from last year was gone. Maybe the stranger in the mirror wasn't so bad after all. Maybe I was going about it all wrong. Instead of trying to run away from this new person, I should embrace her. She had some things about her that were worth embracing or those guys wouldn't have reacted to me the way they did.

I took off at a full run for Kris's house, tossing the dress I was saving for my funeral in the Goodwill bag. It was the first "adult" dress I'd ever owned, bought right at the end of sixth grade. It was the one I was wearing in my coffin in my near death experience dream. After the dream, I never wore it again. Otherwise, it might be in the wash when I died. But there was no sense in dying now!

I knocked in great excitement, the aluminum storm door rattling in its frame. I heard a few muffled thumps as Kris bounded down the stairs to answer the door. When she opened it, she stood there, aghast, momentarily at a loss for words. I just backed farther into the sun and grinned.

"Oh my God. What did you do?"

"I dyed it. Do you like it?"

She stepped outside, and turned me around slowly. "Oh boy. Does your mother know about this?"

"Of course! How do you think I got the dye?"

"Well, it does look really natural. I mean, surprisingly natural. Even with your eyebrows you can't tell it isn't natural." She shook her head. "But I dunno. Is that permanent?"

"No, she wouldn't let me buy the permanent stuff. So I'll have to do it again in a month."

"Still, why?"

"Red hair fits my personality better."

She rolled her eyes. "That, I'll give you. C'mon. Let's go show my mother."

Kris's mother and sisters didn't share her reticence about my new image. Her mother pronounced it glorious and her sisters screamed, "oh my god, did you do that yourself?"

After that we went up to the pool. The warm sun heated up the water and the sound of lawn mowers hummed in the background. I didn't want to go in and risk messing up my hair, or having red hair dye come out in the pool. Mom warned me the first time I washed it, a lot of dye would come out.

"You know you're gonna get ragged on about that if you keep it that way when school starts," Kris advised as I sat dangling my feet in the pool.

"Yeah, I know, but I'm gonna get ragged on anyway. So I figure, what the hell, eh?"

She hauled herself into the floating lawn chair. "You're in a better mood than I've seen you since I can't remember when. I take it you had fun at your star hickey-do?"

"You'll never guess what happened!"

"No, probably not! What?"

I looked around, as if some parental figure could be lurking around eavesdropping. "An older guy *liked* me."

Kris lit up like a Christmas tree. "Nah uh! Come on, you have to tell me everything!"

"Well, I went to that astronomy party last night, and there was this guy there named Rodger..." I retold the story in excruciating detail, so that she could ferret out his motives at each word, each facial expression.

She rested her chin upon her knees and thought a moment. "When will you see him again?"

"Well, that's the problem. He could come to any star party, so I guess I have to be ready at all of them."

"When's the next one?"

"Two weeks from now."

"Hum. That gives us some time. We're gonna give you a makeover! Come on!"

So, I attended each star party that summer, tanned, powdered, painted, and dressed with the utmost attention. I was a work of art designed by Kris! A new time began with a new goal. I'd gotten this crazy idea, nurtured by Disney stories, that if I could just find one guy who would put his arms around me, press my head gently on his shoulder and say, "there now, I love you and everything is going to be OK" that it actually would be. It worked for Cinderella and Sleeping Beauty, maybe it would work for me!

That was the first summer that seemed to go by faster than it had in elementary school. We did the things we usually did – swam, cleaned and fussed with Kris's pool, rode bikes, had cookouts. One thing that we had done a lot in previous summers that we started to shy away from was playing in the woods. The woods now made me nervous. I couldn't explain why at the time but looking back I know it was because of the events of the previous summer. I also found I could not accept rides from Lee, Kris's next door neighbor anymore. I struggled to find a reason why I felt uncomfortable with him even though we'd known him since we were old enough to go outside by ourselves. For years we'd played in the woods and ran around doing Halloween pranks with him. Now, he seemed a lot older than us, especially with the driver's license, and the one time he rode us down to Ben Franklin I was so consumed with anxiety I thought I'd throw up in the back seat.

The Fourth of July came and went with the usual family picnic, the high water mark of the summer. The high from the first star party began to wear off. Despite Kris's unbounded optimism, I knew deep down that there was no way that guy could just come knock on the front door and invite me to the movies. A college guy going out with an eighth grader? Even in my over active imagination, I knew that was not ever going to happen. These guys were just too much older to ever become boyfriends.

The weekend after the fourth of July was the next star party. I went down to Kris's early that morning – early for summer that is – to begin preparations. We stood in front of the washing machine, the heat from the water making the air even more humid and unbearable. She put my jeans in and slammed the lid shut.

"Are you sure you know what you're doing?" I asked. "If we ruin those, my mother will flip."

"I know exactly what I'm doing; I've done this a zillion times. The jeans need to be tight. This is the best way to get them there."

And tight they were! I had to lay down on the bed in order to pull them up. They felt like a corset. Decades later, I can say that spandex is the best thing that ever happened to jeans!

"Don't worry, they'll relax a little bit once you've had them on for a while," she explained as she stuffed the fashionable top over my head. Then came the makeup and hair. It was only about 15 minutes before we had to leave when I got home.

"You have GOT to be kidding me," Mom said when I walked in.

"But Kris said ..."

"I don't care what Kris said!" She rolled her eyes and handed me a Kleenex. "Lose the lipstick. Get in the car or we're gonna to be late."

Reid Moore, the host of this star party, was another elderly dude, but like George he was no ordinary one! Between the driveway and the back porch was a pole I assumed was a flag pole or some such thing, so imagine my shock when Mr. Moore came out of the garage with a huge telescope balanced over his shoulder. The thing had to be at least twelve feet long! He climbed up a ladder and fitted it onto the top of the pole. Unless you were looking at something overhead, you had to use the ladder to look in it, too!

I stood in the driveway with Chuck and Jeff anxiously watching the sky. It was a little bit cloudy. Not enough to cancel the party but enough to have everyone worried we would not see much that night. A field stretched out lazily below us in the shadows. A slate colored road, winding its way among dark blue-green pines huddled in clumps, disappeared on a hilltop below the inky horizon.

"It's not a reflector like ours," Keith said. He must have seen me staring at the telescope all agog. "It's a refractor. That's why it's so huge. The only place I've ever seen a bigger one is down at the Allegheny Observatory. Which reminds me, I think we're planning a field trip down there this winter. Hopefully you can come."

"It won't be MY problem to organize it," said Chuck as he elbowed Keith in the ribs. "Cuz I won't be the club secretary no more." He grinned at me. "Actually I was thinking of nominating you."

"What? Me?" I wondered if I was being setup for some kind of mean joke. "Really?"

"Sure why not?"

"So when does all this happen?"

"The first business meeting in the fall. Then we vote on it in

November, and swear in the new officers at the Christmas party."

"Hey come on over here," my mother cut in. I hobbled over in my too tight jeans. She stood beside the picnic table. I hoped she wasn't going to try and get me to eat because I wasn't sure I could actually sit down. "There's somebody you might know from school here tonight."

My blood turned to ice water!

She moved sideways and there he was. "This is Randy. I think he's a grade ahead of you."

"Yes I'm going into ninth," he managed to say. He was every bit as panicked as I was, but I was too freaked out to realize that. After a few awkward seconds, he held out his hand, I shook it. My mother, satisfied, headed off.

Yes I recognized Randy, but I didn't know him. I had no idea if he knew about all the rumors swirling around me at school or even if he knew I was an untouchable geek. I was not aware of his place in the social pecking order either, but I knew he was a gifted kid, so it was pretty unlikely he was going to end up as the next star quarterback.

"So how long have you belonged to the club?" I asked.

"About a year. Frank and I joined around the same time." He nodded towards another younger boy setting up a telescope some ways away. I recognize him from school, too. What's worse, he rode my bus! I swallowed hard. As with Randy, I didn't actually know him.

"Hey Frank," Randy called as he walked past us. "This is Laura. She's new." Frank nodded and mumbled something but didn't make eye contact. I was just as much a threat to their social safety bubble as they were to mine. If there'd been any big rocks nearby all three of us would have dashed for one to crawl under.

Randy and I stood there awkwardly as neither of us could think of a damn thing to say. Then I noticed someone else new. A blonde guy who seemed younger than Chuck, Keith, and Jeff. We made eye contact and he held it. My stomach flipped over.

"Who's that?" I asked Randy. "Does he go to our school?"

"Well, yes and no. That's Martin Robinson. He goes to our school but he's at the high school. I think he's going in to eleventh grade. That's his little brother Doug." Doug looked as young as I actually was. Maybe even younger.

"Here it is!" Mr. Jack gestured impatiently. "Quick, anyone who wants to look! It's a high magnification and it will be gone in a minute!"

That gave Randy and I the opening we needed to disengage. I stood in line and then climbed the ladder when it was my turn. The planet hung in space like a pendant, its bright turquoise color the most evident feature.

As I turned and stepped away from the telescope, I noticed that Martin had joined Chuck, Jeff and Keith who were horsing around with a couple of other guys. For a moment, I was hesitant to go back over, afraid of looking eager. They were talking about cars. My jeans were chafing me and my made up face itched.

"...Rodger has that old junky Volkswagen..." said Chuck, watching me.

He was baiting me. How to appear nonchalant? Acting as if I hadn't been paying attention all along, I yawned.

"Have you seen Rodger lately?" asked Martin.

"No, actually we haven't," said Chuck. "He is in Colorado jumping out of airplanes. Air Force ROTC." He sneered at me. "So he won't be coming to any more parties this summer, unless it's by parachute."

This jibe was thankfully lost on everyone else, except maybe Jeff, who didn't say much of anything. I shrugged and wandered over to the food. As I took a bite out of my hot-dog, Randy appeared beside me.

"Are you going into eighth or ninth grade?", he asked. He sounded friendly, like he didn't know anything about me or my past. At least I hoped so.

"I'm going into eighth. I think we had the same lunch period last year." It was true, I remember seeing him there now that I'd had time to think about it. He sat with a bunch of other boys who had a reputation for being 'brains'. It seemed as if everyone sported a label in junior high, 'brain', 'retarded', 'popular', 'jock'. I was not entirely sure what the word for me was, 'pariah', perhaps. Who was I kidding? He had to know.

"How do you like junior high?" He must have seen my expression as I searched for something noncommittal to say and quickly added, "It can be a trial at times."

"That's for sure," I agreed.

"I hear you have one of those Astroscan telescopes, do you like it?"

"Oh, yes, actually I do. It gets a really sharp image, but the higher magnifications give me trouble."

"That's always the case. The smaller the aperture the less light."

"I can't find things really well, like your friend Frank can", I admitted. Frank could find anything, just ask him and he would point the instrument at the sky and there it was.

"He's had a lot of practice."

I relaxed in the technical banter, temporarily forgetting about possible bad first impressions produced at school. I had much in common with him, being interested in science and stuff, which was a change since Kris got bored when I talked about such things. The party ended early after the clouds returned with reinforcements. Several times during the course of the evening, I felt watched and turned to catch Martin looking at me. He was not shy about it. I met his gaze for a few seconds before someone came along and interrupted one or the other of us.

When I got home I rummaged through the pile of calendars and papers pertaining to household management that my mother kept in the telephone nook looking for the club newsletter with the star party schedule. The next start party was at Martin's house! Then, I realized that our family vacation to Washington, D.C. fell on the same weekend as Martin's star party. There was no way they were going to move the vacation since my mother wrote four months in advance for tickets to tour the White House, so it seemed that getting to know Martin would have to wait. Which wasn't necessarily bad since I really needed to have another birthday before I ended up in a situation where I had to tell him how old I was!

CHAPTER 9

At The Aunt Farm

The cigarette smoke level at the Aunt Farm dropped precipitously that year when Aunt Gerk bought her amazing table top air purifier. It sat humming quietly to itself on the carved antique side board, out of place and out of time. Antique side boards, I thought to myself, were places for silver tea sets and crystal, not plastic air filters, half-finished crossword puzzles, and junk mail.

Still, there was no denying how much a little clean air improved the place. We all sat around the table, the summer sun streaming in the window where Aunt Biggie's enormous white Persian cat lounged like some pompous Roman god. It was promising to become a large Sunday night crowd: the three aunt farm aunts: Gerk, Biggie, Margie, my mother, Aunt Marion, Aunt Lo-Lo, and me. Aunt Marion and Uncle Stacey were visiting that week so Aunt Lo-Lo stopped up for dinner. Dad and Uncle Stacey were in the living room watching TV. It was still early. Some of the cousins would turn up for dinner, guaranteed.

"I fold," I grumbled, tossing my cards on the table.

"I'll see ya and raise ya five pennies," my mother parried.

"Last hand before we clear the table for dinner," warned Aunt Gerk. Meals and sleeping were only temporary interruptions in the card game that had been going on for over 20 years. It went on for another fifteen before they started to die off.

Everybody tossed in their five pennies and laid their cards down.

"Mar's pot, as usual," said Aunt Marion. The rest of the room groaned in unison. "It's your fault, Snooks," she said to my mother. "You dealt me an awful hand. Not even one wild card!"

"Oh well," sighed my mother as she scraped her pile of pennies together and swept them into an empty coffee can. "Sometimes they just don't go to people."

"They go to dogs?" Aunt Marion snapped.

Everyone laughed. I laughed so hard I almost peed myself. This was all typical when the Staceys were around. They were hysterically funny! They lived in Illinois on the shores of the Lake of Egypt in a Spanish- looking house with a huge porch. We often went there – along with lots of other cousins – to visit in the summer, to fish and hang out on the lake.

In the cramped kitchen, the windows were cloudy with steam as a large pot of gravy boiled on the stove. Aunt Gerk scooped out some beef bouillon and stirred it into the pot. "So," she said, noticing me loitering in the doorway. "What's new with you?"

"Boy trouble," my mother answered for me, brushing past me with the bread tray.

"Oh!" She took the sugar bowl, the salt and paper shakers, the butter dish, and a dish of jelly out to the lazy susan in the middle of the table. "So, what's the problem?"

"She can't get a date," Mom answered for me.

Aunt Lo-Lo laughed. "What do you mean she can't get a date?"

I rolled my eyes. "Don't talk about me in the third person when I'm standing right here!"

"So why do you even need a date?" asked Aunt Marion. "You know men are nothing but big pains in the ass." They all looked at each other knowingly and laughed.

"That's for sure," agreed Aunt Lo-Lo tapping a cigarette on the table.

"Besides, you're not supposed to go out on dates until you're sixteen," said my mother.

I rolled my eyes again and sighed. "Most people in my grade already have steady boyfriends. A girl without a steady boyfriend is like a dog without a bone!"

"That may be but that doesn't mean their parents let them go out on dates. I doubt it's most of them either. A few of them maybe. Kids your age aren't even old enough to drive, so how can they go out on dates?"

"What does driving have to do with anything?"

"How do they get to wherever the date is?"

I stared at her, unable to comprehend how she could be so dense. "Their parents drive them."

She shook her head. "Then it's not a date."

"It is so! A guy and a girl who like each other go somewhere together. That's a date."

"Well I don't consider it a date until they can go on their own. It's not a date if your parents drive you. It's ... having your parents drop you off at the movies." She turned and retreated to the kitchen to fetch a dish of peaches. I had her though!

"So if I get invited to get dropped off at the movies, you'd do it since it's not a real date?"

They all laughed when they realized how she fell into my little trap.

"We'll worry about it IF it happens," she recovered.

I crossed my arms in a huff. "You wouldn't ruin my one chance, would you? I'd be branded a failure. You can't just let me die an old maid!"

She stopped what she was doing and looked at me. "Must you always be so melodramatic? First of all, as I've told you a million times the other kids at school aren't thinking about you – they're too busy worrying about their own problems. It's not your only chance. You need to understand: men are like streetcars. There's always another one coming down the line."

"You're not taking this seriously!"

"There'll be plenty of opportunities when you're a little older. If you've set your cap at any of those guys in the Astronomy club you can forget it. You're too young. They won't ask you because you're only twelve, no matter how much they like you."

I slumped at the table. It seemed so unfair spelled out in black and white like that.

"I'll be thirteen in two months," I offered.

"Aw honey, that isn't gonna improve things much," said Aunt Lo-Lo.

"And that isn't entirely true. There's one who might ask. And he's younger than Chuck and those guys." I didn't tell them that younger meant sixteen. I'd done a little more research and now knew that Martin was a year older than Kris – he was in her older sister Sue's yearbook. This coming fall, Kris would be at the senior high with him. Sure, I hadn't actually talked to him yet and there were no more star parties scheduled for what little remained of the summer, but the club business meetings would be starting up in September and I was really hoping he would show up. Kris thought the situation had great potential.

The sisters exchanged wary glances. The aunts knew a lot about boyfriends, both good and bad.

By the time I knew her Aunt Gerk had a boyfriend: the card sharking Aardvark. I can still see them now in a room full of smoke. The Aardvark would sit down at the table and Gerk would pour him a glass of bourbon. The game would still be rolling full steam when we left at midnight.

Biggie also had a boyfriend during the time I knew her. He drove a Cadillac and gave her expensive jewelry, but didn't hang out at the Aunt Farm much. She was a widow and that uncle had died before I was born.

Aunt Lo-Lo promised me she'd ask me to be a flower girl in her wedding when I was in elementary school. Kris got to be one and I was pea green with envy. Mom warned me never to trust anything Aunt Lo-Lo said. She eventually made good on that promise and a couple years later, I got to be a flower girl. Since then, she'd divorced that guy. I didn't even realize he was gone until I asked why we never saw him anymore.

"So, whatta you think would happen if he did ask you out?" asked Aunt Gerk.

"I hope I'd be allowed to go!" It made me giddy just imagining what it would be like, sitting next to him in a movie theater or at McDonald's.

"No, I mean what happens after you've gone out with him? The next weekend, and the weekend after that? Whatta you expect to happen?"

Geez, I'd never even thought of that before! You go out on a date, and eventually you get married in a cloud of white lace and tulle, like happily ever after and all. So what of the nebulous and uncharted territory between the two? It took a minute to muster my defenses.

"Wouldn't he'd ask me out again?" Doubts began to percolate in my mind. He wouldn't stop liking me after the date, would he? What if I said something stupid? Maybe just getting the first date wasn't enough to ensure perpetual bliss. My mother must have read my expression.

"This is why people wait until they're older. You have no idea what you're getting involved in. When you're a little older, you'll have more experience."

"If you never let me out of the house, how will I ever get any experience?" I parried.

The aunts looked at my mother like they were watching a game of tennis. "True, but most people do this a bit more gradually. They start by going out in mixed groups of boys and girls their own age."

"I don't have enough friends to make a group," I snapped. "And boys my own age are useless!"

"I'm with her on that one," Aunt Biggie chimed in. "Thirteen year- old boys are not worth much."

My mother laughed. "OK! I concede that point but anyone older is not likely to ask."

"Why?"

"It's not gentleman like," Aunt Gerk said. "They could be accused of taking unfair advantage."

"You make it sound like some sort of game." I knit my eyebrows together and wondered, take advantage of what? I was just as smart as they were, wasn't I?

"Well it kinda is," said Aunt Gerk. "It has rules and, you kind of have to learn them as you go."

"Rules like what?"

"Like not going out on a date until you're 16," my mother scored. They all laughed. I scoffed.

"You think the rules are bad now, you should've seen what it was like when I was young," said Aunt Biggie. "When I was in college, we had this nasty old lady who was our dorm mother. Had eyes in the back of her head and radar like a bat! You know what?"

"What?" said Aunt Marion. They all sniggered.

"She didn't allow us to wear black patent leather shoes, because boys might see our underpants reflected in them!"

They all burst out laughing again.

"We were all over eighteen and still weren't allowed to date," she went on. "Boys weren't even allowed to knock on the door of the girls' dorm. Not that it stopped us. We just went to the boys' dorm, instead. Naturally, we weren't allowed in there either, but they didn't have a babysitter, so it was a lot easier to sneak in. There was a guy on the lower floor who was a bootlegger. We would all put our money in a basket and lower it out the window. He'd take the money and put a little bottle of whiskey in the basket. We each got about a thimble full."

"I don't really think this is helping," my mother warned.

"You know what I'd do in your situation?" said Aunt Gerk. "I'd be very kind and nice to them anyway. Because that way, they'll say to themselves, gee, she's such a wonderful person, I'll ask her out as soon as she gets a little older."

I sank. "That doesn't help me now."

"Sure it does! You go to your meetings, parties, whatever. Have a nice time treating them in ways that will make them genuinely like you. Time will pass before you know it. When you're a little older, you'll have laid the groundwork. You'll have lots of dates."

"You should listen to your Aunt Gerk," Lo-Lo agreed. "She's always had lots of dates. Way more than I ever did." She winked at my mother.

"So what are all you ladies carrying on about out here?" asked Uncle Stacey from the living room doorway.

"I was just trying to remember that new joke you told me," Aunt Marion said. "But I can't tell it as good as you can."

"Well I'll tell you what," he said. "I'm thinking of making some daiquiris. Once they're all ready, I'll tell it. You have a blender?"

"Of course we have a blender; what do you think this is?" laughed Aunt Gerk as she took him into the kitchen and got him started. Soon, the sound of the blender made it hard to hear anything. Everyone else waited in anticipation.

"Can I try one?" I asked Mom.

"They have alcohol in them."

"So?"

She sighed. "I suppose. A very SMALL one. You might not even like it."

I did like it! We all sat around the table sipping away, quietly waiting for him to start.

He looked at my mother. "This isn't exactly PG."

She waved him on. "Go ahead."

Uncle Stacey's jokes were always much more funny when he told them because he was so completely deadpan. I don't think I ever saw him crack a smile in all the years I knew him. He lit his cigarette and began. "Well, there was this young girl from the backwoods somewhere, got married. A few days before, she went to the doctor and asked if there was anything he could give her to prevent her from getting pregnant. So the doctor gave her a diaphragm. A week later, she comes back. 'I'm sorry doctor, but this doesn't work right', she said. The doctor asked, 'well what kind of jelly have you been using?' She said: grape!"

The room burst into hysterical laughter. I laughed too, even though I didn't get it.

"Tell the one about the snail!" said Aunt Marion.

"So one day this snail walks into a car dealership and says, I wanna buy a brand new Mercedes. The salesman says what do you mean? Snails don't have any money! So the snail whips out this huge chunk of cash and slaps it on the table. Well, this one does. The salesman counts it and gives in. Okay, then what color do want it? Bright red, says the snail. And I want you to paint a big white S on it. The salesman asks why would you want a giant S painted on your Mercedes? And the snail says, so that when I drive by, people will say look at the S car go!"

The all howled with laughter again.

"I don't get it," I said.

"Oh well, I'm sure you've never had it but in France snails are considered a delicacy. They cook them with butter and garlic and call it escargot. Get it? S CAR GO?"

"Okay. Whatever you say."

After that, they broke out the cards and we didn't get home until after midnight. It was progress that I'd had a daiquiri and they didn't send me out of the room when my uncle told a dirty joke. That's got to be a brick on the path to adulthood, right?

***

It was a cool, rainy day in late August when my mother drove me into Pittsburgh. The windshield wipers swished back and forth with a prematurely shed oak leaf, damp and limp, trapped under one of the blades. Mrs. Fine had referred me to a psychologist for some tests and we were on our way to the appointment. I was not in the best of spirits since the weather reminded me that school was not far off. I'd be on my own this year since Kris would be at the senior high.

I thought about all this as we rode along and I looked out the passenger side window. It seemed that life was quiet before I ever entertained the possibility of boys liking me. Sure, it was also dull and kind of hopeless, but at least it wasn't so confusing. Deep down, I knew that Aunt Gerk was right, but I just didn't see how I could survive feeling so terrible for another three years. I'd been having a pity party ever since that night at the Aunt Farm and I really just wanted my mother to bring the balloons.

"My life is a rotten, stinking, heap of trash. I wish things could go back to the way they once were. It sucks now."

My mother suppressed a grin like she always did when I was about to launch upon some tirade. "It could be worse."

"I don't see how."

"Well, what happened to you last year - and I assume that's what we're talking about since we're on our way to see the psychologist - did happen only once. How would you like it if it had been someone in your family, someone you couldn't get away from, and it happened over and over again? There are people in the world with worse problems than you."

She assumed wrong. I wasn't thinking about that at all!

"You know, I'm really sick of you bringing that up all the time! And I don't see how what happens to somebody else has anything to do with me. Just because someone else might have worse problems, does that suddenly make my problems disappear?"

"I wasn't implying that your problems should just disappear. I'm just trying to point out..."

"Every time I try to talk about my problems, you try to talk me out of having them and make me feel as if I'm some sort of selfish idiot."

"That isn't my intention at all! I'm trying to give you some perspective. You either totally deny your problems, or else you think you have the worst problems that ever existed. You have to understand that everyone has problems of some kind, some worse than others, but that no one has any unique problems. No matter what problem it is, somebody's had it before! You would be a lot farther along if you could learn to be at least be a little bit thankful once in a while."

I scoffed. "For what?"

"How about for having parents who are willing to drive you all the way to Pittsburgh? Do you think my mom and dad would have done that for me?"

"You're just doing it because you have to."

"No, I don't have to! I want to! I read in an article that it takes at least a year for someone to get over something like, like what happened to you. Know that your father and I will stick with you, no matter how bad it gets, until you get through it."

After a brief pause, my mother continued, her face set stout in grim determination. "It'd be a lot easier if you'd listen once in a while. I should've made you listen that day!"

"How would you know what was going to happen?"

"I was warned!" she snapped, her knuckles turning white on the steering wheel.

"Warned by who?"

"Grandma!"

Well, that was the last thing I was expecting and it shocked me into silence.

"She warned me the Saturday before it happened! You and Noelle were walking out to the car. Grandma got all upset when we were ready to leave. She was crying and shaking and we had a hell of a time getting her settled down. She just kept telling us over and over to keep you and Noelle away from the bridge. All the time we're thinking, what bridge is she talking about? Eventually, she settled down a little and told us she had a dream. She said if you went to the bridge, you would both die."

The hair on the back of my neck stood up. I was right in thinking I should have died. So why didn't I?

"We tried to reassure her," my mother continued, "and she made us promise not to let you go near the bridge. We still couldn't figure out what bridge she was talking about. I had a bad feeling that day. That's why I told you not to go. I remembered what Grandma said and realized, the bridge! When I looked up, you two were already gone. So then I thought, the whole thing is just nuts. I mean, Grandma's pushing 90. Do I really wanna chase after you in the car, because of a dream? So, I dropped it. And I have regretted it every damn day since then."

"Well, that's all fine and interesting, but when I started this conversation I wasn't even talking about all that. I was talking about boys."

"It has everything to do with boys," she insisted. "Because what you don't understand is that all men are like that. You can't trust them. So you remember, when you do start to date, that boys are only after one thing. You're a lot prettier than I was, so you'll have a lot more trouble. Boys tried to do that to me, too, but I outsmarted them. I would never go anywhere alone with them. So remember that. Never go anywhere alone with one."

"Are you implying that happened because I'm stupid?"

"No, I'm not! I'm talking about men, and being safe around them."

I rolled my eyes. "Don't you think that maybe you're exaggerating, just a tiny little bit?"

"No."

"Really, all men are like that? What about Dad?"

She sighed and glanced at me out of the corner of her eye at a stop light. "I'm talking about men and sex! And you're Dad, well ... he's a man! On some level, all men are rapists."

I sat there with my jaw in my lap. This wasn't the last time I'd hear this claptrap. You hear it over and over again from some therapists who specialize in "women's issues", no matter how warm and fuzzy they project themselves. I could never buy the idea that every man walking on the face of the planet would hurt women or girls if given the chance when they knew they wouldn't get caught.

"That's like saying all women are bitches," I argued. "There are plenty of girls in school who treat boys like garbage. So it would seem to me that neither gender is all good or all bad. So you shouldn't just paint everybody with such a broad brush."

She pulled into the parking lot. "Whatever. I'm sick to death of this conversation. I've done my best to warn you and that's all I can do."

I may have acted disinterested, but what really struck home in this conversation was the intelligence about Grandma. So this stuff happened to her too? Precognitive dreams and ghost visits? Well then, it was time to pick her brain about it. I just had to be careful how I went about it. If I ended up telling her what happened to me, my parents would have my hide.

We went into the building and after a silent elevator ride, arrived at the psychologist's office. I spent what seemed to be hours looking at Rorschach's ink blots and filling out questionnaires. The fluorescent lights were bright and buzzed loudly while I stared at the ink blots. The psychologist was a nice woman with curly blonde hair, not the least bit the kind of adult who talked down to children. She promised to explain it all to me, afterwards.

When the tests were complete, the psychologist went to talk to my mother in the waiting room while I sat in her office. I slid backwards on the large leather couch until my feet wouldn't touch the floor. She must make a decent living to furnish an office like this. A large potted plant stood by the window, and pictures in brass frames adorned the walls. I sat gazing at a print of Monet's Water Lilies when I heard voices drift in through the door which had been left slightly ajar.

"The test results will take about a week, but I can tell you a little bit. She certainly doesn't have any symptoms that would indicate a psychiatric disorder. Research into this area is really only just beginning and I would love the opportunity to talk to her if that is okay with you."

"You're welcome to try," answered my mother, dryly. "Don't be surprised if you get your head bitten off."

"She doesn't talk about it?"

"Sometimes – but she gets really angry at you if you bring it up."

I sat back on the couch, annoyed. Granted – anytime the topic was discussed it lead to a fight. That wasn't because of talking about it, it was because I always felt like she was blaming me for it. I had no time to contemplate as the door opened and the psychologist returned. She placed her notebook on the desk, took her glasses off, and sat down in the chair opposite of me.

"I was just telling your mother that your results will take about a week."

"Then I can see them?"

"They'll go to Mrs. Fine, since she requested them, and so you can talk about it at your next appointment with her."

"Will it say what's wrong with me?"

"I can tell you right now that there is nothing wrong with you," fingering imaginary quotation marks in the air about the word wrong. "Mrs. Fine categorized you as having Generalized Anxiety Disorder." I got the feeling she was aware of my textbook reading and self-diagnosing habit and was treading cautiously. "At least that is what it has been called up until quite recently. There is a lot of research going on with people who have had experiences like yours. We see these symptoms in Vietnam War veterans, people who have been held as hostages, and other catastrophic events. We now call it Post Traumatic Stress Disorder, or PTSD for short."

"So you would call what happened to me a catastrophic event?"

She looked surprised. "Yes, of course. Given what happened to you, you are completely normal. In other words, anyone who experienced what you did would likely have these symptoms."

"Then, the million dollar question is, how do I get rid of the symptoms?"

"Most patients with PTSD benefit from the type of therapy like you are getting from Mrs. Fine. Has it improved since you started seeing her?"

"Yes. But it hasn't completely disappeared either. It happened a year ago! When will it go away?"

"I can't give you an exact answer. It varies from person to person. But I see no reason to think you are developing any kind of psychiatric illness. You seem to be making progress, maybe not as quickly as you would like, but progress nonetheless, with your current treatment. So my advice is to continue it. There are some psychologists who specialize in treating PTSD, but not anywhere close to here."

She seemed to know way more than anyone else I'd met. So I decided to take a chance and ask her about some of the more bizarre parts of it.

"I can't explain this very well, but maybe you can tell me why it is. When I woke up in the ER that night, I felt like I wasn't the same person that I was before."

"Can you tell me more about that?"

"I can't put it any other way, it's as if ... my life before it happened and my life after it happened don't belong to the same person. It isn't that I didn't remember my name or my parents and all that stuff it's just that I ... well ... I didn't know who I was anymore. I felt like ... someone else. When I look in the mirror, a stranger looks back. I don't know who I am anymore." I looked at her doubtfully, as I didn't seem to be making my point. "You probably think I'm nuts."

"No, I don't. There is a term to describe this: disassociation. Please go on."

"I'm not a child anymore. As of that day, I'm not a child anymore, but I'm not an adult either so I don't belong anywhere. I suppose I've learned to live with it," I shrugged, "since no one ever really has understood me anyway. I was different before any of this ever happened."

"How so?"

"It's hard to explain, I just always have been. It's most obvious in school. I don't think like the other kids, I don't talk like them, and I'm not interested in the things that they are. I just don't fit in."

"Do you have friends?"

"Yes I've always had friends, but most of them are either older or younger than me. I don't get along very well with kids my own age."

"You definitely are not typical. You have an unusually large vocabulary and seem much older than you are. I would also say from these results that you have a rather high IQ. Often people like that describe the same kinds of school experiences."

"Even my dreams are different," I offered.

"How is that?"

"Well, I dream in the same places. Not physical places, but dream places. This is so difficult to explain. It's like there really is such a place, and I have another life there, because when I dream about one of these places I can remember all the other dreams I had before, like memories. They are not repetitive dreams – each one is new, they just happen in the same place. I started calling them "dreamscapes" when I was little because they're like dream landscapes. I know I'm dreaming when this happens because I recognize the place. I don't know of anyone else who does this. The other kids think I'm lying."

"Actually what you are describing is called lucid dreaming. We now know it's a real phenomenon. There's someone studying it at Stanford University, in fact. I read an article about it, very recently. I don't know how common it is, but there are other people who experience this. They say it's associated with creativity."

On the way home in the car, I watched out the window and thought about what I'd learned. Lucid dreams! Now there is a wonderful thing! A name for it! If a psychologist in Pittsburgh said that lucid dreams were real, then there was no way anyone out in the God forsaken boonies where I lived could accuse me of making it all up! I related everything I'd been told to my mother and she had a lot more respect for the dreams from then on.

The opening strains of *The Lawrence Welk Show* always remind me of Grandma, my father's mother. Every Saturday night, we went to visit her at precisely 7:00 PM and were greeted by The Lawrence Welk theme song blaring from the TV in the corner of the cozy living room in her little rented one-bedroom cottage. If we were even five minutes late, she assumed we'd been in a car accident and proceeded to have a hissy fit. She had a good reason.

My father, the only boy and the second youngest of five siblings, was born in what around these parts is affectionately known as a mine patch. A mine patch is a little town that grows up around a coal mine. Usually the houses are owned by the mine and rented to the miners and it has a company store like most industry towns. This particular one, Kinlock, was attached to the Western end of New Kensington.

They lived in the far end of complex of row houses known collectively as The Titanic. His father – my grandfather – was the Kinlock coal mine's fire boss, which is what they would now call a safety inspector. He was considered to be part of the mine's management and that entitled him and his family to the coveted end house with windows on the one side. The Titanic, like its namesake, succumbed to disaster. It burned to the ground sometime in the 1970's.

Being a part of the mining community, particularly with the memories of the nearby catastrophic Harwick mining disaster, which was one of the ten worst mining disasters in American history, Grandma always lived with the very real possibility that her life could be changed in a moment by an accident and her husband might not come home.

Dad also had a younger sister named Nelly Jean who was killed in a sled riding accident – involving a car – a few days before her tenth birthday. Looking back, I can't understand how I never made the connection between Nelly Jean's accident and Grandma's habit of freaking out if we were late.

I still remember that house; the texture of the gray carpet in the living room, the satisfying rattle of the aluminum screen door, the Mellon Bank calendar hanging in the pantry, and the drawer where the tea spoons were kept in a green plastic utensil holder. Sitting in that living room, I was content listening to old time songs on the Lawrence Welk Show. The performers were men in ruffled tuxedo shirts and women in frothy rainbow colored organdie dresses. I especially watched it for the dresses!

That Saturday began like any other. The aroma of freshly baked pies engulfed us in a cloud of warm, damp air as we came in. Grandma stood at the sink with an apron tied around her waist, washing several large mixing bowls in the sink while the tea kettle steamed contentedly on the stove.

"Coffee?" offered Grandma, wiping her hands on her apron. "I have rhubarb pie, if you're interested." Nobody made better pies than Grandma!

The evening sunlight diffused softly in the cheery yellow curtains above the kitchen sink. Grandma stood slicing her warm pie. I moved up to the counter and gawked about hopefully.

"I made you your favorite treat," she said, anticipating what I was looking for. Whenever she made pies, she took the leftover crust and rolled it out. Then, she would bake it in a little tin pan, sprinkled with cinnamon and sugar on top.

I made myself a cup of tea while Grandma served pie and coffee to my parents. I took my pie crust and sat down next to Grandma's chair in her little space between the kitchen and the living room, a cozy spot with the phone nearby and an unobstructed view of the TV.

Grandma sat down in her chair and picked up her crochet. Her hands were twisted into claws by arthritis, but she never lost her skill. She made all sorts of things, but I particularly remember the afghans and baby booties. All of us had at least one of her afghans. The cheerful and bright baby booties she made by the hundreds. She packed them in plastic bags and donated them to the local hospital maternity ward. I can hardly fathom the number of parents who took their new babies home in Grandma's booties. I often eyed them enviously for my baby dolls, but Grandma was adamant that dolls could easily get on lacking booties, while newborn babies in hospitals would surely catch pneumonia without them.

Lawrence Welk ended, and *Hee Haw* came on. "I wish they

hadn't taken *Wonderful World of Disney* off," I complained absentmindedly.

"Yes, TV just gets worse and worse," agreed Grandma. "I don't watch most of it, with people shooting at each other and such nonsense."

My father, no doubt tired to begin with, had that glassy- eyed hypnotic TV look about him. That mood indicated he could watch for hours. My mother sat absorbed in a new, glossy magazine.

I'd had more dreams about Grammy and the weird repeating digits and the smell of rose water showing up at odd times. I didn't understand anything about the dreams but they made my parents very uncomfortable. Since what had happened the previous summer, I'd stopped having dreams in my usual dreamscapes I'd had since I was a baby. The only lucid dreams I had now always took place in a version of the Aunt Farm, and were often dark and sort of scary. I often heard the whistle of a steam engine, but never actually saw it.

"Tell me one of your ghost stories", I asked during the lull. Grandma could tell the best ghost stories about banshees and other weird things. I'd always enjoyed them but in light of my recent experiences and dreams, I was even more curious. I knew Grandma Mason had seen ghosts and had psychic experiences. I'd been waiting for a good night to pump her for information about it, when my parents were not paying close attention.

"Well", she began, her crochet hook sliding rhythmically through the colorful yarn, "when I was a little girl we lived on a farm in Ohio. Every fall, they cut the corn stalks down, and left behind in the ground were stalks about three or four inches high, very hard and sharp. In those days, there were no public cemeteries like there are now. You buried your dead on your own property, and we had our own little cemetery on the far side of the corn fields. Anyhow, one day my brother and I were playing and we stopped to rest on one of the head stones. We took our shoes off to empty pebbles from them, and we were laughing and talking. Then suddenly, from somewhere behind the head stone came a voice that said: 'Please go away and let me rest'. We were so scared that we ran across those sharp corn stalks in our bare feet, leaving our shoes behind!"

"Did you see anything?"

"Not that time, but my sister did. She and her beau were sitting on the back porch one evening after dark, and you could see the cemetery from the porch. They saw two shadowy white figures appear in the graveyard and walk right through a split rail fence."

"Do you think dead people are aware of us and can sometimes come back?"

"Maybe." Her crochet needle halted and for a moment, she was lost in thought. "Probably. After all, the Bible says we are surrounded by a great cloud of witnesses. I've never really thought about it much, I suppose. It's happened to me, and to a lot of other people I know. I don't think anybody really knows what they are."

"Are you ever afraid of them?"

Having finished the baby bootie, she tied it off and tied the pair together before answering.

"Sometimes. But I don't think they can actually hurt you."

"Why do you think ghosts come back? Do they want something? Or are they trying to tell us something?"

The television blared on, and Grandma regarded me with a penetrating stare that seemed to say, so you've seen something. In that look I sensed I'd touched upon some raw nerve. Grandma was always a private person, quite the Victorian lady who had a very well developed sense of propriety. Her husband – my grandfather – died several years before I was born. Years later, my sister told me that the day after he died, she walked into her bedroom and saw him standing by the foot of the bed in broad daylight. Of course, none of us will ever know what transpired between them, as they faced each other for the first time separated by a veil of death.

"There are really no solid answers for those kind of questions. The Bible says: *For now we see through a glass, darkly; but then face to face: now I know in part; but then shall I know even as also I am known.* To see through a glass darkly is ... to see through a glass darkly. There's just no way to know that, until the day comes when you can ask God face to face."

"Noelle says there was a ghost in her house. She says Linda's roommate got rid of it by casting a spell on it to make it go into a glass of water and flushing it down the toilet."

Grandma laughed. "I don't believe that." She reached into her bag and pulled out another brightly colored skein of yarn, her mood altering with the color of her crochet. "Is Noelle coming to visit this summer?"

Dad blinked wearily. "I'm not sure she wants to come this year."

"Well I can't say I blame her," I began without thinking.

He sat up and pinned me down with a dirty look. "She's getting older and doesn't want to leave her neighborhood friends," he explained.

We both looked at Grandma, still hooking away, to see if she noticed. There was no reaction, one way or the other. It was as if she hadn't heard any of it. But did she?

I changed the subject. "What about things like, fate? Are some things just meant to happen? Even if you know about them in advance, maybe by dreaming about them?"

"Yes, I do believe in fate. I don't believe the future is set in stone though. Some things seem to be meant to happen and you can't change them no matter what you do, and other things are not that way. It is hard to tell the difference. The things that are fated - only God can change those things. Or at least, he can transform them. He can use them. Come on in the bedroom," she offered. "I've something to give you."

I followed her into the dim bedroom, lit only by a little lamp on a table next to her bed. She ambled slowly, cane in hand, past the blanket chest and towards her dresser, where she always kept a stash of candy and Juicy Fruit gum. I ask about ghosts and she gives me candy?

She drew something out of the top drawer. "I've been meaning to give you this. This is an old Bible; I've had it for years and I'll not have need of it much longer. I know it isn't much, but, I still want you to have it. I want you to keep it. Because, experiences like that - ghosts, dreams, or whatever - they come into your life like a dollar you find lying on the sidewalk. You can leave it there and walk away, or pick it up and use it for something. You don't know for sure where it came from, and you sure don't know where it's going. But this," she put her hand softly on the worn leather Bible, "you can trust. And you may not know it yet, but sometimes you need that more than the dollar on the sidewalk."

To be sure, I didn't know much about either God or ghosts at that point, but I'd figured out a few things. Like not all ghosts are the same. Some – like the spooky thing we used to encounter in a certain place back in the woods – were always in the same general place and felt scary, as if they were stuck there. Others – like Grammy – could come and go wherever or whenever they wanted, and tended to be 'warm fuzzy' dispensers on some sort of a mission.

CHAPTER 10

Fall of 1982

The summer faded into fall and school started again. Even so, in our corner of the world we look forward to a time called Indian summer, when the leaves are bright and the weather is mild. It was on an Indian summer day that Kris and I set out into the woods with a picnic basket.

"Do you remember when we first found this place?" asked Kris as we tramped along.

"Yeah! And you used to call it winter wonderland because we found it sled riding? Hey! Let's see if there are any more raspberries!"

The journey to this place took us through somebody's back pasture, where there was a huge patch of red raspberries. At one time, there was also an enclosed field with a friendly pony, but he was gone by that summer. As were the raspberries, as they were the old fashioned kind that have one bonanza in July.

After inspecting the barren berry bushes, we spread out our blanket in the middle of the field and lay down on it, hands behind our heads. It was at the top of a very long hill. You could see for what seemed like miles back then, the view unmarred by housing developments. Below us, the woods blazed fall colors. I could smell the familiar musty odor of fall as all around us a breeze caressed the drying field grasses, rippling them like brown silk. It reminded me of part of a poem I read somewhere ... *when summer's purple heather has gone to autumn rust.*

"Someday when I have a yard of my own, I want to grow a garden of purple heather," I mused.

Kris sat up and opened the basket. She took out two strawberry jam sandwiches and handed one to me. "Why?" she laughed. "That's a funny thing to grow in a garden."

"It reminds me of my grandmother. You know, Robert Burns, Scotland, and all that."

We sat admiring a particularly large oak tree on at the top of the hill behind us flashing many shades of red, its huge limbs outlined against the bright blue cloudless sky.

I sighed deeply. "School sucks without you guys." I missed Kris and her friends now that they were at the senior high. I hadn't seen any of them since we went out for ice cream after the freshman farewell dance this past May.

"Don't worry! It won't be long until you'll be at the senior high with us."

"I hope so, because it's really dull at the junior high. I'm not going to any dances this year."

"I don't blame you. I wouldn't go either. Junior high dances are babyish." This was a new attitude – the past year she dragged me to every single one of them.

I rolled over onto my back and gazed up at the sky. I closed my eyes in the bright sunlight as the warm breeze touched my cheek.

"We ought to do a skip day this year, like we used to", I said.

"You mean the sled riding skip days?" She tilted her head back and laughed, her honey blonde hair alive with highlights in the sun. "Oh, yes!"

In elementary school we used to skip school once per year and go sled riding. We would go up to the bus stop and hide among the gravel piles until the bus went by and her mother left for work. Then we would go to her house, get dressed in our snow suits, and spend the morning sled riding in the woods. The woods were silent in soft, fluffy snow and it felt like we were the only people in the world. Cold and hungry, we would return and sit on the warm cellar stair peeling off layers of wet clothes. Then, a feast: hot chocolate with marshmallows and a spaghetti dinner, eaten in front of the TV while watching reruns of *Bewitched*, *My Three Sons*, and *I Dream of Jeannie*. Then we would clean up, put everything back exactly as before, and return to our hiding places at the bus stop until it was time to arrive home from school. Never once did we get caught.

She reached into the basket again. "Do you want something to drink? I brought a bottle of Pepsi."

"Sure."

"Sorry I don't have any ice."

"That's all right. I don't need ice. Band is really a drag this year. They're going on a band trip but I have already made my excuses. I don't want to be somewhere away from home with no friends."

"Well, I can't blame you. You need to stay in band now or you won't be able to be in it in senior high. And you might like it better." She glanced down at my arm. "That's a nice watch. When did you get it?"

"I got it for my birthday." When my parents asked me what I

wanted for my birthday that year I told them I wanted a fancy gold watch. *Cosmopolitan* said that a classic gold watch made a much more elegant look than an armload of cheap costume jewelry.

"How did you ever get your parents to buy you something like that?"

"Well it wasn't that expensive. It isn't a name brand or anything. But it does look good."

"It ought to look good for the next star party! Now that it's fall, are there any more star parties? Or is that it for the year?"

"No more star parties but there are business meetings at the senior high. Sometimes Mr. Jack shows movies that he has for his classes." That, of course, reminded me of some exciting news! "And Chuck nominated me for club secretary!"

"Do you think you'll win?"

"I think so. Chuck was the secretary before and he says he is sick of it. I hope I'll see Martin again at one of the meetings. "

She thought for a moment. "Which one is he?"

"I saw him at one of the star parties this summer. Not the first one. I think it was the one after that. Anyway, he's blonde and really nice looking. I didn't actually talk to him, but all evening he kept looking at me. He's younger than Chuck and Jeff. Maybe the same age as Keith or even younger."

"You and all your men! Do you know where this Martin goes to school?"

"No. I don't really know anything about him except that he has a brother named Doug. His address on the membership roster is in Avonmore."

"I'm pretty sure that's part of our school district. I'll do some discreet asking around and see if I can find out more about him." She poked me in the ribs. "So when do I get to meet all these cute guys you're always talking about?"

I sat bold upright. "You could come to a business meeting!"

She wrinkled up her nose. "No thanks. When will there be another star party?"

"Not until next summer. But we're going to have the Christmas party! Maybe you can come to that." I leaned back on the blanket again, my feet pointing downhill. Near the bottom of the hill was a large stand of pine trees. At the edge of this thicket sat an old car. I'd seen this old car plenty of times before but today it gave me an idea. I sat up and turned towards Kris. "Let's go see that car."

"That nasty old thing? It's probably got hornets in it, or worse!"

"There are no bees this time of year! Let's go. I have an idea!"

"Oh, all right." The car sat at the edge of the thicket, creeping farther in with each passing year. One window was broken and leaves and sticks littered the back seat and floor. One back wheel was missing. Despite the dirt, I could tell that it had once been a nice shade of blue. I stood totally infatuated.

"So what's you great idea?"

"We could restore it! Then we would have our own car!"

"Fix up this thing? You must be out of your mind!"

"No! Look how neat it is! It has fins! Let's check under the hood!"

"Not me! There could be an animal in there!"

But it was too late. I was already groping around the front grill. Poor Kris stood several yards away, her arms over her head in defense of whatever life form emerged from the engine compartment.

"Just tell me when it's over!"

To tell the truth, I was a little scared myself. I slid my hand through the grill in the middle where I thought the hood latch should be, hoping there was not a big hairy spider under it. The latch clicked and the hood shuddered, dislodging dirt.

"I got it!"

"OH Gawd!" She wrapped her arms more tightly about her head.

The rusty old hinges groaned as I lifted the hood. It took all the strength I had to open it. Sunlight touched an engine that had not seen the light of day in a long, long time. I wiped my hands on my pants. "No creepy crawlies."

Kris approached the car warily. "Doesn't look like there is much else, either."

"Well, the belts and hoses are gone, but the engine is there! I think the radiator is gone too."

She wandered around to the driver's side and peered in the window. "So is the radio."

"Well, how hard is it to find a car radio? It probably only got AM anyway."

"Do you really think your parents are going to let you drag an old car home from the woods? How are you going to get it out of here?"

"I'm not sure but I'll think of something. I wonder what kind of car it is."

"I have no idea, but we better get going. It's almost time for dinner."

From that day forward, I loved the old car with a passion formerly reserved for stuffed toys and favorite cartoons, but for now I kept my mouth shut until my plans had time to congeal in my mind. The very next day I awoke to frost, confirming my suspicions that it would be impossible to get the car out until spring. I used the intervening time wisely, to interrogate my father on the finer details of how cars work and to read my brother's discarded auto mechanics books.

***

I lay on my mother's bed while she was reading, staring up at the plaster swirls on the ceiling. This is how we had most of our meaningful conversations. The late September night was hushed and dark outside the window. A few distant porch lights winked in between the near naked branches of the trees as they swayed in the breeze. The lamp next to my mother's bed cast a warm circle on the ceiling. A few wisps of steam drifted up from her cup of decaf Sanka sitting on the nightstand.

I flopped over onto my stomach and faced her. "This Thursday is the Astronomy Club meeting, and Chuck said he was gonna nominate me for secretary! He says he's been secretary for the last two years and he's sick of it. Do you think I'd be any good at it?

"I think it would be a great opportunity for you," she answered. "It will get you more involved and teach you how organizations work."

"What exactly does a club secretary do?"

"Well, for one thing they keep the meeting minutes."

"What's that?"

"Notes basically – you keep a record of everything that was discussed at the meeting. So you've got two basic categories. Old business is anything that was discussed at the last meeting. New business is anything new that comes up at the current meeting. So you keep track of what was discussed, what motions were made, who made them, who seconded them, and if they passed. I also imagine you would keep the membership roster up to date and distribute newsletters and star party schedules. And read the minutes from the last meeting at the start of each meeting. It really isn't all that hard. I'm sure you could do it with no problem."

"Where did all this stuff come from – new business, old business, passing motions and all that stuff?"

"It's called Robert's Rules – most clubs are run that way. You'll run into it over and over again. That's why this is such good experience. You can use these skills in any organization for the rest of your life."

"The newsletter says we have to decide where the Christmas Party will be this year at the next meeting. Can we offer to have the Christmas party this year? No one else has claimed it yet! We joined too late to have a star party this past summer, so can we host the Christmas party?"

"I don't see why not. I was also going to volunteer for a star party, but we'll be on vacation for most of the summer. So it will have to be in September."

I was not expecting such a positive response and squeezed my hands together with delight. Naturally, my first thought was, "What should I wear?"

"I saw a great outfit in Family Circle I could make for you. It had a very full black taffeta skirt with a wide red satin cummerbund, and white blouse that kind of reminded me of Lady Diana's wedding dress. We can get you a pair of black patent leather pumps to go with it. What do you think?"

The night of the Astronomy club meeting I hurried down the darkened hallway towards Mr. Jack's classroom. My footsteps made eerie echoes up and down the dark corridor. We usually parked in the upper parking lot outside the library and came via what was known as The Back Hallway. Mr Yijko's classroom had no windows whatsoever as it was located in the center of the building. The cinderblock walls were painted beige which cut the glare from the florescent lights somewhat. A huge poster of Mount St Helens hung on the wall above the table for the refreshments; it had erupted about a year and half before and figured heavily in his Earth and Space Science lesson plans. On a bulletin board to the right of the blackboard hung a large cartoon of his dog Spot looking through a telescope and recording his discoveries in a notebook. One of his past students had drawn it for him.

I slipped into the room and took a desk next to Chuck, Jeff, and Keith. My mother arrived a few seconds behind and began talking to a group of parents on the other side of the room.

"So, what's new with you?" asked Chuck.

I pulsed with adrenaline and could hardly wait to tell him about my plans for the car, but I didn't want to overplay my hand and look childish. So I said as calmly and nonchalantly as I could, "I found an old car in the woods."

Both of their eyes perked up. "Do you know what kind?"

This was EXACTLY the reaction I was looking for. I folded my arms on the desk, and blinked at them innocently. "Why no. Actually, I was hoping you guys might know."

"What's it look like?" asked Jeff.

"Well, it's a four door sedan; it has chrome around the windows. It's fairly long, it's blue. I don't know what else you need me to describe."

"That could be a lot of things. Does it have any fins?" asked Chuck.

"Yes, but they're small."

"Look around on the dashboard. It should at least give you the maker", suggested Jeff. "Does it say anything along the back, on the rear fender, or on the trunk above the bumper?" I wasn't going to tell them that these places were covered with moss, but I resolved to go scrape it off at the first available opportunity.

"Did somebody buy a car?" asked Bruce.

Chuck gestured towards me. "Naw. She found it in a bush." All of us laughed.

"It's not in a BUSH, it's in a field," I corrected, as if that made much difference. "It belongs to a friend of my brother."

"How old is it?" asked Bruce.

"I'm not sure. It's at least from the sixties. Maybe older."

"Wow, what if it's a '57 Chevy!" suggested Bruce. "They're worth a lot of money, you know. If you're really interested in fixing it up, you should pursue it. Even if it's something else, there are a lot of old cars worth money these days."

Just then, Martin Jamison and his little brother Doug walked in. Even though I had only seen him once and that was six months ago, I recognized him. He came over and took a seat behind me, Doug trailing along behind. I wiped my sweaty palms on my jeans and tried not to jiggle my leg with nervousness.

"So what's up with you, Martin?" asked Chuck.

"Oh, not much", he answered with a shrug.

"Have you met Laura?" asked Keith. "She's a new member."

He turned to me and smiled. "I don't think we've officially met but I remember seeing you at someone's house this past summer. Over at Moore's maybe."

"Well then, Martin, this is Laura, and Laura, this is Martin."

"Nice to meet you, officially", he said as he shook my hand. Smirks sneaking across their faces, Chuck and Jeff exchanged a look. I wondered if they knew I liked him. How did they know these things?

"So what have you been up to? We haven't seen you in a while", continued Keith.

"It's been a pretty busy summer. Things have calmed down since school started. I don't think I told you guys, I'm at Kiski this year. The teacher's strike went on so long my parents lost their patience and sent me to Kiski Prep."

My eyes widened. Kiski Prep was a boys only private boarding school in the area. No wonder Kris couldn't find him at the senior high! Granted, we'd only been back at school for a few days. The strike went on for weeks that year. We wouldn't be out of school until the end of June! My parents were very unhappy because they were planning a long involved car trip to California and wanted to leave as soon as school was normally out. They told me we'd be gone most of the summer and I was seriously bummed at missing so many star parties. Thanks to the teacher's union, I wouldn't have to miss George Bailey's, which was always the second Saturday in June.

"Geez you're not boarding there are you?"

"No, I just go during the day like regular school."

"How do you like it?", asked Chuck.

"It's all right, I guess. Some of the people I've met are pretty cool but it's a little too stuffy. I'm going back to Kiski for my senior year."

Chuck grimaced. "Do they make you wear uniforms and stuff?"

"A jacket and tie every day."

Chuck shook his head. "I couldn't deal with that." Jeff nodded in agreement.

Bruce, who was club president at the time (he and Mr Jack flip-flopped between president and vice president every year) took a quick visual survey of the room. "It looks like everybody's here. I'm going to call the meeting to order."

As soon as Bruce approached the podium, everyone scrambled for a seat and the room grew quiet. "Let's call the meeting to order. Does anyone have the time?"

Chuck waved at him without looking up from scribbling in the club notebook. "I've got my watch on."

"Let's start with old business. Chuck, would you like to read the minutes from the last meeting?" Chuck responded by reading off a litany of all the topics discussed at the last meeting.

"Are there any additions or corrections to the minutes?" No response from the peanut gallery.

"Is there any other old business?" Again silence. "Okay, then. New business. First off, we have to decide what to do about the Christmas party. If no one else wants to host we can have it at my house again."

My mother raised her hand. "We can have it at our house. You can also put us down for a star party, but we'll be out of town most of the summer so I'd like to have it in early September."

"Great! Early September is no problem – we don't' have any other star parties scheduled in September yet. What day do you think is best for the Christmas party? Saturday, December eighteenth maybe?"

"No that's too close to Christmas", complained Chuck.

"OK, what about the fourth?"

"I'm working that day," someone said.

"How about the eleventh?" Everyone looked at each other but nobody had any objections. "That settles it. Since we're having the party that month there will be no business meeting on December second. We'll hold the December meeting at the Christmas Party."

"Anyone else who wants to have a star party this summer, let me know by the Christmas party. So far I have George, Reid, Randy, and Bob. There is still room for one or two more if anyone is interested. So I suppose now we can move on to the big agenda item for the November meeting - nominations for new club officers. Who wants to make the motion to open the nominations?" A hand went into the air. "Who will second?" Another hand went into the air. Bruce turned to the black board. "Do I have any nominations for president?"

Chuck grinned. "I nominate Bruce!"

Bruce suppressed a laugh as he wrote his own name on the blackboard.

"I nominate Bob Jack", chimed George. Silence followed.

"OK. Since the second runner up is vice president, we can move on to Treasurer."

"Bob", came a nomination from the other side of the room followed by silence. Bob grinned. He'd been treasurer for years. "Doesn't anyone else want to run?"

"How about secretary? Any nominations for secretary?"

Chuck raised his hand. "I nominate Laura." My name joined the others on the back board.

"I nominate Chuck", said Jeff, kicking Chuck's chair.

"I decline", said Chuck, "it's time I handed this over to someone new."

"Aw, come on Chuck! If you don't run, then we'll have two whole categories with only one person running!" protested Bruce.

Chuck rolled his eyes. "All right. I'll run. But nobody better vote for me."

"Do I have a motion to close the nominations?" A hand went up. "Second?" Another hand went up. "OK. Nominations are closed. Is there any other new business?"

"Yeah," said Mr. Jack, "who is bringing the refreshments to the next meeting?"

"I'll bring them!" said George.

"OK. Do I have a motion to close? Someone to second it? With that, I'll turn things over to Mr. Jack. He's got a movie for us."

"It's a film on quasars", explained the nonchalant instructor as he wheeled the projector into position and threaded the film through it. "My students stayed awake for it, so it can't be too bad. Can somebody pull down the projector screen?"

With that, the lights went down and the movie started. I rather liked it, as quasars were a new discovery back then and I had not read much about them. Several times during the movie I sensed that something was going on in back of me, and when I turned around in the dim and flickering light Chuck and Jeff were both giggling silently. Once I caught Martin's glance when I looked back at them, a glance that seemed to say 'what's their problem?' I really liked Martin.

When the movie ended and the lights came up everyone began gravitating towards the doughnuts and soda pop. As he stood up, Chuck waved the red club notebook at me.

"Just think, jailbait! Next month, this will be *all yours.*"

"Only if I win."

"Don't worry, you will."

As I poured a glass of bright orange pop my mother appeared beside me. "Looks like you'll be elected."

"I'm running against Chuck so I could lose." I took a bite of a soft, sugary doughnut.

"Nah. They'll all vote for you because they know he doesn't really want it. Besides, I think you'll make a better secretary than him, and I wouldn't be surprised if everyone else does, too."

"You're running for secretary - that's great", said Randy as he pulled a chocolate doughnut out of the box.

"Oh hello, Randy. It's nice to see you again. How have you been?" said my mother.

"Pretty good."

"Where have you been sitting?" I asked. "I haven't seen you all evening."

"Oh, I've been over there with them." He gestured towards the back of the room where Frank and Doug sat watching Randy, their faces turning red. Whenever I was around, they all became mute and awkward. Randy was the only one I was friendly with.

As my mother wandered off with Bruce talking about the Christmas party, I leaned towards Randy and whispered, "Do you know Martin very well? This is the first time I've actually talked to him."

"Not really," he answered with a hint of sympathy.

"Does he usually come to the meetings?"

"Last year, he was fairly regular."

"What are you two whispering about?" demanded Chuck.

"We weren't whispering," I defended. "We're just talking, why?"

He retreated, leaving Randy and me alone again in front of the doughnuts. I squeezed my Styrofoam cup until it crackled. The atmosphere had grown awkward. When the movie had first ended, I was so excited that I thought I would burst. Now I wondered if I said something wrong. I grappled for something to say.

"I got a new stereo last week. Early Christmas present."

The awkwardness faded in an instant. "Really? Where did you get it?"

"Montgomery Ward. It has an AM/FM radio, a record player, a cassette deck, and an eight track player."

"That's great! You can record from the radio so much better that way!" From across the room Frank threw Randy an impatient look from behind his freckles and bright orange hair. "I think our ride is here, and Frank is getting ready to leave without me. See you in school?" he asked.

"Sure." He scurried off. Martin came over to the refreshment table to grab a doughnut for the road. He already had his jacket on and his car keys out. I'd better act fast or my opportunity would be gone. I tried to appear relaxed. "So, when will I be seeing you again?"

"Well," he mumbled with a mouth full of doughnut. Holding up a finger, he wiped the powdered sugar off his face. "Unfortunately, I won't be at the Christmas party. My family is going to New Orleans for the holidays." Doug appeared behind Martin and stood with his arms crossed, staring at the ceiling during the entire conversation.

"Really? Do you have relatives down there?"

"Yeah, my mom grew up there. I'm really sorry to miss your party, but I'll be back in time for the January meeting. Good luck in the elections! You'd get my vote. I'm sure you'll win." Doug sighed and shifted his weight from one foot to the other. Martin ignored his impatience.

"I hope so," I added.

"Have a nice Christmas." He smiled before turning to leave. Doug trailed behind him, obviously relieved.

"You too," I called after them.

***

It was not long before I found myself packing my little duds for a weekend road trip, this time to my brother Bob's house. Bob was living in a new town and I wasn't too sure I liked it as well as Columbus, Ohio where he'd been living for the last eight years while getting his his Ph.D from Ohio State University.

Bob graduated that summer in an uneventful ceremony in the University Gymnasium. Soon after that, he was offered an assistant professorship at Bowling Green University, which was about another hour's drive northwest in Ohio.

The new house was more of a craftsman style, nothing like the spectacular Victorian that had been his home for the past several years.

Now here he was, in a plainer house, in a new town far away from our favorite Chinese restaurant and the frozen yogurt stand. Bowling Green was dull compared to Columbus. For one thing, it had no bicycle paths. Yet, I was looking forward to seeing my brother again. That same weekend there was a symposium and a faculty reception at the home of the head of the Political Science Department. Since we would be there, we were graciously invited. So off we went on another excursion in vacation land: begging my father to stop and let us go to the bathroom, arguing about where to eat, and wondering if we should have gotten off at the exit we just passed.

I didn't really have anything to wear to something like that so my mother let me borrow one of her dresses. When she saw it, she told me I looked too 'matronly' and tried to persuade me to wear something else, but I refused to budge. It was an opportunity to interact with the world free from my past and anxiety be damned, I was determined to make the most of it.

The lecture went completely over my head. I didn't know anything back then about politics and still don't. A cold drizzle fell outside. I was glad I had the new raincoat my mother made for me. I sat during the lecture and admired the shiny gray fabric as it lay across my lap, thinking about all sorts of things. The gray reminded me of New York City, the color of the sky scraper in which Bob lived back in the 70's where the traffic drove beneath it all day and all night. I must have been three years old the year he lived in New York. We used to visit him and I remember the round, globular street lights and Dad refusing to let me spit off of the observation deck of the Empire State Building.

My brother, seated next to me, rose his hand slightly to wave at a man I recognized from moving day, and I emerged briefly from my thoughts to rub my eyes, yawn, and glance at my gold watch. The sound of applause rose all around me. Bending as gracefully as possible, I picked up my purse and stood with the crowd, smiling and shaking hands with people as we moved towards the exit.

After a short ride, we arrived at the dean's house. It was a large, Georgian style house, immaculately furnished. It just oozed money. Designed for entertaining at their social position, my mother would say.

We were greeted at the door by his wife. She smiled warmly, took our coats, and directed us towards a table full of hors d'oeuvres. I had just crammed several of them into my mouth when she reappeared with a red-haired girl.

"I'm so glad that you could come tonight. This is our daughter, Jennifer." I smiled, nodded, and did my best to swallow the evidence of my gluttony as inconspicuously as possible.

Jennifer held out her hand. "I'm glad you came. There usually isn't anyone my age at these things. I just got a new Atari, would you like to play a game?"

"Sure! I've played it before! There is this guy in our neighborhood who has all of this electronics stuff," I prattled on as I followed her into a library, "he has a short wave radio, a computer, and an Atari. Sometimes he lets the neighborhood kids play with it."

The library was a warm, dark room, with a fire burning cheerfully in the fireplace. Two overstuffed leather sofas sat facing each other in front of the fire. We sank into them, one of us on each side, facing the TV opposite the fire.

"Which game would you like to play? We have chess, backgammon, tennis, and that space invaders thing."

"Let's play space invaders."

She popped the cartridge in and the game began. We sat for quite a while, shooting at the rows of spaceships on the screen, until I lost for the fifth or sixth time.

"I guess I'm not too good at this."

"It takes practice. Sometimes I spend entire days playing this. If you don't mind my asking, how much age difference is there between you and your brother?"

"Nineteen years. I'm thirteen."

"You're kidding me! I thought you were at least my age and maybe older. I'm seventeen. Are all your other brothers and sisters that much older than you?"

"Yeah pretty much. I was sort of a post-menopausal accident, I suppose."

Jennifer stifled a giggle. "Maybe you seem older because you have been around adults so much. I spent most of my time around adults, too. I'm an only child."

I enjoyed being with Jennifer. She seemed to understand, somehow, even though I had just met her. I sunk back into the sofa, relaxed. "I love the color of your hair! Would you believe I dye mine? My mother will only let me use that temporary stuff and it isn't nearly that pretty..."

She ran her fingers through it. "Thanks, I, ... I need to have it cut! I just got back, you see, I was in rehab. I was using cocaine, it was terrible. Don't ever try that stuff..."

"I'm so sorry!"

"No, that's okay. I'm just glad it is over. My mom would probably kill me if she knew I was talking about it! Things have been so nice since I got home! I have to make all new friends now. They're sending me to a new school. I start next week."

"You are so lucky."

"How is that?"

"Something bad happened to me, too. I was ... I dunno how to explain it ... abducted by this guy? It was last summer, but ever since then it's be awful. I'm anxious and afraid all the time. I think the other kids know something. It's like, *The Scarlet Letter* that we read in English class. Well, I'd give my right arm to start over in a new school. Just think! You can be anybody want to be! When you walk through those doors, you have no past. Nobody can judge you for being anything other than what you make up your mind to be that first day."

"Wow I guess I hadn't thought of it that way," she said. "I was too busy worrying about missing my old life. But you're absolutely right! It's like, a clean slate! Why don't your parents send you to a new school?"

"Well, we pretty much live in the middle of nowhere, and I don't think there is anywhere else. But I have this Astronomy club I belong to now that isn't part of the school. It's my way of starting over."

Jennifer's mother appeared at the door. "We're serving a light dinner if you girls are interested. Come on out and have some." She waved a tea towel at us cheerfully. Jennifer and I exchanged glances and headed for the buffet table.

"I remember you", came a voice from behind me, "you're Bob's sister." I turned to face him, and he shook my hand. "I was at his house to help the day he moved."

"Oh I remember you now. Gregg?"

"That's me." He grinned and gestured to a nice looking man beside him. "And this is Paul, one of the other Assistant Professors in the department."

Paul nodded a greeting and smiled warmly. "I didn't realize that Bob had family nearby."

"Well, we're not that nearby; we're from Pittsburgh."

"Oh really? I was in Pittsburgh not too long ago. It's a nice town. Hey Brian! This is Bob's sister from Pittsburgh."

"No kidding! I never knew that Bob had a sister."

"Jeff is a graduate student. Your brother's slave", teased Paul.

"In political science?"

"Yes. I'll be finished in about a year."

"And what is it that you teach?" I asked Paul.

"Linguistics."

"So then I guess you speak a lot of languages?"

"Ten: Spanish, French, Portuguese, German, Russian, Mandarin Chinese, Latin, Arabic, Yiddish, and of course, English."

"Say something in one of them!"

He thought for a moment before uttering something totally foreign. The other two men laughed.

"What did he say?" I glanced back and forth between them. "It must have been bad."

"No", he reassured. "It wasn't that bad. All I said was 'How are you?' in Russian." Somehow I didn't quite believe him. "So what is it that you study?"

"Science. Chemistry, and I enjoy amateur astronomy." This guy was flirting with me!

Paul grinned widely, his eyes glistening with the excitement of the chase while the other two men stood by and watched the game from the sidelines. I just hoped to God that my mother wouldn't show up. "You have a telescope?", he asked.

"Why yes, actually, I do. A reflective telescope."

"There are different types of telescopes?" Just then, Gregg handed me a glass of wine.

"Yes, thank you." I reached out and took the slender glass of burgundy wine from Gregg's hand.

"There are actually two types of telescopes", I began, taking a sip of wine. The hair on the back of my neck stood up as I tried to swallow it without making a face. I turned and grabbed a napkin from the Chippendale sideboard. "Excuse me. I think I'm going to sneeze", I lied from behind the napkin. I had never had wine before and gosh, that stuff was awful! It wasn't anything like the daiquiris!

Doing my best to smile, I forged onward. "The earliest telescope design is the refractive telescope, which was invented by Galileo. It consists of lenses arranged in a tube with the eyepiece at one end and the lens at the other. It is what most people think of when they hear the word telescope. A reflective telescope, on the other hand, is a much more recent technology that uses mirrors in addition to lenses, and the eyepiece is at the same end of the body as the lens. The opposite end is closed off. Reflective telescopes are much easier to use."

"Fascinating", he said. "So you look at what types of things? The moon? Planets?'

"Oh yes, and much more. There are galaxies, nebulas, star clusters, ..."

Jennifer stood talking to another group of people at the other end of the room, and when I caught her glance she gave me the thumbs up. I stood and talked to them about astronomy and every other imaginable topic, still holding the glass of wine since there was no way I could drink it.

"Where did you go to college?" one of them finally asked me.

Oh shit, now what? I decided now was as good a time as any to lower the boom on them. "Nowhere yet. I'm still in high school." I just left the junior part out.

The three of them gasped in unison. "No you're not! She's just kidding us," said Paul.

"Check her driver's license", Gregg suggested.

"I don't have a driver's license! It's true. If you don't believe me, ask my brother."

"Wow." Paul scratched his head and looked puzzled. "I thought you were around the same age as Bob." Out of the corner of my eye I noticed a look of admiration in Brian, the graduate student's eye.

Just then Mrs. Merrel entered. "I don't believe you have met my husband yet, Dr. Merrel."

"No I haven't, as a matter of fact." I followed her through a doorway into the living room and in the resulting confusion I managed to discretely dispose of the wine.

"Howard, here is Bob's sister. This is my husband, Dr. Merrel."

"How do you do? I hope you are enjoying your stay at Bowling Green." He smiled warmly and was obviously a very nice man.

"Yes, very much, sir", I answered, kind of intimidated.

"Who knows, maybe one day we'll have you as a student here What would you like to major in?"

"Chemistry, I think."

"Well you have a few years to make up your mind, but chemistry is a good field. We have a strong chemistry department here, so please do consider us."

"I will."

Then I noticed the magnificent Steinway in the corner of the living room. "What a beautiful piano!" I said.

"Do you play?" asked the dean.

"Well, sort of ..."

"Please." He gestured towards the piano.

I sat down on the bench and spread my fingers over the smooth, ivory keys. I drew in a deep breath. This was it! I played "The

Entertainer" by Scott Joplin, my best piece at that time. When I was done the room broke out into applause.

"It's time to go," said my mother, my coat draped over her arm. I was sorry to go! It was the most fun I'd had in a long time! Jennifer and her parents saw us to the door. Just as we were about to go, Greg appeared.

"That was the theme song from my favorite movie. It's a pity we don't have more pretty girls like you in Bowling Green."

"Good heavens! You'll inflate her ego so big we won't be able to live with her,' said my mother as she shoved me out the door.

"You know," she said to me once we were outside, "you shouldn't go around playing other people's pianos."

"I'll have you know I was invited by the dean himself!

"Oh, leave her alone, Mum!" My brother came to my rescue. "They loved it. What's the harm in that?"

So that was the subject of my English essay, the ubiquitous *What I Did Over the Summer*. The teacher called my mother about it.

"Do you know your daughter makes up stories?"

"What kind of stories?"

"Well, she turned in an essay about what she did over the summer, some crazy story about attending her brother's doctoral graduation and then a reception at a university dean's house."

"That is what she did over the summer," my mother said.

Silence. Mom said she could hear the woman thinking to herself, the parents lie, too!

***

A week or so before my party, the outfit was done and Kris came up on a nasty, rainy Saturday to check it out and help clean my room. We were up in my bedroom, having just moved the furniture around again. We never seemed to be able to get it arranged exactly right. Over the past year, my mother replaced the frilly, little girl bedspread and canopy cover I'd had for most of elementary school with something more sedate. The canopy was now a sheer woven lace and I had one of her homemade artistic quilts for a bedspread.

You would think with all that storage my room would be super organized, but it never was! It was usually an utter disaster. In contrast, Kris loved to clean and was a superb organizer so when my mother started the clean-your-room-or-else threats she came up and we did it together. This irritated my mother to no end, but she'd given up fighting us years ago since it produced results while forcing me to clean it alone never did.

We now had the bed with its headboard along the inside wall sticking out into the room. This made it easy to listen to the stereo in bed with headphones, since I wasn't allowed to blast my music and force my parents to listen to it.

I snatched the new outfit from the ironing board and put it on, then held up the picture from *Family Circle* magazine of a similar outfit.

"Very nice!"

"Do you think it will be OK for the Christmas party?"

"I'm sure it'll be a huge hit."

I flopped down on the bed. "I wish you could be there."

"Yeah, me too. Bad year for my family to decide to go to Florida for the holidays! But I'll come to your party this summer." She picked up the latest *Cosmopolitan* from my organized desk. "Let's see ...' How Well Do You Really Know Him? A Quiz That Could Lead to

More Questions!' I'll read the questions out loud. You actually to talked to him so you should ace it!"

Mom was not happy about our obsession with *Cosmopolitan*. I started reading it because my sister-in-law read it, and she used to give them to me after she read them. Unfortunately, I'd lost her to divorce the previous year and now I had to fight my mother to buy them. She thought *Seventeen* was more appropriate. We compromised and subscribed to both.

In the end, this really helped my cause, as I was developing two personas. The first was the fashion model teenaged girl – this was initially Kris's creation, but I was a quick study and my teenybopper wardrobe was filling out nicely. I was now dressing this way at school and had faced down the fallout over the red hair. The kids at school were calling me 'Princess Dye' which honestly was an enormous improvement over 'Hey Ugly'.

The second was discovered by accident at Bob's University party, I managed to fool all of those people into thinking I was the same age as my brother! Without even trying! I'd realized that the image one projects can be quite powerful. So I was also developing – with the assistance of Cosmopolitan – a thirteen going on thirty wardrobe.

The day of the party, I spent pampering myself. My mother spent it cooking.

I got dressed early and spun in front of the mirror listening to the rustle of the taffeta. The elaborate blouse with tucks and lace was found on sale at Horne's. My mother made the full tea length black taffeta skirt and bright red satin cummerbund. Then I sorted through my drawers until I found a suitably full petticoat.

A soft flurry of snow powdered the darkening winter landscape outside my window as I sat in front of my dressing table mirror.

Much to my surprise, my hair cooperated. I leisurely put on my new Merle Norman makeup and went downstairs to the kitchen to see how things were coming along.

"Who are you? Rudolph the red-nosed reindeer with lips?" howled my brother, John as I came downstairs. Hearing John's outburst, my mother emerged from the kitchen wiping her hands on a dish towel. "Oh! That red lipstick is too bright! Go upstairs and blot it."

"Yeah! Your friends will go blind looking at you!" giggled John.

My eyes began to sting.

"It's not that bad," consoled my mother as she waved the tea towel in front of her. "You just need to tone it down a little. Don't get all upset over nothing."

John said, "I'm just teasing you! I'm your brother! It's my job!"

I just turned and run back upstairs. From my room, I could hear them talking downstairs.

"What's her problem?"

"Just let her alone. She's having this party tonight and she's all worked up."

Upstairs in the bathroom I scrubbed the lipstick off with a tissue. I put on some bubblegum lip gloss instead. No way was I going to cry and ruin my makeup! I turned out the lights and lay down on my bed to do some Mrs. Fine deep breathing.

I was almost asleep when I was jarred by the abrupt sound of the doorknocker. Somebody's here! I stood up in the darkened room, my heart pounding. Then came the sound of the door opening ... who was it? I wandered out to the top of the stairs and peered down. It was Randy and his parents.

"Hi", he called, looking somewhat uncomfortable in his outfit that seemed to say, my mom picked this.

I smiled and floated down the stairs on a cloud of fabric, somewhat less confidant than before but willing to try again. My brother had gone home. It was my father who ruined my dramatic entrance by lobbing a pile of coats at me.

"Take these upstairs and lay them on the bed. Thanks."

Randy threw me a sympathetic look and followed me upstairs. "Wow! You guys have a lot of gifts!"

For a moment I couldn't imagine what he was talking about, until I realized that all the Christmas presents had been wrapped and stacked in the corner of my parents' bedroom. The week before a large box of gifts had arrived from Linda's. It was a pale substitute for their presence at Christmas. Sitting there, all stacked up, with all the other presents my parents had bought, they did look kind of a lot.

"All of my family doesn't come home for Christmas anymore", I explained. "They send us a box of gifts and we send them one. They were all down under the tree but my mother decided it would be better to put them away for the party. They were taking up a lot of room."

Randy looked a little perplexed. "They don't come home?"

"Yes, my sister and my niece. They live in California. Can't afford plane tickets. My brothers still come, and my other niece, who is my brother, John's daughter. She's three."

Standing there talking about it, I found myself missing Noelle. Missing the old days when they still lived in Boston and they came home every holiday. When Noelle and I would hardly be able to stand the excitement. Then it would all get overwhelming and I would have a meltdown. It happened every year like that. I snapped out of my reverie and I remembered my manners. "Would you like to see my new stereo?"

"Sure!"

I lead him down the hall and into my room. For once I was glad it was clean, thanks to Kris!

"This is cool", admired Randy, pressing buttons and turning knobs as I discretely kicked a pair of underwear into the closet and closed the door.

"Hey you kids!" called my mother from the doorway. "Frank is downstairs, so scram."

I cringed. There was nothing I hated more than her calling us kids!

When we entered the living room, I was struck by its brilliance. The Christmas tree glittered brightly in the corner and the big table had been set out and lavishly decorated. As I grabbed a cookie from the silver tray I noticed Frank running the electric train under the Christmas tree. Tam, the Siamese cat, had found refuge behind the couch but was captivated by the train going round and round under the tree. Inch by inch, he ventured closer, out from his hiding place, his crossed eyes following the train intently. With a burst of energy, he lumbered over and derailed the entire operation; Frank groaned in disappointment.

"He does that", I consoled, crunching down on the floor beside him in a cloud of poof.

"That cat is cross- eyed," observed Randy.

"He's a Siamese." I retrieved the train and stuffed more crinoline under my ass to keep it off of the tracks. That's when I noticed the cat, sitting with his back towards us, had his tail draped carelessly across the tracks. I elbowed Frank and pointed.

Frank grinned. "Yeah!"

"Aw, it won't hurt him, will it?" asked Randy.

"Nah. I hate to ruin the suspense but the train just stops. The tail is too big for it to run over. The look on his face will be priceless!" I placed the train back on the track and jacked the throttle up the whole way. We all waited in tense silence as the train approached the tail. When it got there, it bumped against it with an audible mechanical groan. The cat turned around and looked in surprise, then flicked his tail away. "RAOWW!"

"What are you doing to my cat?" demanded my mother from the other room.

Another knock came at the door and a large crowd of people entered including Chuck and Jeff. Rather than be seen sitting on the floor, I settled myself into a chair for the duration of the business meeting. There were some new faces. One was a woman in her twenties named Susan, who I had heard the others talking about but had never met. She was working at a local nightclub at the time. She had to go to work after the party. She had her uniform on.

As Chuck predicted, I was elected secretary that night. Full of a warm excitement, I sat with the heels of my new black patent leather shoes anchored on the chair rung. When I looked down I could see the reflection of the multicolored Christmas lights blinking and dancing on their shiny surface.

When the meeting had concluded, Chuck approached me.

"As I predicted, it appears that the best man for the job, or should I say the best woman, has won." My cheeks burned. "Here's the club notebook. It's all yours!"

"Congratulations!" added Bruce, shaking my hand. "I think you'll do a great job!"

"Why don't you play us something on the piano!" suggested George Bailey loudly enough for all to hear.

"All right", I agreed, secretly pleased. I descended into the basement and launched into the third movement of Beethoven's 'Moonlight Sonata', a lesser known, but still powerful piece. When I arrived at the end of the piece, I became aware that Bruce, Chuck, Jeff, and Keith were all standing behind me.

"How do you do that ... when you run up and down the keyboard so fast," asked Bruce.

"I don't know", I answered honestly. "I just let my mind go blank." I paused for a moment and spun on the stool to face them. "Have you guys ever heard of the centipede's dilemma?"

"Huh?"

"The centipede's dilemma. One day another bug asked the centipede how he coordinates all of his one hundred legs to walk, but after he thought about it, he could never walk right again. It's the same way with how I play the piano. I thought about it once, and I couldn't play for a whole week."

Later, I was talking with Randy, Chuck and Jeff when Randy mentioned my new stereo. They seemed quite interested.

"Would you like to see it? Come on, I'll show it to you", I offered, turning and bounding up the stairs. A few moments later Chuck, Jeff, Randy, Keith, and Bruce were admiring my new stereo and checking out my record collection, which was not all that impressive given my allowance at that time. Those were the days when I used the stereo as an oracle. This one had a turn table, a cassette tape player, an 8 track player, and an AM/FM radio.

"Where did you get it?" asked Keith.

"Montgomery Ward in Lower Burrell. I was glad we could find

one with an 8 track. They're getting harder to find but I still have a lot of good 8 track tapes I listen to. They were my brother John's but it's classic stuff, I think."

He picked one up off the desk. "Jefferson Airplane. Cool!"

"You should record those onto cassettes," advised Randy. "Now that they're not making 8 tracks anymore, it won't be long before they stop making the players too."

Mom appeared in the doorway. "We're serving the food now, so come on down."

We filed out of the room and went downstairs to eat. We were joking and talking and having a delightful time, and it wasn't until later, after the guests had disappeared into the still, snowy night when my mother accosted me in the hall.

"How could you take those guys up to your room!"

"What? Who?"

"Bruce, Chuck and those guys! Who else?"

I had no idea why I was in trouble. "Why? They just wanted to see my stereo. What's wrong with that?"

"You know exactly what's wrong with that!"

"No, actually I don't. You didn't complain when I had Randy up there earlier in the evening."

"That's different."

"How?"

"Randy is your age. The rest of those guys? They're men!"

"Well, not really! Bruce is, I suppose, and Chuck might have turned twenty but the rest of those guys? They're teenagers, same as Randy and me."

"We'll they're much older."

"A couple years. So? What's that have to do with the stereo? What are you talking about?"

"You know exactly what I'm talking about! How could you be so stupid? Do you think that Susan – who was here tonight - would have done a thing like that? If any of those guys took a step towards her bedroom, she would've told them where to go!"

Now I was really confused. "What does any of this have to do with Susan's bedroom? You never care when Kris is up there? And you didn't care when Randy was up there. What's the difference if the older guys are up there? Geez, there were a whole bunch of us!"

"You know exactly what the difference is! Bruce is married and has two kids. He wouldn't touch you if you were Marilyn Monroe!"

"What?" I stared at her in horror! My own mother had a dirty mind! How unbelievably creepy! "If I'm getting in trouble for something, I at least have the right to know what it is!" I yelled.

She scoffed at my righteous indignation. "I'm not explaining this to you when you know darn well what I'm talking about!" she spat. "You just remember what I said. I better never catch you doing something like that again!"

She stormed off in a big huff and I stood alone in the hallway, stunned, trying to puzzle out what I had done wrong. She assumed that I knew all sorts of things that I didn't! When I tried to ask, she just got mad at me because she thought I was being facetious; she didn't believe me when I tried to tell her that I just didn't know!

I had no connection in my mind between bedrooms and boys, and I didn't know that adults had sex in bedrooms. For my whole life prior to that night the bedroom was where all of your toys were: electronic games, board games, fish tanks, pet snakes, books, stereos, etc. I was never allowed to deface the living room with my junk, excepting Christmas, and neither were any of the other kids I knew. Whenever you had a friend over, regardless of gender, you went and played in your room. We were TOLD to go play in our rooms! Now all of a sudden the rules of the game had changed? I didn't get it!

CHAPTER 11

January of 1983

Tim had a mischievous grin on his face as we sat down at a school cafeteria table by the window, clutching our brown paper bag lunches. We'd been eating lunch together all that year. After banding together in gym class last year, he was the one person at my lunch period I trusted. Sometimes, we would just sit at our window table and look out at the grassy fields and trees and wish we were out there, instead of in school.

Today was a bright and sunny day, even if freezing cold, a beautiful reminder that summer lay somewhere beyond the horizon waiting to liberate us from these dark halls. It was a warm thought to chase away the post-Christmas blues.

"Guess what I brought for lunch", said Tim

"What've you got? Leftover fruit cake? Stale Christmas cookies?"

"Better!" He pulled a medium sized plastic bag out of his backpack. "I swiped these last night. They're rum balls!"

I looked at him doubtfully. "You mean they have, like, real alcohol in them?"

"Of course! Try one."

The rum ball practically melted in my mouth, the odor of rum tickled my nose. "You know what? These aren't bad."

"I like them," Tim laughed as he had another.

"Guess what? The next astronomy club meeting is next week, and Martin should be back from New Orleans! I hope he goes to the meeting. I wonder what I should wear?"

Tim scowled. He was not a fan of my salvation-by-boyfriend plan.

"What? Don't you want me to be happy?"

Tim popped another rum ball into his mouth. "Of course I do. I just don't want to see you get hurt."

"Why would he do that? He likes me."

"But he IS in eleventh grade!"

"So what? If he likes me for who I am, then it shouldn't matter."

"Well, just the same, don't count on it, OK?"

Some kids behind me did something stupid and Tim burst into an uncontrollable fit of laughter.

"What's so funny?" asked a slightly overweight boy sitting farther down the table. Tim continued to laugh, his head down on the table as he pounded his fists up and down.

"Nothing", I snapped. "What are you doing to your tray?"

"Cookie a la gravy", he answered in a mock French accent.

"That's revolting!" In response to my criticism of his food mixing, he dropped his mouth open the whole way in mid- chew. "Do your knuckles drag on the ground? Tim! Why do we sit near these pigs?"

"Huh?"

"You wonder why I don't like boys my own age. Give me some more of those rum balls."

"I'm a boy your age, do you hate me, too?"

"No! You're different."

"Well then you can't say you hate boys your own age. You just hate most of the boys your own age. You are right, I am different. So are you. Neither one of us fits in around here. We're misfits."

"But don't you see? That's why I need the boyfriend."

"No I don't see."

"Well, if someone like that liked me, then nobody could say I was a geek anymore. How many other people around here do you know of going with someone in eleventh grade?"

"Yeah, but is that a good enough reason?"

"Well it's more than that! If I had a boyfriend, I'd feel better. I'd be confident. I'd be going somewhere in life. I wouldn't be alone anymore."

"How do you know that's how it would be?"

"Well I almost had a boyfriend once or twice, and it was pretty amazing. I was on cloud nine for a long time after that, and it was only one for evening. Imagine if it were all the time!"

"I wish you luck, I really do. To me, it doesn't seem worth the risk. I mean, yeah, you might feel great for a while. What if he dumps you for someone his own age? Then, you're gonna feel even more like shit, and humiliated when you get laughed at for it."

"Well maybe," I conceded. Truthfully, I hadn't thought of that, but he was right, even if I didn't think Martin was enough of a scumbag to do something like that. "I have to do something! I can't just get picked on and laughed at in school forever while living in fear and sleeping on the roof until I go to college."

"What?"

Oops! Maybe there really was alcohol in these things!

The bell rang and we went to art class. The rum balls were in full force and we both kept getting the giggles. We sat way in the back to avoid drawing any attention to ourselves. Being this uninhibited, I asked him something that had occurred to me over the years I'd known him.

"How's come you stay over at your grandparents' house every weekend and come to our church?"

He stopped giggling for a moment and looked out the window.

"Problems at home. I like to get away from my dad and step-mother for the weekend."

I was stunned. "I'm so sorry! I shouldn't have asked you that."

"No, I'm glad you did. I never told anyone before. My grandparents are cool! They really care about me. I wish I could live there all the time! They're my mom's parents, so they don't have any particular loyalty to my dad. Since I am there every weekend, I go with them to Puckety Church." That was the mild part of what he told me that day. I was afraid to ask him where his Mom was. Later, I learned she had drug problems and was pretty much out of the picture by then.

"What were you talking about when you said living in fear and sleeping on the roof?"

"Well ..."

"You don't have to tell me if you don't want to."

But I found I did want to. He'd trusted me with his terrible secret, so I trusted him with mine. So, I told him everything, even what that man did, how everybody treated me, all of it.

When I was done he said, "If anybody says those things while I'm around, I'll punch them out."

"Well, my mother would be proud of me today," I said sarcastically.

"Why's that?"

"She told me never to tell anyone. This is the second time I've blabbed it. I told Kris not long after it happened. She cornered me; I had no choice, really. So, I'm sure she'd flip if she knew I'd disobeyed her TWICE now! Unless she does know. Sometimes she knows things, and you don't know she knows them, until she's ready to spring the trap on you."

He laughed. "I like your mom. Though, I wouldn't wanna get on her bad side, either. Does the school know?"

"Oh good heavens, no! Give them more ammo to persecute me with? No thanks."

"So how do you deal with the weekly therapist appointments? Don't they ask questions?"

"Ha!" I pointed to my braces. "Cover! I was getting my books out of my locker the other day right before my early dismissal, and the home room teacher says to me, hey, that's quite a thing you have going with those teeth there! And I'm thinking *teeth*? Yes, teeth! Quite a thing with the teeth, ha ha. So that's what they think, I guess."

"That's brilliant!"

We agreed that day to keep each other's secrets. We would report any gossip we heard about each other, hence keeping tabs on what other people were up to. Us against them!

We were developing a new problem. Already as we sat there plotting this all out, our classmates were checking us out, pointing and sniggering.

"What if people start to say we are going together?" I whispered. "You know that's what's going to happen. The teasing will be relentless. They'll graffiti our lockers with hearts and flowers. They'll sing that sitting in a tree thing at us all day. It'll be unbearable."

"Will you be my cousin? Family is supposed to always stick together and if we tell everyone that, they won't be able to say we're going together."

"It's a deal, cousin."

"Thanks, cousin." We shook hands on that day, in eighth grade art class, and so began a kinship that lasted for the rest of our lives so far.

***

Calling boys.

This was the new frontier of conflict between my mother and me.

"Nice girls do not call boys on the phone!" she insisted.

"But it's 1983 for God's sake! Not 1893! That's sexist!"

"But nothing! I don't care what year it is; nice girls do not call boys on the phone! Boys are supposed to call *you*. Not the other way around! Men need to pursue. If you do the pursuing, they will think you're desperate, fast, and that there's something wrong with you."

"That's true to some extent," Kris agreed. "It's called playing 'hard to get'. What you need is a reason to call them."

Then, like magic I had a reason – I was the club secretary now!

Mom and I were upstairs in her bed organizing the club notebook.

"Geez," she said. "He's not the greatest note taker, is he? Look here it just says 'meeting brought to order 7:11'. What? The meeting was brought to order at the Seven Eleven?"

We both laughed.

"Look here, though, this is the schedule for who is bringing the refreshments to the business meetings. January is Chuck. You should call him and make sure he can still do it and hasn't forgotten."

"But wait, I'm not allowed to call boys!"

"Well this is different, this is club business."

Right.

"Also your dad and I have a meeting at the church on Thursday night so I won't be able to drive you to the astronomy meeting. I thought maybe we could arrange for you to get a ride with somebody. Since you have to call Chuck anyway, why don't you see if he can pick you up and bring you back? I was going to ask Bruce but Chuck is closer and doesn't have to go as far out of his way."

I stared at her. Had aliens taken her over?

"I know you're still kind of nervous getting in cars with men. You need to get over that. I know Chuck well enough by now to know he's okay. You don't have anything to be afraid of from him."

She was misattributing my look of utter shock, but I decided not to enlighten her.

So I did it. He wasn't home and I left a message with his mother. Which was a bit of a letdown!

Back in the day we had party lines, which were anything but!

Basically, you shared a telephone line with a few of your neighbors. So you had to wait for them to be done if they were already on the phone, and often while you were talking, you heard them pick up the phone and then slam it back into the receiver when they realized you were on the phone again! We all had separate phone numbers so if someone called you it only rang at your house, even though the line was shared. You had to pay extra for a private line, which Kris's family did as they had so many girls that nobody else would ever get a phone call if they didn't. Later that year, her older sister Sue got a separate telephone line in her bedroom, and to save money that phone was a party line. It was the same party line as us! So when I called boys, Kris could pick up Sue's phone before they answered and listen in. This saved a lot time since I no longer had to repeat entire conversations verbatim to get her opinion on how things were going.

To my surprise and delight, Chuck called me back the next day. Since he called me, Kris wasn't on the line. I was on my own. My parents acted like Chuck's calling me was no big deal, but I was nervous as hell.

"I just wanted to remind you about the refreshments for Thursday," I said. "And I have a little bit of a problem."

"What's that? And no problem about the refreshments, my mom is picking them up from the store on Wednesday."

"Well, my parents have a meeting that night so I don't have a ride. Would you be able to give me a ride?"

"Your mom's okay with that?"

"Actually, it was her idea. She was going to call Bruce and ask him, but remembered that you live closer."

"Sure, I don't see why not then. I'll pick you up a half hour before the meeting."

Immediately afterwards, I called Kris. "Oh my God! This Thursday, I'm riding to the Astronomy club meeting with a *guy*!"

Thursday came much faster than I thought it would. Kris stopped up after school to help me get ready.

"I still think you should wear the jeans and the sweater," she said.

"I know, but he's been out of high school for a few years. I don't wanna look like a kid!" For once I'd over ruled her. I was wearing a new plaid wool skirt and blouse from my thirteen going on thirty wardrobe. "Besides look, this outfit in Seventeen is just like it."

"OK then wear the granny shoes with it, not those pumps. Like they show here."

Fair enough compromise.

"Remember what I told you about talking to guys", she cautioned as she wound my hair around a curling iron. "You don't want to sound dumb, but you don't want to sound too smart, either. Just be cute and let him do most of the talking. Also, don't start talking about all that science stuff."

"But it's an astronomy meeting."

"That doesn't matter! Flirting is flirting. Guys don't like girls who are smarter than they are. So play it cool and don't act like a tomboy. Now close your eyes so I can finish your mascara. There. You're perfect!"

She stepped back to admire her work, then handed me my glasses.

"I have to go home for supper, but good luck! This is your first one of these as secretary, right?"

I nodded.

"Knock 'um dead!"

"What time is he picking you up?" Mom asked.

"5:30." I said.

5:30 came, then went. By 5:45 I was really nervous. By 6PM, I was bawling face down on the bed.

"I'm so sorry," Mom consoled. "Do you want me to call and see if something happened?"

"No!" I wailed. She and dad exchanged a helpless look.

Six o'clock came. I guessed the meeting was going on without me. Would they wonder where I was? How would I ever take notes for the February meeting? Would they think I was a complete flake? I went over to my desk and flipped open the club notebook to the page I'd prepared. And that's when I noticed the time. I ran downstairs.

"Mom! Mom! I was wrong about the time! He'll be here in fifteen minutes! The meeting's at seven, not six! I have to wash my face! What am I gonna do?"

They both dropped their newspapers onto their laps. "Wait, you're kidding me! You mean you didn't bother to double check the time before you went to pieces? What are we gonna do with you?" They both cracked up.

"I thought you had a meeting at the church," I said.

"Not until seven-thirty. You better get movin' if you're gonna get your act together in the next fifteen minutes!"

In a flash, I did it. When Chuck pulled in the driveway in his new red Trans Am fifteen minutes later and honked, I looked like nothing ever happened, aside from the slightly stuffy nose. Mom walked me out. He rolled down his window. Duran Duran's *Hungry Like a Wolf* blared out from the radio.

"Meeting and back. Nowhere else," she warned us both as I

climbed in the passenger side.

He saluted. "Aye, aye, captain."

The car looked like the dashboard of a 747. Dials glowed orange everywhere I looked. I laid the club notebook on my lap and pulled the seatbelt around, then looked for the other side to hook it into.

"Allow me," he said. I handed it to him and he fastened it. I was thrilled! If the kids at school could only see me now! Riding to a club meeting with a friend like this! Then he put the car in gear and took off like a bat out of hell, spraying gravel into the yard. I could feel my father cringe inside the house. He hated it when people peeled out in the driveway and disturbed his meticulously raked gravel.

I hated to admit it, but my mother was psychic. Once we were on our way, the familiar panic feeling rose up inside of me. I looked over at him. "It's shorter if you go that way," I advised, pointing down Shearsburg Road past Morrison's pig farm. "Back roads."

He shrugged and followed my advice. I felt slightly relieved. I didn't know if it really was shorter, but didn't want to drive past the bridge! My hands shook so I sat on them. I took a few deep Mrs. Fine breaths and reminded myself, this is just Chuck. Chuck, my friend I've had for almost a year now. The worst thing Chuck does is tease people. He's certainly not a ... rapist. So I don't need to act like a frightened jack rabbit!

He glanced over at me quizzically. "You alright?"

"Yeah I'm fine! I'm great! How are you? I'm sorry I forgot to ask! Anything new and exciting?"

"No, not really" he said, not sounding very convinced. "You just seem a bit, I dunno, tense."

"Tense? Me? Nah, no tension here."

A few minutes later we arrived at the upper parking lot. He got the refreshments out of the trunk and I helped him carry them down the back hallway. The bright lights in Mr. Jack's classroom burned my eyes after being outside in the dark, and then in the dark hallway. We sat the bags down on top of the bookcase that ran along the side of the room.

"So, this is it", teased Chuck. "Your first meeting as secretary! You dunno how glad I am that it's you and not me." He grinned. "I see Martin Jamison is here."

I betrayed myself with a florid blush.

"Oh, I see now!" he laughed. "It seems we have a crush."

Well, he was right about that and I was relieved to realize he was writing off my strange behavior in the car to the situation with Martin. My real secret was safe for the time being. I was still really annoyed he'd figured out about Martin. Now he'd tease me about that, too.

"Does he know you're jail bait?" he asked.

"Leave me alone!"

He sniggered.

Martin came over and joined us. "How was your Christmas party?"

"Oh, it was very nice. How was New Orleans?"

The conversation continued, albeit rather awkwardly, until the meeting came to order. I read Chuck's minutes from the Christmas party, and the rest of the night flew by.

"You ARE going to show up next month, sir, after you volunteered to bring the refreshments?" I teased Martin afterwards. I was trying to flirt like Kris taught me, but it felt really awkward.

"Oh don't worry, I won't forget."

The next step was to get him to call me. "Do you want my phone number in case something comes up and you can't make it?"

"Sure", he said with a hint of shyness. I scribbled my number down on a scrap of paper from the club notebook; he took it and put it in his wallet. Then he herded up his little brother and left.

"So you gave him your phone number, you little tramp!" teased Chuck as we were leaving. Did he ever miss anything? Did he have eyes in the back of his head?

"In case he can't come next month! He's bringing the refreshments."

"You're in the membership roster you know, the one that's attached to the newsletter?"

"Oh." I forgot about that. "Well, what if he lost it?"

Chuck rolled his eyes.

The fear did not come back again on the way home. Not even when we drove past the bridge.

***

I took advantage of some sunny winter days to visit the car. I needed to find out what kind of car it was. After crunching through the thin, crusted snow I arrived at the car's resting place in the copse of evergreens. I tried to open the driver's side door and found it to be stuck. The passenger side door opened so I climbed in and sat warily on the seat. Being in the dead of winter, I didn't expect any spiders or animals, but you can't be too careful.

A musty, mildew smell rose all around me. A bucket of pine cleaner could do wonders around here, I thought. I looked around the dash board for an indication of the car's manufacturer and there in the middle of the steering wheel, encrusted in dirt, was the word

FORD. Score one! When I climbed out of the car it took several slams to get the door to stick. Terrific. One door won't open and one door won't shut.

Walking around the back I bent back some pine tree limbs and exposed a rear fender with chrome letters on it: GALA. As I brushed away the pine needles and accumulated dirt more letters emerged: XIE. Ford Galaxie! What an interesting name for a car that might belong to amateur astronomer!

So who did it belong to? Someone had driven it up here, parked it, and forgotten all about it. It most likely belonged to whoever owned the field. I suspected it was Copeland's. Figuring now was as good a time as any I started down over the hill to see if they were home.

The hill down to Copeland's yard was rather steep, and I had to walk sideways to keep from sliding down the hill on the crusty snow. At the foot of the hill was the end of their driveway. The house hid behind a mass of scraggly bushes. A few birds that stayed behind for the winter flew out as I passed by. I walked up to the porch and knocked on the door, and Mr. Copeland answered.

They were a delightful elderly couple living in the woods in the middle of nowhere and as it turned out, they knew my parents and my brother, Bob. One of their sons had been Bob's best friend in high school. I didn't stay long as it was threatening to get dark, but he agreed to give me the car as it wasn't worth anything anyway. He confirmed it was a 1962 Ford Galaxie and promised to hunt the keys and title. He said he would help us get it out in the spring. It was time to approach my dad about it.

I bounded all the way home, up the steep hills and slippery slopes. When I arrived home, my parents were sitting in the living room reading the newspaper.

"Guess what?" I blurted, gasping with exertion. They dropped their newspapers and started at me like, "oh shit!" This scenario had occurred many times before and usually preceded something bad, at least from their perspective. "Mr. Copeland gave me a car!"

"A what?"

"A car!"

"What kind of car?"

"A 1962 Ford Galaxie!"

They exchanged bewildered looks. "Where is it?"

"Out in the field above their house!"

They rolled their eyes and sighed. "Am I correct to assume it doesn't run?"

"Well, not right now."

"Then how are you gonna get it here?"

"Well I was kind of hoping that Dad would know of a way."

"What do you want with an old junk car?"

"I wanna restore it."

"With what money?"

"My allowance." Laughter followed.

"Do you have any idea how much that will cost? Mechanics are expensive ..."

"No, I was planning on doing the work myself."

"You don't know anything about cars!"

"Well, there's books! I've already read a couple. It shouldn't be that hard! I can get the parts from the junk yard up in Apollo."

They exchanged a look of despair. It was usually impossible to do anything with me when I got an idea like that into my head. "All right. When spring comes, I'll go down and look at it with you. Maybe I can pull it out with the truck and tow it home," Dad offered reluctantly.

"Can't we go sooner?"

"No! My truck could get stuck in that field! You'll just have to wait until spring. Until after the mud dries up."

On my way upstairs, I could hear my mother getting on my dad's case.

"Why are you even thinking of letting her drag that thing home?"

"You never know, she might learn something useful. Even if she only learns to change a tire it's probably worth it. Besides, we let John work on an old car."

"John was older."

"Not by much."

"Yeah, well need I remind you of what happened with that?"

That gave him pause for a few minutes. They let John get a junk car when he was fourteen, thinking he'd never get it running. But he did, and he backed it up the driveway and into the neighbor's parked car. He spent the next two years working his ass off to pay for the damage.

It was a clear, chilly night when my dad dropped me off at the senior high school for the next astronomy club meeting. I left home with soaring spirits, as I had managed to unload the old lady for the night. When my dad dropped me off, he gave me a look that seemed to say DON'T make me regret this.

"I'll be back at nine o'clock. Be here."

"Can't you come at nine-thirty?"

"No. You have school tomorrow."

"OK! OK!"

I skipped along the hallways giddy with excitement. When I got there, Martin was nowhere to be seen. I was early.

"So where's Martin?" asked Chuck with the same old sly grin on his face. "I thought he was bringing the doughnuts."

I shrugged nonchalantly. "I dunno, as far as I know he is still coming. I brought my camera, so say cheese!" He grimaced as I snapped his picture. It was fun to catch him off guard for once. A few minutes later Martin appeared with a box of doughnuts under one arm, a brown paper bag under the other, and Doug trailing behind him.

"Do you need any help with that?" I asked.

"No, my mother packed everything for me." He smiled as he pulled three two liter bottles of pop out of the bag, followed by a package of napkins. Then he stared for a moment at the bottom of the bag.

"I don't believe it! She forgot the paper cups! How are we going to have pop without paper cups?"

Chuck held out his hands cupped together. We all cracked up.

"I don't think so!" Pretty sticky!"

"We could run and pick more up at Fisher Big Wheel," I suggested. Whoa! Where did that idea come from? I was learning to think on my feet!

"Good idea! Let's go now and no one will even notice." He turned to Chuck. "We'll be back in a few minutes, you'll keep an eye on Doug for me, right? Thanks buddy!"

Martin was out the door and I was right on his heels. Chuck was still standing there with his mouth open. What an opportunity!

We slid into the front seat of his parents' Honda. I batted my mascara at him.

"Nice car."

"It does its job. I have a 1963 Buick Rivera that I'm trying to fix up. It would be really cool."

I tensed with excitement in the passenger seat as all Kris's painstaking advice about talking to boys took flight from my mind. "I'm working on a 1962 Ford Galaxie. It's missing a lot of parts, though. I need a radiator, a carburetor, new intake manifold gaskets ..."

"How do you know so much about cars? I never met a girl who knew how to work on cars."

Then I remembered Kris's warnings. "My dad taught me. I have some books, too. That isn't weird, is it?"

"No. Actually, it's kind of neat. Maybe I'll teach you to drive sometime."

"Really? That would be fun!" This was heading in the right direction.

He pulled out onto the main road. It was only a very short ride to Fisher Big Wheel with one stop light at the bypass. Up until quite recently, it had been all farm land. I used to watch the lazy cows dotting the surrounding hills during boring classes. We passed the McDonald's and the brand new shopping center going in behind it. Mr. Jack sure was pissed about that! He'd lobbied for years to have an observatory built in the high school courtyard. A year after it went in, so did the shopping center and the light pollution from it rendered the observatory unusable.

The new McDonald's had become the unofficial kid hang out, sort of a teenage Chuck E Cheese. My social anxiety made me avoid the place like the plague. Half the school was in there on any given Friday and Saturday night, so a stray booger, a silly comment, or a piece of toilet paper stuck to your shoe could destroy your life in the space of a few seconds, but I'd have walked in there with Martin without a second thought. With him, I didn't feel like a failure. I felt like I could do anything. The magic was working!

Fisher Big Wheel was in the older shopping center on the other side of the bypass. It also contained the movie theater, a Pizza Hut, and a strip mall with a grocery store, a pet store, and a furniture store that used to sell those weird 70's scenic lamps with oil that ran down strings to look like rain.

We arrived in the parking lot and got out of the car. What to say to take it one step farther?

"Can I ask you kind of a stupid question?" I demurred.

"Sure, why not?"

"What do you do when you like somebody? I mean, how do you let them know?"

"That's not an easy question." He smiled a mischievous smile. "Sometimes, I try to set up these little schemes ..."

"I know, I do that too!" It felt like the oneness of a drop of water returning to the sea. He held the door open for me. "Now I have a stupid question for you. What do you do if you're thinking about asking someone out, but she is say, maybe about four years younger than you are and you're not sure if you should."

"I wouldn't let an arbitrary thing like that hold me back. The only thing that matters is whether or not you like her."

"Hum, well maybe I will, then."

"Can I help you?" interrupted a sales lady.

"We need some paper cups," he said. She took us to the right aisle and we grabbed a package of them and headed for the checkout. I was relaxed with Martin now. That little conversation got rid of any residual awkwardness. It seemed natural to just hang around and talk now. We hurried back into the school and slipped quietly into the meeting. Chuck was barely suppressing his giggling and Jeff was grinning like a chipmunk. I threw them a dirty look while Martin put the package of cups next to the drinks and we slid into our seats.

After the meeting, we all had refreshments as usual, other than me running around snapping photos. I'd seen Bruce and Mr. Jack do it so why shouldn't I?

I sat with the guys eating doughnuts and talking about school. "When did you graduate, Chuck?" asked Martin.

"Two years ago. In '80. Both Jeff and me. You planning to come back to Kiski for your senior year?"

"Definitely. I've about had it with this private school."

"Do you think you'll take Astronomy with Mr. Jack? Most people take it as juniors, but it isn't mandatory that way."

"If I have room in my schedule."

"Oh, you have to! Remember all the fun we used to have in his class, Jeff? He used to tell those stories about his dog, Spot."

"Yeah, about how Spot stands up and looks through the telescope!"

"And the dog orgy."

"OK", said Martin looking somewhat doubtful. "Dog orgy?"

"Oh, he shows all these great movies every Friday, like In Search of Ancient Astronauts. We had a good time in high school. Once we skipped out at lunch time and went to Monroeville mall!"

"You couldn't do that now. The place is like a fort," said Jeff.

"Escape from Alcatraz." Martin and I said it at the exact same time. We all laughed.

The night was over far too soon. It was ten to nine and I had no intention of pissing off my father with things going this well.

"I have to go, my ride will be waiting," I told him. "My dad will have a cow if I'm late."

"I'll see you at the next meeting, won't I?" asked Martin.

"Sure! I have to be here. I'm the secretary, remember?"

"Maybe I could give you a lift home."

"I have to ask. How about I call you and let you know?"

"Sure."

With that, I left the most successful night of my teenage career. Boy, did I have a lot to tell Kris!

***

Right after that memorable night, I came down with the flu. Once I was on the road to recovery, it was time to broach the subject of Martin driving me home from the next astronomy club meeting. I'd lost quite a few days to being sick and I was afraid he would start to think I wasn't interested. So I cornered her in her den – reading in bed – where she would be most receptive.

"Can I ask you something? And this is really important so don't laugh!"

"I won't laugh, I promise."

"Martin asked if he could drive me home from the astronomy

meeting."

"And you told him what?"

"I told him I'd have to ask first." I thought maybe I would get brownie points for that.

My mother dropped her book onto her lap and suppressed a grin. "And who, might I ask, is Martin?"

I squirmed beneath her penetrating gaze. "Well, you know, he's one of those guys in the astronomy club. The one with blonde hair, who's star party we missed because we were in Washington, D.C?"

"Isn't he a little old?"

"No he isn't! He's nowhere near as old and Chuck and those other guys."

"I take it he drives, though?"

"Well, yeah, just barely." Yikes, that didn't come out right! "I mean he's sixteen. He can drive just fine."

"You aren't supposed to date until you're sixteen."

"Driving home from the astronomy club meeting isn't a date."

"It could lead to one."

"Well that's sort of the idea. And if it happens, I hope you will consider ditching this arbitrary rule! He's here right now. I can't put him off for three years. If you had any idea what this means to me! It's not just some stupid kid thing! I really like this guy!"

"Alright, we'll discuss it when the time comes. You don't have a date. Yet. Martin can drive you home." She raised her finger. "But no McDonald's or driving around. You come straight home! You cross me on this, I swear to you that's it!"

So now I had to call him and let him know we were on! So I called Kris first.

"Mom says he can drive me home. I need to call him and let him know."

"Give me the count of 25 to get upstairs and then dial it."

So I did. And it was ringing. Where was Kris? If she picked up the line after he answered, he would hear it for sure.

Click.

"Hello?"

"It's just me!" she whispered. The ringing continued.

"Maybe nobody's home," I whispered back.

"Hello?" I stood stunned for a half second.

"Um ... Is Martin there?"

"Which one?" Here was a contingency I hadn't thought of.

"The younger one?"

"Hold on."

"Hello?" said Martin's voice.

"Hi!"

"Hey! How are you? I was wondering what happened to you!" Phew. He sounded happy to hear from me and I didn't have to tell him who I was.

"I got the flu. Sorry that held things up for a few days. I wanted to let you know the good news, which is that my mother said it's okay if you drive me home from the astronomy meeting. The bad news is they'll be timing us with a stop watch." Martin chuckled in response. "We're not allowed to stop anywhere or drive around."

"That's alright. It's a start."

"So how have you been?"

"Oh, pretty good."

This small talk continued as Kris secretly interpreted it. After the call was over, she called me from their regular phone. It was really annoying trying to talk over the dial tone on the party line.

"I think he definitely likes you," was her conclusion.

"What should I do now?"

"Are you kidding? Reel him on in!"

***

My dad dropped me off at the next meeting. Instead of being my usual social self, I sat at a desk while the rest of the crowd horsed around. The recording barometer ticked loudly every few minutes. It was nearly time for the meeting to start and Martin was nowhere to be seen. Was he standing me up? I didn't have any other way home. I'd either have to bum a ride from someone else - and have them know I'd been stood up - or walk up to McDonald's and use the pay phone to call my parents. Neither were enviable options.

"You're certainly in a foul mood," observed Chuck.

"I'm tired," I lied. "I have exams this week and the flu before that."

"Where's Martin?"

"Do I look like his mother?"

Chuck regarded me with an amused smirk and wandered off. But just as I had accepted my fate as inevitable, Martin dashed in with Doug in tow. He slid into the seat behind me.

"Sorry I'm so late," he apologized. "The meeting hasn't started yet, has it?"

"No. You're good."

"You weren't worried, were you?"

"Nah, I figured you ran into traffic or something."

The meeting started and as I sat there, aware of his presence behind me, I started to calm down. It was one of those times when I wished my mother had been around. Once I left with Martin tonight everything would be public knowledge, at least in the club. Chuck suspected but after tonight there would be no more doubts.

Although my spirits lifted and the earlier unpleasantness had faded, I still just wanted to go. I didn't feel like hanging around at the meeting and risk losing my nerve. While I waited for Martin and Doug, I had a doughnut and talked to Randy for a few minutes.

"Are you ready to go? "asked Martin. Randy looked at me as if to say, 'Are you sure you want to do this?'

"Yes! I'm ready." We were on our way.

It was a clear night and Orion the Hunter hung above the senior high like a sentinel, his arrow pointing down at the muddy landscape. Martin opened the door of the pickup truck for me, gesturing me inside before crossing in front and climbing in the driver's side. Doug climbed in behind me. He sat with his arms crossed the entire way home, frowning. As Martin and I giggled and prattled on, he rolled his eyes and sighed.

When we arrived at my house, Martin climbed down from the driver's side and opened the door for me. He took my hand as I hopped down from the truck and landed precariously on the gravel in my high heels. When we arrived on the porch he turned to me, quite naturally, and took both my hands.

"Why don't we go to a movie in a week or so? It's almost spring and, you know, that means prom time will be coming up as well."

"I'd love to on both counts. I just need to settle a few minor details with my mother."

"Yeah, I probably should too." I was glad that he came from a good enough family for his parents to care who he was running around with and made a mental note to use this in my negotiations.

"I'll call you in a few days. Good night!" He hesitated long enough to smile again, and then left. I slipped in the front door and stood leaning against it. I heard him drive away. My mother dropped her newspaper and eyed me suspiciously from her chair in the living room.

"So how'd it go?"

I grinned widely. "I have a date."

"Oh GOD help us!"

CHAPTER 12

March of 1983

Negotiations about the date went on late and were intense. Lots of arguing, lots of tears. Finally, she arrived at her verdict.

"I've decided to let you go. She held up her hand to silence my ecstasy, "But there are going to be some strict rules."

"Whatever they are, I'll agree to them!"

"You better listen before you go agreeing! First of all, you can go for something to eat and then to the early movie, but I want you straight home afterwards. You can do your canoodling in the TV room. Under no conditions are any boys allowed upstairs. If you go to his house, his parents have to be home. Don't think I won't call them and make sure. He has to pick you up here and when he does, he needs to knock on the door. Not just honk in the driveway! And one last thing. If you cross me so much as once, that's it. It's over! Understood?"

"You know you're the best mother in the world!"

"I just hope I don't live to regret this," she mumbled. "It seems to me that for better or worse you've reached the point in your life where you need to start coming to terms with relationships and boys. Putting it off and frustrating you is probably not going to improve anything. If you give me one good reason to think you don't have the maturity to handle it or can't be trusted? I mean it! I'm not even gonna listen to any discussion again until you're sixteen!"

A couple days later after school, I stood in front of the full length mirror in my parents' bedroom trying on a prom dress. I frowned as the stiff peach taffeta pooled on the bedroom floor. It would not do! The peach color made me look like I had the complexion of an oompa loompa. This gown was a hand me down from one of my older cousins. Frothy pastel prom gowns were in but they were not good colors for me. The magazines always insisted that redheads shouldn't wear red but I wore red anyway and people told me I looked good in it. I wondered if my mother could dye the dress red. If not, I was going to have to pitch a fit for a new one.

The phone rang and I almost jumped out of my skin. I knew it was him before my mother even answered it and called me downstairs with a look of amusement on her face. I could tell from the sound of his voice that something was wrong.

"Well," he sighed, "we have a teeny weenie little bit of a problem. It's my mother. She says I'm not allowed to go out with you until you're sixteen."

I couldn't think of a thing to say; it seemed as if I'd been kicked in the stomach.

" I don't think she'll hold out that long," he went on, trying to fill the silence. "Just give me some time to work on her. She'll soften up! In the meantime, I could meet you at McDonald's on Friday. If we both go there and hang out, there won't be any problem."

"I don't think my parents will go for that. They said you have to pick me up at the front door."

"Just say you're going to hang around at McDonald's with some friends and have them drop you off."

"That won't work. I've never hung around at McDonald's before, so if I suddenly asked them to drop me off there? They'd know I was trying to circumvent the rules and meet you."

I heard a disappointed sigh, and felt a little encouraged.

"It almost sounds like they got together and planned this," I tried to joke.

"I don't think they did, but it sure does seem that way! At any rate, we don't want to get caught lying to them, or there'll never be any chance of changing their minds. It's not the end of the world. We can still talk on the phone, and I'll see you at the next meeting in a couple weeks. And at all the star parties for the rest of the summer."

I sighed. "Well, for the beginning of the summer. I don't get out of school until the end of June, and right after that we're going on this huge trip to California and back. There is no way I can get them to call it off. I sure wish it wasn't this year!"

After a few minutes of small talk about the trip, the line grew silent again. "I hope you're not mad at me," he finally said.

"Oh, no! I'm not mad at you. I'm not really mad at anyone. I guess it's just that I don't seem to have very good luck with relationships."

He laughed. "Aw sweetie, you're awful young to go making big broad generalizations like that. Geez! Give it some time. You're doing better than you think. I'll work on my mother, I promise."

"I don't understand why doesn't your mother like me. Was it something I did?" The possibility of being rejected by a guy's mother never really crossed my mind.

"It isn't that she doesn't like you, she doesn't even know you. She just thinks you're too young. If she gets to know you a little bit, she might change her mind." There it was again. I was being judged on account of my age. Nothing else seemed to matter.

"Why does everyone always make such a big deal about that?"

"You really don't know, do you?"

I was really ashamed to admit it. "No, I don't. I mean, isn't it more important to judge somebody based on who they really are, and not just some arbitrary thing like how old they are?"

He gave a nervous laugh. "OK I can try to explain this, but you have promise you won't get mad. Because I'm gonna have to get, kinda blunt. I don't how else to explain it."

"Go head. I promise I won't get mad."

"All right, I'll try. Again, pardon me if this is a little too crude but I don't know ... okay. Let's suppose we go out. We have a nice time, we go out again. We keep going out. Then after a while, we decide to go steady. You follow so far?"

"Yeah." This sounded reasonable. Granted, I hadn't thought much about it, but this chain of events sounded perfectly desirable to me.

"Now this is where you don't yell at me. Remember, this is all hypothetical. But say we go steady for a while, and then eventually start having sex maybe once or twice a week."

"Excuse me?" I coughed. I had just been kicked in the gut again. After a few seconds of silence, I swallowed hard and recovered myself.

"I'm not saying this to insult you! I would never ask you or want you to do anything you didn't feel comfortable with. This is often how it goes for people, so everyone just sorta assumes, after you've been together for a while, that you ..."

"But why would anyone think I would do something like that? I would never do anything like that!"

"I know that! And I'm not saying that you would. It's just that's ... how people think."

"Well then people have dirty minds!'

"Yes, they do! That's my whole point."

I wiped my eyes on my skirt and did my best to hide the fact that I was crying. Sex was not part of the plan. It was never part of the plan. "It still doesn't explain the age thing."

"Well there are laws against older people doing that with younger people. They call it statutory rape. I don't know exactly what the ages are, but you are under it, I'm sure. That's why Chuck calls you jail bait. Didn't you know that?"

"No!"

Now I was really furious at Chuck. "If you knew all this, why did you ask me out in the first place?"

"Well, I didn't think the issue would come up for a really long time and you'd be older then. I guess I was just adopting a wait and see attitude. Please don't be upset with me. I didn't mean to hurt your feelings."

"I know. But why would anybody ever do THAT with someone they were dating?" I spat the word out with disgust.

He laughed. "Because they would eventually want to."

"Why?"

"Well, that's something I can't explain. Let's just say when you're together for a long time its gets harder and harder to NOT do that. You'll just have to wait and see what I mean."

"Don't hold your breath!"

"You promised you wouldn't get mad."

"I know, I'm sorry. I'm not mad."

"And the unfair thing is, it is just nature taking its course. But when nature does take its course, for the guy it's all pats on the back and high fives. But the girl is a slut. That's the double standard. It's not fair but it's just life. And on that note, can I give you some advice?"

"Sure."

"When Chuck calls you jail bait – or worse – a little tramp? Whatever you do don't laugh. It isn't funny, and it isn't very nice."

We talked for a little while longer and he promised to call in a few days to let me know how things were getting on. I told my mother I wasn't hungry and didn't want any dinner. I didn't initially want to share my burden but she seemed to have already guessed what happened. She didn't dance a jig or say I told you so. She told me she was truly very sorry, and reminded me that my problem would eventually solve itself if I could just learn to be a little more patient.

She didn't know about the huge education I'd just been given. I lay upstairs on my bed staring at the ceiling as the sun set outside my window and turned the shadows blue, then purple, then black. It took a while for it to sink in. It did sink in and I started making connections. Connections like realizing why did that ER doctor asked me if I had a boyfriend, and why the police asked my mother if I hung around with older kids. They thought I was the rapist's whore! How could I have been such an idiot! Now I saw what my mother was trying to protect me from, why she yelled at me for having the older guys in my room to see the stereo. It wasn't about me at all. It was about what other people would think! It was about other people making very bad judgements about me because of what happened two summers ago.

Now, I saw the giant flaw in my plan. I thought that being seen on the arm of an older boyfriend would prove I was worthwhile and lovable, but was I ever wrong! If I'd done that, I would've been doing what they now call feeding the trolls. Giving them ammunition. I was really glad we hadn't walked into McDonald's together. For the time being, I would keep this relationship to myself, other than a few trusted confidants like Kris and Tim. Both of them already knew enough to bring me down in flames. If they were gonna do that, it would've happened long before then. So I trusted them.

I turned over and sobbed on the bed. The smell of rosewater appeared.

"Why does this have to be so hard?" I asked her. "How am I gonna face this down alone? And will I ever be able to have a boyfriend? Or will I be alone forever because of this?"

Silence. Not even the TV was on downstairs. Grammy's ghost was an endless well of empathy and warm fuzzy feelings, but sometimes I really wished she could answer me.

"You're dead! If you were alive you'd be 100 years old, so you have to be smarter than me," I argued. "I need you to tell me what to do! Or at least tell me my life isn't completely over!"

I listened hard. More silence, then an over whelming compulsion to turn on the stereo. I slapped my headphones on and pushed the ON button. The lyrics of a song came through loud and clear with her answer:

> *When the night has been too lonely,*
> *And the road has been too long.*
> *And you think that love is only*

For the lucky and the strong.
Just remember, in the winter,
Far beneath the bitter snow.
Lies the seed that with the sun's love,
In the spring becomes the rose.

✳✳✳

April came that year, bringing with it the blooming of daffodils and the forsythia hedge along the driveway bursting forth in cheerful yellow. A veil of green haze spread through the woods, and down by the creek, the skunk cabbage came up along with the bulbs circling the foundation of the long lost log cabin. The pig and sheep farm on the next hill over honored their annual tradition of spreading manure over the fields where they grew feed corn. The resulting poop miasma forced us to spend the better part of a week indoors when we wanted to run free outside again and feel the warm sun on our faces. It's hard to be sad with life renewing itself around you. It also helped to have new perspectives. It was good to know that if nothing else, he liked me. No matter what else happened, he still liked me.

There was also the Galaxie to think about. Now there was something with needs even greater than me! So I threw myself into the project with renewed abandon. Every nice day after school I walked down through the woods to visit it. Sometimes I took a bucket of water and a scrub brush and began cleaning and tending it here and there. I took the front wheels down and put them on and watched to make sure they didn't go flat again. As I walked home one evening near dusk, I remember looking up over the hills and seeing the sun behind a haze of clouds. It was low in the sky, and was a brazen reddish orange. I thought of the words of a song I that I once knew: *I think I'm gonna be all right. Yes, the worst is over now. The morning sun is rising like a red rubber ball.*

***

I'd never seen my brother John laugh so hard as the day he first clapped eyes on my Galaxie. He could not stop laughing as my father tied an old tire onto the back of the truck so that the car didn't rear end him during transit. It was a warm, sunny day, the first summer-like day of the year.

"Here! Take this chain and hook it to the car," Dad told him. John took the chain reluctantly and headed towards the Galaxie. "Make sure you hook that to the FRAME!" Dad called after him.

John waved him away like a horse fly. "Yeah, yeah."

The preparations were complete. We took our places: Dad driving the truck, John and me in the Galaxie. I wanted to drive it but Dad refused. "If something goes wrong, I want someone who knows what they're doing driving that thing", he insisted.

We lived in the land of long steep driveways and the Copelands' was no exception. The driveway emptied out onto a steep hill. At the bottom of the hill it curved like a black ribbon and crossed the creek before starting up an even steeper hill on the other side.

"Are you ready?" Dad called, starting the truck.

We were ready.

My father put the truck in gear and started out, Mr. Copeland watching anxiously. I rolled down the passenger side window and leaned out. With a loud squeak, the Galaxie came to rest against the tire on the back of the truck as we went down the driveway. We skidded to a stop briefly at the bottom of the driveway. So far, so good. Dad stuck his head out the window and gave us the thumbs up. Carefully, he pulled out onto the road. I watched the chain pull taut. After a couple of loud mechanical groans, we were sailing smoothly up the hill.

"I feel like I'm raising the Titanic," grumbled John.

Then there was a loud bang and we started drifting backwards. The chain lay behind the truck like road kill.

John and I looked at each other. "This thing doesn't have any brakes, does it?" I shook my head. He looked around. "Aha, parking brake! Hope it holds."

It did and the Galaxie ground to a stop and we all got out to inspect the damage. We missed a really cold bath in the creek by about sixty feet. My father, who had been watching the show in his rear view mirror, backed up to where we were. He got out of the truck and shook the chain at my brother.

"Goddamit, John!" he fumed. "I thought I told you to fasten this to the frame? It pulled right through the bumper! What the hell were you thinking?"

He fastened the chain himself and we started out again. It was smooth sailing from there. Back at our driveway a small crowd of neighborhood kids gathered to cheer us on. Dad unhitched the car and pulled the truck out of the way. Then he pushed the car and it drifted down the driveway. With some difficulty, John steered it to its designated place behind the shed.

The Galaxie came to rest over top of the old bonfire pit where we had neighborhood bonfires during the summer, where we used to sit around roasting marshmallows and talking late into the night. In time, the Galaxie took over the role of the old bonfire pit and became a neighborhood icon in its own right.

Tending to the Galaxie continued to dominate my time outside of school. I cleaned it, fixed the doors, learned to sand rust and repair with fiberglass, to remove stubborn bolts with WD-40, and a million other tasks. I researched at the library and spent many Saturdays in deep concentration, working wordlessly with my Dad nearby.

***

One afternoon as I wiped my hands on a gasoline soaked rag, I noticed that something was going on over at the neighbor's. Laughter and squeals of delight floated across the orchard. There was a group of kids playing kickball at Lisa's house across the street. I decided to take a walk up and see who all was there.

Lisa was three grades behind me, which, due to the way the grades were divided up in the junior and senior high, meant that we were never at the same school building again after elementary school. Lisa and Tabitha, another neighbor who lived at the end of the cul de sac, were the same age as Noelle. So we did hang out, but I saw them less often in those days than I did Kris, simply for the reason that Kris and I rode the same bus.

As I crossed the muddy road, I recognized several kids from as far away as the crossroads. There was an older boy with them who appeared to be same age as me or a little older. I wondered why he would be playing with a bunch of elementary school kids.

"Hey! Can we go in your laboratory?" asked Lisa.

"Yeah! Can we?" echoed several others.

I rarely played with the chemistry set anymore so the laboratory had become more of a hangout for us few neighborhood kids. When Lisa's family got new carpet, we took the old carpet and installed it up there, so it now had wall to wall carpeting. We often sat around on the discarded living room furniture and watched the old black and white TV, played games, ate snacks, and generally hung out like you would in a basement game room.

"Sure. It's probably really dirty from sitting all winter, but why not."

"Oh, by the way, this is Davie Jones," added Janelle, one of the kids from the crossroads. She gestured towards the older boy who nodded. He must be a cousin, I thought.

Up in the laboratory we carried on, talking, giggling, and telling jokes. Before long, the crowd got rowdy and Davie Jones was swinging from the rafters like an orangutan, the younger kids applauding with delight.

"Does this kid live up at the crossroads?" I asked Lisa.

She shrugged. "I don't know, he came with Janelle and Jesse."

So I cornered Janelle. "Who is this kid?"

"Oh, I don't know."

"Lisa said he came with you."

"Well, he followed us here. He came over to our house with Amy."

"And where's Amy?"

"She didn't come down. They're going away."

"So, nobody knows him?"

She shrugged. "I guess not."

I was a little more suspicious. So I questioned him directly. "Excuse me, I don't mean to be rude, but, who the hell are you?"

"I'm visiting some people who live a couple houses down from Janelle and Amy."

"So you're new to the neighborhood?"

"Just passing through."

"Where do you actually live?"

"It doesn't matter where I live, 'cuz I'm running away. I don't suppose you'd let me stay here? I won't make a mess, I promise, and I'll be gone first thing in the morning."

"How old are you?" I demanded.

"Sixteen. So how old are you?"

"Thirteen."

He smiled at Lisa. "And what about you?"

"Eleven."

"Hey you guys! We gotta go home for supper!" called Janelle from the outside door.

"The next one of you to stick your face in here gets it kicked!" hissed Davie. She threw us a frightened look and ran. Lisa and I exchanged worried glances, realizing we were the only ones left in the shed with Davie.

He grabbed Lisa and pinned her to the makeshift couch. "If you give me a kiss, I'll let you up!"

"No! Get off me, you disgusting pig!"

"Don't you talk to me that way! I don't want to have to hurt you ..."

"Let her up, now!" I demanded. As a criminal, this kid did not impress me much. He came across as amateurish and didn't seem very smart, even if he was obviously pretty crazy. But I could tell Lisa was terrified. So my plan was to get him to let her go and then deal with him by myself.

He regarded me with amusement. "Why should I?"

"She's just a kid. Why bother with her? Listen! Her mother's calling her for supper. If you don't let her go, they'll be over here and you'll be in trouble. But my parents? They don't eat for another hour."

He got off her and stood nose to nose with me. "I don't hear anything."

"Maybe you're not listening close enough? You wanna take a chance?"

"I hear her!" said Lisa, inching towards the trap door. She got as far as dangling her legs over when he noticed.

"Freeze!" he yelled. She froze.

"Come on, let her go. What would you want with her anyway? Her parents are gonna show up any minute. And I'm not defending you when they do." A long silence followed.

"OK. Get out of here!"

Lisa bolted for the exit.

"So? You have a boyfriend?"

I returned his steady glare. "Yes."

Sure, wasn't the last time I'd say that in my lifetime to get rid of a creepy unwanted guy. It's a sad commentary on society when plain statement 'go away' isn't enough. Outside the window, it was getting darker. I'd be expected for dinner soon. Worst case, I just needed to stall this kid long enough for my mother to come bang on the door.

"Well he ain't here now, is he? So what sort of things do you do with him, when you're alone?"

"That's none of your damned business."

"Oh yes it is, because you're gonna show me."

"And if I don't?"

"You aren't going home until you do."

I laughed. "Well, I hope you're prepared to starve to death in that case. I thought you were on the run and leaving tomorrow? Huh? But if you'd rather sit here and wait to get caught, fine by me."

It is entirely likely that he misinterpreted my pressuring him to let Lisa go as some sort of suggestion that if he did, we could have a 'some fun' or whatever. I doubt it occurred to him that the sight of him forcing my eleven-year-old friend to kiss him, thereby scaring her shitless, would put me in a state where there was no point below which I would not stoop to ensure that he got absolutely nothing of what he wanted. We sat there like that for a while as it grew incrementally darker, until I started to get hungry myself. At which point, I decided I'd had enough of his bullshit.

"Look, this is a stupid game, and I'm leaving!" I started towards the trap door, but he stopped me, gripping my chin with his hand.

"You are a stubborn little bitch, aren't you? But you are kind of pretty." I shook him loose. He grinned and attempted to put his hand down my shirt. Something inside me snapped, and I threw a punch, knocking him off balance. I'm not even sure where I hit him, as I was almost as surprised by it as he was.

"Ow! Don't do that! I have a bad back!"

While he was busy whining, I climbed down the ladder and strode confidently across the makeshift kitchen on the lower level. I heard a thud as he jumped down and tackled me from behind. I kicked him hard in the shins and we both fell on the floor. I rolled on top of him and grabbed him around the throat with both hands, then started to squeeze. He gagged and tried to pry my hands loose, then found enough strength to flip us both over. I still had him tight by the throat and while he could breathe without my weight behind my stranglehold, he was not having an easy time finding his balance to escape from it, either.

I heard the barn door of the shed roll open. "What's going on in here!" bellowed Mr. Lawrence from down the road. He stood in the doorway brandishing a 22 gauge rifle.

Shocked, I let go of Davie and he fell back against the wall. "Nothing!" he gulped, and looked at me as if I would actually help him out.

My memory of the next few seconds seems to last far too long, as I wondered which of us was going to juvenile hall that night. Was the official story going to be the juvenile delinquent who attacked a girl or the crazy 13-year-old bitch who beat up an at-risk youth? I'd just been busted red handed with another kid in a chokehold! I decided if I was going to juvie it was still worth it, and I didn't regret a thing.

At last Mr. Lawrence spoke. "You, son. Stand away from that wall. Keep your hands where I can see'um!" Several other neighborhood fathers appeared with their 22's and they and took him away. Mr. Lawrence turned to me. "Are you OK?"

I almost laughed with relief! Bringing my hand to my face, I realized that I, too, had a bloody nose. "Yeah. I'm fine."

He dropped the rifle and pulled me towards him. "Did he hurt you? Did he..."

"Hell no! I kicked his ass!" Like my mother would kick mine, if she heard what I just said! He nodded and followed after the others.

Meanwhile the unbridled rage that nearly lead me to strangle a wannabe rapist was still coursing through my veins and pounding in my temples. I paced the shed like a caged animal until Lisa and Tabitha returned.

"Are both of you okay?" I asked them. They nodded. "I'm glad you thought to go get help. Thanks for that. This place needs a lock!"

I stomped off to my dad's workshop on the other side of the shed and got a hammer, some large nails, a chain, and a two keyed padlocks. On the inside, I pounded the nails in on either side of the sliding door, bent them, and fastened the chain to them. Now I could use the chain with the padlock to secure the door from the inside. The outside had a latch that would accept the other padlock. After that bit of work, we sat outside on the stoop.

All this time I'd been told, don't tell anybody! All that time, I'd worried every day what might happen to my friends, or even my enemies! They didn't know! They NEEDED to know. Consequences be damned, it was time to end this.

"I have to tell you guys something," I said. "This is NOT the first time something like this has happened. I should've told you a long time ago but my mother forbade me to tell anyone. But I can see now that's a mistake. I can't just let you keep on thinking it's safe around here." I told them what happened two summers ago. Not in huge detail, but enough that they were warned.

Their eyes grew huge. When I was finished, Lisa said, "I think we saw that guy. We were up at the crossroads, sitting on that big tire that used to be a bus stop at the end of Janelle's driveway?"

The tire in question was at Shearsburg Crossroads, which was only a few hundred feet away from the bridge where I was attacked.

"This guy drove past, who looked like that. I can't remember the car exactly but it was some kind of souped up muscle car. He stared at us all funny when he drove by and he went a little way down Finnin Road. Then he slammed on his brakes and turned around. We took off running! I mean, we really took off! When we were rounding the blind curve I saw him drive all the way through Janelle's yard! We didn't stop running until we got home. He didn't see where we ran I guess, cuz he didn't follow us. We haven't been back up there since."

We agreed after that to not go anywhere alone and to report any strangers seen in the neighborhood. Lisa said she could get her mother to drive them to and from the bus stop every day. This alleviated some of my worry about the elementary school crowd.

About an hour later, my mother returned from the great gathering of parents up by the mailboxes. They always discussed problems by the mailboxes, as if standing there next to the road were some sort of neutral territory. She came into my room where I was still trying to settle down.

"That boy today? Lisa's mother remembers seeing him in a class for emotionally disturbed children. Apparently, he was in a foster home over the hill and he ran away from it. Amy's mother found him hiding in her bushes and gave him something to eat. That's when he followed Amy next door and then came down here with the rest of the kids. The men have returned him to the proper authorities. He's out of that foster home, and he won't be anywhere around here again." She looked at me long and hard. "So what did he do to you?"

"Nothing!"

"Oh, come on!"

"I told you the truth! Nothing!"

"I'm not judging! I just want to make sure you aren't pregnant."

I held up my hands in front of her face and yelled, "I told you nothing! Do you see these hands? I was strangling that son of a bitch! If Mr. Lawrence hadn't interrupted me, I'da killed um! And you know what's worse? I think I would have enjoyed it!"

She backed warily out of the room and closed the door.

I was too wound up to sleep. I took a hot bath, I tried to watch TV. I tossed and turned in bed thinking about it, all over and over again. The anger finally wore off and I was left with the anxiety and the shame from having my mother and the neighbors think, even for a short time, that I'd let some piece of shit kid do something like that to me. I'm not saying that to put anybody down who would've been intimidated into complying with him – Lisa was certainly terrified of him. But I hadn't been. He put me in touch with my inner bad ass! I honestly don't know if I would have killed, or even seriously hurt, that kid if nobody had intervened. It is entirely possible that we would have fought until he got tired of it and then left on his own. There is really no way to know.

Near midnight, all the dogs in the neighborhood started barking and barking. First one dog, then another, then another, until they were all barking. I began to panic – was it Davie come back with a weapon to take his revenge? Or was it the original rapist come back to finally finish me off?

I ran downstairs and grabbed the phone, then crawled under the telephone desk and pulled the chair in so nobody could see me. Due to the way the angles were that particular spot couldn't be seen from either the living room or kitchen windows. If somebody was out there, it was too late to escape to the roof. I had to talk to someone! It was too late to call Kris; her parents would kill both of us. So in desperation I dialed Martin instead. If I got an angry, groggy parent, I could always hang up and they would never know it was me.

"Hello?"

"Martin?"

"Hey! What are you doing up so late?" he half whispered. At least he seemed happy to hear from me.

"Having a nervous breakdown. What are you doing?"

"Watching a really lousy movie. What's the matter?" I burst into a terrible crying jag, sobbing and sobbing into the receiver. "Shhh.

Come on, you've got to tell me what's wrong," he urged.

"I, I don't even know where to start," I sniffled. "It's such a long story."

"Just calm down, and start at the beginning."

"I'm afraid if I tell you, you won't like me anymore."

"Bull. Now go on."

I fidgeted and twisted the phone cord around my finger, hesitating above the abyss before leaping in. "All right. Well, you see, when I was eleven, I was, um, abducted by a stranger."

Stunned silence. "When did this happen? Where was this? And what happened?"

"Two years ago. My niece and I were out riding our bikes, and he abducted us at knife point, and took us into the woods."

"And then what happened? Did he stab you?"

"No"

"If you don't tell me, I can't help you."

My cheeks began to burn. "I can't say it, can't you guess?"

"Not really."

"Well what do you think happens to people who are abducted?"

"You've got to at least give me a clue or something."

I thought for a moment. "Okay. Think of a large primate, then put and 'R' in front of it."

There was long moment of silence, followed by a stunned, "Oh." It was really awkward for a few minutes. Then he cut the tension with some humor. "You know, I actually sat here for a few minutes and thought, runkey?"

We both laughed and then the silence returned. "So do you still like me?" I finally asked.

"Of course. Why would that change anything? I just don't really know what to say. It's not as if it was your fault."

"Well, that depends entirely on who you ask."

"You've just got to ignore people like that. That's sick. Did the police ever catch this guy?"

I began to shiver again. "No. We saw the guy all over the place, but nothing ever came of it. So we all tried to ignore it, just live life like it was before, but it doesn't work."

"Do you remember much about it?"

"Heck yea! It's surprising what I remember, although it's disjointed. I try not to think about it. Then something happens and ... and it's all right there again." I went on, and the floodgates let loose. I told him about all of it: what happened, the things people said, the nightmares. All of it up to and including the fight I was just in. "When that kid tried to pull that on me, I got so mad, and I realized that I would rather kill, rather die, than go through that again. In fact, I'm sorry that I didn't die the first time around."

"Don't say that! If you'd died in the woods that day, we would never have met. What about your family?"

"I'm not convinced that it's worth it. We're all miserable. I've come to realize that what I'm really worried about is it happening again to someone else. I mean, what happened to me is over and done with, there's nothing anyone can do about it. Isn't there some way to stop it from happening to the next person?"

"Lock that guy up and throw away the key, that's the only way I can think of. Do you feel any better?"

"I think so."

"We've been on here for over an hour, and I don't want to get you in trouble over the phone bill. I can't go to Crooked Creek next weekend, but I'll see you at George's star party."

"After this mess, you probably think I'm really crazy."

"No, I don't. You're like a breath of fresh air, sweetie. That's one of the reasons I like you so much. You're tough as nails, and yet there's a kindness and innocence about you I admire. I hope you don't ever lose that."

CHAPTER 13

The Girl In The Woods

Obscure distant cousins showing up at the Aunt Farm was not a rare happenstance in those days. Sometimes, they visited once and never again, others visited more regularly. It functioned as a home base for a very wide extended family that shared common ancestors as far back as my great, great grandparents. So, it was really not out of the ordinary to arrive there one Sunday and find two girls, I assumed I was related to somehow, sitting upstairs on Aunt Gerk's bed. The weather was nice for very early spring. The air smelled like fresh soil and the evening sun slanted in through the large window in the bedroom, making hazy patterns on the worn rug.

"Haven't seen you for a long time," said the girl sitting on the rounded top of the foot board. She was different, like me. She had straight dark brown hair, freckles around her nose, and was not particularly attractive or unattractive. I felt an immediate bond of kinship with her, yet felt hesitant to get too close, because the first thing someone would notice about this girl was her anger. It flashed behind her eyes, almost frightening in its intensity. She was dressed simply in jeans and a red striped T shirt. She was very familiar and I didn't want to let on that I couldn't remember her name.

"No, I guess not. So who is this?" I gestured at the other little girl.

"That's Millicent," she said.

Millicent reminded me of a little girl I'd encountered in the church nursery a long time ago who incited an insane sort of jealousy in me. She had long blonde pipe curls and wore a lacy pink dress with white socks that turned down with lace around the cuffs and black patent leather mary jane shoes. I couldn't imagine why someone would show up visiting at the Aunt Farm like that. Maybe they came straight from church? Maybe it was Easter and I missed it? It reminded me of the Easter outfits they used to sell for little girls that were all fluffy and frilly in pastel colors. I was dying for a walk in the woods, but wasn't sure they would want to go given her attire.

"Oh I don't know," said my supposed cousin, sliding backwards onto the mattress. "Do you have any ideas? I'm bored."

"Do you want to go for a walk in the woods?" I asked, casting a glance at her as if to suggest that Miss Muffett here might morph into a suitable playmate if we got her covered with enough mud.

"Sure that sounds like fun!"

"Are you OK to go dressed like that? You won't get in trouble? It might be muddy," I said to Millicent.

"No I'm fine, let's go."

We went downstairs and found the aunts and my mother sitting around the dining room table as usual. I wondered where the parents of these two girls were.

"Can we go outside?" I asked.

"Sure, just don't wander off," my mother answered.

Before anyone else could question us further, we took off. The wooden screen door banged shut behind us.

"If you're up for it, we could go all the way to the big creek," I suggested. "That's always fun."

"Do you know the way?"

"Sure I've been there a zillion times."

We started off through the woods, dodging puddles and prattling about all sorts of nonsense. It was too early for tadpoles but I checked all the puddles, anyway. We arrived at the T.

"It's this way," I said. "See the fence? The fence runs all around it, but there's a gate up here that's almost always open."

We walked up along the fence but to our disappointment, the gate was locked.

"Now what," the girl muttered. "This isn't very fun."

"There's no leaves on the trees, if we climb a few feet up the fence we'll be able to see it."

We did, and the big creek was full of water that day, only a foot or so below the dam. It sparkled and shimmered like a lake.

"Well, this is boring. There's no way in? Do you have any other ideas?" she asked.

"Hum. We could walk around it and see if there's any other gates?"

"Have you ever gone the other way?"

"What do you mean?"

"The path back there. We went to the left. Have you ever gone the other way?

"Actually, no."

"Do you know what's down there?"

I shook my head.

"Then let's check it out. It'll be an adventure!"

We started out down the unknown path, our curiosity piqued. The woods became denser after we rounded a curve and we could no longer see the path back home. It started down a steep hill and as we plodded along silently, I started to worry a little. After walking for what felt like a very long time, we came to an old railroad track running on top a bank.

"Wow, I didn't know this was down here," I said. "I thought the railroad tracks were long gone."

I'd always been fascinated by the railroad track near the Aunt Farm. No trains had been on them for a very long time. I could remember being very little – young enough to be in an infant seat between my parents in the front seat of the car – and seeing the black diesel engine with its cyclops headlight eye crossing the road in front of us at the bottom of the hill. Even though I knew the train was long gone, part of me still looked for it every time we drove over that crossing. It was a tight spot. The train tracks crossed the road and went across the small trestle over the creek immediately on the other side. The creek did a meander there so the car bridge was on the other side of the tracks, making the car bridge and the train trestle almost at right angles to one another. By that time the tracks were gone and all that was left of the trestle was the stone piers with two wooden beams going across where the rails used to be. This had to be part of the same train track.

The shrill call of a steam locomotive echoed down the valley, startling us.

"I thought you said there were no trains anymore," my cousin said.

"I didn't think there were! That sounds like a steam engine. I wonder where it is and what it's doing here?" I heard diesel whistles around the Aunt Farm often since the Conrail main line ran along the north bank of the Allegheny River and the Bessemer line crossed over the river a few miles away in Harmarville. Both were plenty close enough to hear train whistles. My dad swore the steam engines were long gone by my time.

"So you're sure there isn't a train coming?" she asked.

"Impossible. The bridge farther up the track is falling into the creek. There hasn't been a train on this track for at least ten years."

"Want to follow it and see where it goes? Or do you know where it goes?" she challenged.

"It goes ... it goes up to the road and crosses it. I don't know where it goes from there, honestly. It's probably really far to the road crossing."

"Let's just follow it a little way then."

"OK, but it's getting late. We need to leave enough time to get home before dark. I sure don't want to be here at night!"

So we followed the track for a while. The valley was steep and full of shadows as the sun dropped lower in the sky. The creek bubbled along beside us.

"Look over there!" said Millicent. Maybe 20 feet away from the tracks was a large bushy pine tree. It was almost oval shaped and looked more like it should be in someone's yard. Peeking out behind it was an old railroad push car.

"Wow. I bet we can ride on that! Let's try to push it away from the tree." Try as we might, it was too heavy for three little girls, and we could not budge it.

"Hey, you're not pushing fair. I am doing all of the work," complained my cousin.

"No, you're not. It was a stupid idea to come here anyway. I want to go home," said Millicent.

"Leave her alone, let's not fight. It's getting dark. We should go home." I said.

Giving me a shove, she said, "Why don't you make me?"

"Hey!" I shoved her back.

The next thing I knew we were all shoving each other, half playfully. It was almost a game until Millicent lost her balance and fell backwards, hitting her head on the handcar.

"Ouch, that had to hurt," I said. "Are you okay?"

"I think so," she mumbled, sitting up.

"I think she is really hurt!" I said, panicking.

"No she isn't; she is just pretending!"

"I'll be fine. Let's just go," she said, stumbling towards the tracks.

I turned towards my cousin. "What are we going to do? We have to get help! She might not be able to make it home."

We turned back around, but she was gone! We called and called until we were hoarse, we looked all around. Still no sign of her.

"What should we do? It's really getting dark now. Do you think she somehow went home without us? In any case, we need to get help. If we search any longer we're gonna get lost out here!"

We ran most of the way back and were completely out of breath by the time we got back to the house. It was fully dark by then. My parents were waiting on the porch.

"There you are! Where have you been?" Mom yelled.

"We went for a walk in the woods …"

"Well you went too far! It's dark!"

"Yes! "I admitted. "We need help. Millicent is lost!"

"Who?"

"Millicent! The girl who left with us earlier. The three of us! Remember when we came through the dining room and asked you?"

"You went outside by yourself."

"I did not! I had two other girls with me, and one of them is right here." I turned around. Now she was gone, too!

She grabbed my arm. "I don't have the patience for this. It's time to go home."

"But she's lost! She's hurt! She could be dead by now!"

"There's nobody else here!"

"But …'

"WAKE UP!"

Huh? I opened my eyes and I was in my bedroom, in my bed, totally confused.

"You're burning up," mom said. "Put this under your tongue."

"But she's lost in the woods!"

"Stop it! Who? What are you talking about?"

"There's a girl lost in the woods," I moaned. "She's dead. She died in the woods. The girl died in the woods."

"You were dreaming. Stop fussing and put this under your tongue!"

I submitted and shivered, agitated. Why wouldn't anybody listen? She took the thermometer and read it. "104. That's high. You need a Tylenol. It'll take a day or so for the antibiotics to start working." She shook the mercury back down on the way to the bathroom medicine cabinet. I was having a relapse of the bladder / kidney thing I'd had immediately after the rape. Due to the fever and deep sleep I just came out of, I didn't remember getting sick. The rosewater smell came out of nowhere and it was strong, I almost made me gag.

"Grammy is here."

"Grammy died in 1971!"

"Can't you smell that?"

"Smell what? I don't smell anything. You're hallucinating. You have a high fever."

"But I have to find this girl!"

"You're not going anywhere for a few days, at least. I'm telling you, you were dreaming. It's not real!"

"Are you sure? Because I knew exactly who that girl was while I was in the dream, but now all of a sudden I don't know anymore. She had to have been at the Aunt Farm before. She's really familiar."

She returned from the bathroom with the Tylenol and a glass of water. "The one who died?"

I swallowed the pills. "No the one who was with me when it happened."

She shook her head. "Go back to sleep. We'll talk about it later when you're feeling better."

I was exhausted and felt terrible so I gave up and did what she asked. I was asleep before my head even hit the pillow.

***

The Saturday of Hunting and Fishing Day was not the best day for an outdoor exhibit. When I awoke that morning the sky was gray and overcast, threatening our plans with rain. Every year the Kiski Astronomers had a booth at Crooked Creek Park for Hunting and Fishing Day to recruit new members. Since it mostly involved sitting and chatting with visitors rather than doing any astronomy, it was not a popular event. Being a club officer, I volunteered to help out. My mother also decided not to stay either but she did agree to drop me off and pick me back up. On the way up, I told her about the nightmare.

"Was there ever anyone named Millicent over at the Aunt Farm?"

"Not that I know of. You can ask Aunt Gerk if you want."

I described both girls in detail again and still she insisted they did not align with anyone she knew of.

"The other girl, whose name I can't remember, seems so familiar! It's like it's on the tip of my brain and I can't retrieve it. Are you sure?"

"Well not a hundred percent," she admitted. "We had a couple big reunions there over the years. It could be someone you met at one of those, someone who was only there that one time."

"I don't know about that. If it was somebody I met once, why would they seem so familiar? Do any of the events fit? Did you ever see a railroad handcar? Or did anyone ever disappear near there?"

"No."

I looked out the window. Honestly, going to Crooked Creek was making me kind of nervous. The last time I was there it was a long, long time ago. I tried to remember a plastic bucket and shovel and a swimsuit that was white with blue polka dots. Sand on the floor in the car. My brother swimming in cutoff jeans. My mother refusing to wear an orange bathing suit because she thought it made her look like a life guard. Going way out in the water on the safety of my father's shoulders. Stopping at an ice cream stand along the road. These memories came slowly and out of focus. Thinking about them at all was like flexing a limb for the first time out of a cast, awkward and stiff. I turned my attention back to the dream conversation.

"If you do walk down that path away from the big creek, where does it go?"

"You were right about that part. The path does go to the railroad but it's long gone now."

"If you follow it, where does the railroad go?"

"Well one direction, it goes down to the Colfax power plant. That bridge that goes over the road that separates Springdale and Cheswick? The track used to go over that bridge."

Then I saw it: the ice cream stand along the road where we used to stop back then. Or more accurately the ruins of it. Long closed, the huge pink and white ice cream cone sign peeled paint in big strips. The front windows were covered with grime and huge weeds growing up between the cracks in the pavement. I swallowed and looked away.

"What about the other direction?"

"It goes along the valley there and crosses Thompson Run Road, the road the Aunt Farm is on. You know that crossing at the bottom of the hill. From there, it continues up the valley to where the old mine used to be."

"What kind of mine?"

"A coal mine – the Harwick mine. Didn't you know that?"

"No."

"It was still operating when you were born. That's the whole reason the train was there. It was called the Cheswick and Harmar Railroad. They mined coal and transported it to the power plant on the railroad. The power plant owned the mine. It closed not long after you were born. Your dad used to drive through there sometimes.

"I remember that now! There were old railroad cars along the creek."

"Yes, that's where it was. The track went through there and across Tawney Run Road. It made a loop on that far side and then came back across over the trestle that the road used to go under right as you leave Harwick."

I remembered both the road crossing and the trestle.

"Then it went through Harwick and across Pillow Avenue where that railroad crossing used to be. Remember the train engine was along there next to Pillow Avenue for a while, and we took you to see it?"

"Yes I do remember that. It was a diesel train."

"From there, it goes over and connects to the Bessemer line."

"Was there ever a steam engine on that railroad?"

"A long, long time ago. They got the diesel train sometime in the 1940's I think. I was still a little girl."

"Then what does the dream mean?"

She hesitated for a moment and fixed me with a brief, penetrating glaze while at a stoplight. "Dreams are often symbolic. I think the little girl who died in the woods was you."

This was all creeping me out in a million different ways, so I tried to think about other things and keep busy. I hauled tables around while Bruce and Mr. Jack looked at each other helplessly, their offers to do it for me rebuffed. I folded brochures and chased after poster boards when the wind blew them over. It worked. I kept my cover. Keith, and a couple of the other guys showed up, but luckily, not Chuck. I hadn't quite figured out what I should say to him about the while jail bait thing, and that day, I had no wits, whatsoever.

We bought ourselves a few hotdogs from a food vendor at dinner time and settled into some folding chairs where we could keep an eye on our equipment. Right next to us was an archery display with a stack of hay bales covered with a paper bull's eye for target practice.

"Hey, check this out," said Bruce. "I bought one of these last year."

"Did you go out for buck season?" asked Mr. Jack.

"Yeah, but I didn't get anything. Maybe this year." He drew back the bow and let fly an arrow that struck the inner ring of the bullseye with a satisfying thwack. Then he turned to me. "Did you ever shoot a bow and arrow?"

"Actually, no."

"Wanna try?"

I took the bow and picked up an arrow from the table. Try as I might, I couldn't pull it back.

"Hey, wait a minute," said Bruce, taking the bow back. "This is a 45 pound compound bow. That's way too heavy. I should get you a smaller one. This is the same one I have and Amy can't pull it back either."

"You take your wife to target practice?" Mr. Jack asked.

"Sure! All the time."

A communal snigger escaped from the guys. They were always picking on him for the way he treated his wife, meowing and then making whip sounds. To be honest, I was envious of the way Bruce treated Amy. I hoped a guy would treat me like that someday. He was always what my mother would call a gentleman towards her. And for this he was teased! Sometimes he left star parties a little early having promised Amy he'd be home by such and such a time to watch the kids. Sometimes, even Mr. Jack would shake his head and say, with a sardonic grin turning up one corner of his mouth, "you know Bruce, I don't think you're trainin' her quite right." Then Chuck and his minions would shake with malicious laughter. He pretended not to notice but I often saw his eyes dart in their direction.

I wandered off. I hadn't noticed it before, but the meadow around us was chock full of dandelions. They triggered more memories that felt like they belonged to someone else. Playing in the front yard with my brother while he pointed out buttercups. A bright green picnic table I had as a child. A red and white tricycle. The comment my mother made when I told her about my nightmare rang in my ears: *I think the little girl who died in the woods was you.*

I don't know how long I sat there, picking dandelions. I had a huge bunch of them by the time I heard footsteps behind me. It was Keith.

"Your Mom should be here in fifteen minutes or so."

So I'd be leaving. Maybe I'd never be back. "Do you know where the beach used to be?" I asked him.

"Oh yeah, sure! It's down on the other side of the lake. Why?"

"I just want to see it before I go. For a few minutes."

He looked puzzled for a moment. "You want me to take you? Your mother won't get mad?" I shook my head, although I suspected she'd chew me out on the way home. I didn't give a damn if she did. He shifted his weight nervously. "OK. Hold on and I'll get my keys."

We didn't talk at all on the way. We drove down the long, sandy peninsula and stopped. I got out and walked down towards the lake.

Where once bright orange floating footballs marked the swimming area, I saw nothing but sand and water. Where there was once laughter, now only the cries of circling gulls. I dropped to my knees and picked up a handful of sand. There was a time, before. When I was somebody else. When I was a child. I wondered if someday I'd forget who she was. I could have fallen face down on that beach that day and sobbed but Keith was in the car. So I laid the bouquet of dandelions on the sand and left.

CHAPTER 14

On the night of George's star party, it was warm and balmy but clear as a bell. When we arrived, some people were already up in the field setting up telescopes for a good night of clear, moonless viewing. Hot dogs roasted on the grill, the chatter of members' mothers and wives rose and fell as they placed bowls of potato salad, beans, potato chips, and pretzels on the picnic table covered with a red checkered cloth. It looked like the yard and gardens were gilded in the late evening sun.

"Well, well, well! If it isn't Shirley and her lovely daughter, Laura," gushed George in his usual way. He took my hand and patted it.

"How are you, George?" asked my mother as she sat a dish of deviled eggs on the picnic table and began to remove the tin foil.

"Oh, I'm just delightful! Absolutely delightful!" He turned his attention towards my mother, and patted her hand like he did mine. "I hear our devoted President Bruce has a BRAND NEW camera for his telescope. It looks like he couldn't ask for a better evening to try it out. Why did you see that picture he took of...?"

I spotted Martin standing over on the other side of the driveway. I extricated myself and met him on the garden path.

"My parents are here! You wanna meet them?"

"Sure."

"They're up by the observatory."

I glanced up the hill where people were sitting around in lawn chairs. Then, I saw my mother, standing with her hands on her hips and the car door open, looking around for me.

"I gotta help unload the car first. I'll meet you there in a few minutes. If I blow her off, she'll be in a crabby mood all night. OK?"

He gave me the thumbs up and headed up the hill, no doubt to get a barometer reading on his own parents.

"So, how's things?" interrupted Chuck, appearing out of nowhere. Now that Martin explained to me about what being called jail bait meant, I could have just slapped him silly on the spot. Yes, I still liked him in spite of myself, even though he was so infuriating, because he was so funny. Or rather, he was funny when he was digging everybody else.

"Not bad. And you?"

"Good as can be expected. You know those two new guys? I gave them the club telescope." Chuck sniggered. At the last business meeting of the year, two of Mr. Jack's students from astronomy class started showing up.

"You didn't!" laughed Jeff. I rolled my eyes. The club telescope was a standing joke. Really, it was a piece of junk. The intentions were noble enough. It was supposed to be a loaner for new members to help them get started in the hobby. It was awkward, too big, and difficult to use. We used to argue over who had to take it. Chuck insisted I should take it, since I was the secretary. I countered that I t have the space, and my mother wouldn't let me. So he was stuck with it. At least he was until he pawned it off on these two new guys.

"Gee, I hope they come back," I joked. "Are they here tonight?"

"Nope."

"So," said Chuck. Keith and a few other guys had also materialized. "Did you come with your honey tonight?" He gestured towards Martin. I smiled innocently and pinned him with a direct gaze.

"At least I have one."

He stood there dumbfounded. I turned and walked away. Behind me, I heard laughing. But for once the joke was at his expense and not mine.

I carried my stuff up the hill and set up next to Martin and Doug. Both sets of parents settled themselves into a rather serious looking circle of Adirondack chairs.

"Our parents are talking. I wonder what they're talking about," I said.

Martin put his hand up to shield his eyes from the sun and squinted in their direction. "Hard to tell." We exchanged wary glances. "Well, there's only one way to find out." He grabbed my hand and pulled me towards them.

"You've gotta be kidding me! We can't just go prancing up there."

"Why not? I need to introduce you to them anyway."

So I bit my lip and followed. His parents stood up as soon as we drew near. I was as nervous as a long tailed cat in a room full of rocking chairs. Was I dressed like a dork? Or would I say something asinine?

"Mom, Dad, this is Laura." His father shook my hand. His mother smiled thinly. Everyone stood there looking at me, and I froze like a deer in the headlights. My father rescued me by extending his hand towards Martin. "Bill Mason," he said simply.

"Oh, and Mom and Dad, this is Martin."

"We've met," my mother pointed out. "But it's nice to see you again. Have a seat."

Martin pulled out a lawn chair for me on cue. I sat perched on it during a conversation about issues with some of their horses. Neither of us said much. We just watched them talk, kind of like a verbal tennis game. As we stood up to go for the group photo, Martin's father cracked a joke and threw me a quick wink.

"My Dad likes you," whispered Martin.

An old blanket was spread out on the ground beside the telescope. After things were set up, we sat on the blanket and talked. Doug wandered off with the usual crew of younger boys. Laughter flowed down the hill on the fragrant air. The trees, darkened into patches of velvet, stood out against the bright orange sunset.

"So how did you get into Astronomy?" he asked.

"My brother gave me this book for Christmas. It's such a cool book! It has charts that show what constellations are up at what times so I started looking for them. Sometimes I lay on the roof and looked at them. After I got pretty good at finding constellations, I started reading about stars, and how they're formed, and what they're made of, and other objects like planets, nebulas, and I guess the rest is history. What about you?"

"Well, we live way out in the middle of nowhere. My dad has a tree farm. So I spend a lot of time outside, and when you're way up on top of those hills, the stars are just unbelievable. Then, one day we saw a special about it on PBS, and not too long after that we saw an announcement in the newspaper about this club. So we went. It was something Doug and I could do for fun."

"Do you think I made an OK impression?"

"Yeah, I think you did. My Dad likes you, I can tell that much."

"But what about your mother?"

"Ah. She's a hard one to read. But maybe now my Dad'll help me work on her."

"I still don't understand why she doesn't like me. I understand what you told me before, on the phone. But if your Dad isn't worried about it, I don't get it. What's wrong with me?"

"Sweetie, there isn't anything wrong with you. It's her." He looked around to make sure nobody was listening. "Let me give you a little bitta history here. My parents, when they were young, were a couple of party animals."

I looked at him in shock.

"No seriously! They were! They met in a bar one night, then started seeing each other. And, well, one thing led to another and the next thing you know, me!"

"Oh my gosh, Martin, I can't believe you'd say something like that about your own parents!" I laughed, embarrassed.

"I'm saying it because it's true. I was a love child. I didn't come along at a convenient time in their lives. So given her background, maybe you can see why she's a little jumpy?"

"Yeah, but, I don't even know what to say."

"You think just because people are parents, that means they're saints? That they've never done anything wild, or did stuff without thinking?"

"I guess not. I was an accident too. Of a different sort."

"Do tell!"

"Well, my sister and older brother were in college and Mom was working to help pay their tuition. John was still in high school. She thought she was too old to get pregnant, but she did and well, me! I kinda messed up college for them. My sister was ready to graduate so she was relatively unscathed, but my brother Bob lived in abject poverty for his last two years."

I knew there were people who had sex before they got married even before Martin gave me that big education. What I didn't know was how widespread it was. I could remember a time, not too long ago, when Kris and I swore neither of us would ever do that before we were married. Now, there were parents assuming that kids did it and stories about girls we knew doing things that seemed inconceivable as recently as last year. What was wrong was right, what was right was square, and I just wanted it all back the way it was before.

By then, it was completely dark, the kind of soft, enveloping dark that only happens way out in the country. The stars came out and sprinkled themselves across the sky, with the Milky Way drifting through the sky like a magical haze.

"Have you ever seen anything like that?" I said, lying back on the blanket. It looked as infinite as it was.

"Not very often," Martin replied, lying next to me.

"Are you two going to lay there all night, or are we going to find some things?" asked Doug.

Throughout the evening Martin and carried on a subtle exchange of flirting. Near the end of the evening when everyone was busy packing up, he gestured towards me. He stood at the edge of a cluster of tall pine trees. When I approached, him he took my hand and pulled me gently into a spot behind the trees. I could still hear the others, but between the trees and the dark, they couldn't see us. The ground was soft and the aroma of pine rose up as we walked on the fallen needles. He put his arms around my waist and I knew what was coming next.

I had never kissed a boy before. I was anxious and excited at the same time, and I wondered if I would know what to do. Before I had time to worry about it, the kiss just sort of happened. I was weak in the knees, terrified and delighted, and his arms felt strong.

After we got home, I cornered Mom in her bedroom.

"So what did you think of his parents?"

She slipped her house coat over her nightgown and put her slippers on. "They seem very nice."

"Oh come on, what do you really think?"

"They're part of the horsey set."

"Huh?"

"People who own horses live a certain type of lifestyle ... which doesn't really matter all that much, but I can tell you this: they have aspirations for that kid. So, I wouldn't get your hopes up."

"What does that have to do with me?"

"Are you kidding me? They're so worried about his education that they sent him to a really expensive prep school just because of a teacher strike! They don't want him distracted by girl drama, let alone risk getting one pregnant! They want him studying so he can get into a good college. When he comes back in five years with his college diploma all decorated magna cum lade? They'll welcome you with open arms. But now? Don't hold your breath."

"Who said anything about getting pregnant? I just wanna go to the movies and out for a pizza! Why does that immediately make you all think about getting pregnant?"

"Because we know how one thing leads to another."

"Well, not for me! How could you think I would ever do something like that?"

"We've had this discussion before. I can't explain this to you when you haven't experienced it for yourself. You'll understand when you're older and the hormones kick in."

I rolled my eyes. "And they told you all this?"

"No. They were very polite and friendly. But I got the message loud and clear listening to them talk about their plans for him. I'm telling you this because I don't want to see you get all flustrated over this."

One of Mom's boutique words, 'flustrated' was shorthand for both flustered and frustrated.

"It might work out someday, but not right now. You need to learn to relax and go with the flow a little."

"It isn't fair!"

"No I suppose it isn't. Like I said before, men are like streetcars. There's always another one coming down the line."

***

Soon after that, we left for California. I remember leaving school a few days before the last day and picking up my yearbook in the office. Nobody signed it that year because I was gone by the time everyone else got theirs.

We arrived back home in late August and it felt like emerging from a time warp. The locusts were buzzing in the trees to let me know that ninth grade was imminent. Only two star parties remained: Bob Jack's and ours. The evening of Bob's star party was just a scant five days from the end of summer and freedom.

My mother and I rode along the winding country road in the bright sunlight chattering about useless things. A temporary cease fire had graced our relationship since the usual conflicts over clothes, the telephone, money, going out, and cleaning didn't happen while we were traveling over the summer.

It was warm and balmy, but clear as a bell. The reddish orange sunset reflected off of the windows of the red brick house and deep green leafy trees stood perfectly still in the humid air. We sat in lawn chairs on the patio waiting for it to get dark, engaged in an intense conversation about the properties of the Cesium 127 atom.

During a lull in the conversation Jeff asked Chuck, "Do you think Rodger will stop in again?" My stomach flipped over.

"Nah," replied Chuck, pinning me to my chair with his grin. "He had to go back to Ohio."

How to handle this? Chuck was watching me like a cat in front of a mouse hole. I yawned. "I don't remember him coming to any parties this summer."

Chuck's smile widened. "Oh well, it was while you were on vacation. He was at several of those parties."

I felt like he'd punched me in the gut. He was basically telling me that Rodger was avoiding me. Why would that be? Because Chuck was teasing him about me just as bad as he was teasing me about him perhaps? How else could he go from hitting on me to hating on me without having seen me since?

I got up and went to the food table. It wouldn't have bothered me as much if things had worked out with Martin. I hadn't seen him since the night he kissed me. I did send him a postcard. By the time I got back from vacation, he was on vacation. What would happen when he came back? Would he call me again? We weren't allowed to go out. He was probably over me. Did I think he'd just sit and wait for me? No. Even I wasn't that stupid.

Chuck followed me and continued to tease me. "You didn't know that you missed your honey?"

"No and he's not my honey. For Pete's sake, Chuck, I only ever saw him once! I could probably pass him on the street and not recognize him." Expecting that to shut him down, I turned around and started filling up my plate.

Instead he began elbowing me. "Oh, come on. You knew him better than that, I think, you little tramp. Nudge nudge, wink wink."

That was it. Slapping a spoonful of cole slaw down on my plate, I turned towards him in exasperation. "I have absolutely no idea what you're talking about. You go around bugging people all the time and think it's funny. But you know what? It isn't! It's annoying and immature."

Chuck was taken aback for a moment, surprised that he'd managed to get a real rise out of me. Then the sly smile returned. "You DID go somewhere alone with him though, didn't you? You were down by his car for fifteen minutes or so, and that's long enough."

It dawned on me exactly what he was accusing me of. All of the shame pushed on me by other people's reactions to the rape rose up like a geyser. A hot blush swept across my face as my jaw clamped shut and I shook with impotent fury. Several plastic utensils dropped from my plate and clattered on the flagstone walk. The rest of the guys turned and looked at us, wide eyed.

"How dare you!" I finally managed. "I can't believe that even YOU could be that vile! You asshole!" Chuck stepped back and flinched. "Oh, what I'd like to say to you! I can't even think of anything bad enough!"

The other guys hadn't moved other than their jaws dropping onto the flagstone patio.

I turned and stomped off to the umbrella table where my mother sat talking to Randy's parents.

"Home. Now!" Mom excused herself and led me around the side of the house where we could speak privately.

"What happened?"

"It's that ... that CHUCK!" I started to cry.

"What did he do?"

"He," I hesitated. I couldn't very well tell her what he said, what he implied. "He said something awful that I don't care to repeat. He's always teasing me! This time he said something really horrible!"

"Now wait a minute. You can't just let people get you all worked up like this! Who cares what he says? Ignore him."

"I can't!"

"Well what did you say back?"

"I told him off! Now he'll hate me too!" I cried harder.

She rolled her eyes. "One minute you hate him and the next you're worried about him hating you? Good, you told him off. He needed that. He does take the teasing too far. You're not the only one who needs to learn a few social skills."

"But what do I do now?"

"You don't go running away with your tail between your legs, that's what! The world is full of annoying and nasty people. You've got to learn to deal with them. You have just as much right to enjoy this party as he has. I think you should just calm down, go back to the party, and ignore him. Let him stew for a while."

My mother had a gift for common sense and plain unvarnished truth. I wiped my eyes on the back of my hand. "Can you tell that I've been crying? Is my makeup all messed up?" My mother whipped a Kleenex out of her pocket. No crisis ever caught her without one.

"Hold on." She wiped around my eyes, then turned my head to be sure she got everything. "There. You look fine."

The remainder of the evening I spent doing astronomy, rejecting all overtures from Chuck for reconciliation. Several times he approached me and whispered, "I didn't mean it! I was just kidding." I gave him a cold stare and walked away.

✷✷✷

Finally, after much yearning and preparation, the day of my star party arrived. The guests were due any minute. Kris and I sat leaning on our elbows at the kitchen table, carefully dressed and nearly holding our breath while listening for a knock. A soft, warm breeze drifted in through the screen door.

"You've been telling me for a year how cute these guys are," giggled Kris. "I just hope you're right and they're not all geeks or something."

"No! Really, they're cute, I swear! And there are new ones! They're from the high school: Tony and Chris."

"Who are they?"

"I don't know much about them, other than they're seniors. This will be their first star party."

Kris glanced doubtfully out the door. "It's kind of hazy out. I hope they don't decide it's too cloudy and don't show up."

"They'll be here," I reassured, more for my own benefit than hers. I poured Pepsi into each of our glasses and the ice crackled.

Then came the knock at the door.

"They're here!" We gaped wide eyed as my mother opened the door. In walked the whole crew of old retired guys and Bruce!

"Hi Bruce!" I called, forgetting the expectation of cute teenaged boys. I went into the hallway to meet them.

As I shook hands with them all, I became aware of stifled laugher behind me. I turned around to see Kris holding her hands over her mouth. She was laughing so hard that tears ran down her face, but was trying desperately – and unsuccessfully – to hide it. The guys looked confused. My mother looked livid.

"Get her out of here now!" she mouthed to me behind their backs.

"I'm sorry! I told her a joke just before you all walked in, but I didn't think it would be that funny." Still smiling at them innocently, I gave her a swift kick and whispered, "Knock it off!" She continued in her convulsions of laughter. I grinned wider and herded her towards the TV room door. Behind me, I could hear my mother complaining to someone, "I don't know why I ever let her invite Krissy. Between the two of them, they're going to embarrass me all night!"

Downstairs in the TV room, Kris began to recover. "Cute guys! Cute guys!" she stuttered, wiping her eyes. "If ... if that's what you ... think is cute ... you need new glasses! Those guys are old enough to be grandfathers!"

"You're gonna get me in big trouble!"

"I'm so sorry! It's just that ... that ... those square glasses!" She began to howl again.

"It's not my fault they got here first! So they're old! They've got just as much right to use a telescope as anybody else."

"OK, OK! If I live to be a hundred, I'll never forget the ... cute guys coming to your ... star party!" And she howled some more.

When she recovered herself enough, we went back upstairs to find that more people had arrived. Tony and Chris stood in the front yard beneath a maple tree, shifting their weight from on leg to the other, looking kind of uncomfortable. I was redeemed! Tony was more the suave, debonair type while Chris was big and burly; he worked in his father's auto shop and looked the part.

Nudging Kris in the ribs with my elbow, I boasted, "See, I told you they would be here. And there are more coming!"

She stopped and fluffed up her hair. "Now THAT'S more like it!"

I waved to them and they hurried over, relieved to see somebody they knew.

"You guys haven't been here long, have you?"

"Nah," said Tony, "we just got here about five minutes ago."

"You guys wanna see my car? The one I'm fixing up?"

"Sure!"

"I hope you cleaned and de-spidered it," whispered Kris.

I had nothing to worry about. The Galaxie had been washed, waxed, vacuumed, bug bombed, and deodorized. With all that and a new coat of white paint on the 'white wall' tires, it was ready to meet the public. Granted, it still had a few holes in it, but they weren't rusty holes. No sir. I had filed off all the rust just for this occasion, and more than half the holes had already been filled with fiberglass and were painted to match the rest of the car. The various engine components, which my father had so diligently coached me in the removal and restoration, were arrayed on a table inside the shed, painted bright colors with special engine paint.

"Wow, that chrome sure polished up nice!" said Randy, who just joined the group.

Chuck half smiled and shook his head. "Not bad, not bad. Let's see under the hood."

I was still seething with anger towards him. I nodded coldly as he helped himself. Then he walked slowly around the car, inspecting and kicking tires. Luckily none of the white paint came off.

"Hey, wait a minute," said Jeff. "What's all this chrome paint on the leaves under the bumper back here?" Everyone began to snicker, including me.

"All of the chrome was fine except for the rusty back bumper. I touched it up with some chrome paint so it would look decent until I can afford a new one. I guess if I had raked away the leaves, I'd have you all fooled!"

From the exclamations and chattering, I could tell that the others were impressed as they opened the doors and peered inside.

"So, what'd you do with all the parts you removed from the engine?" asked Jeff.

I opened the shed door and made a sweeping gesture. "In here!" The crowd oooh'ed and aaah'ed as they picked up each neatly manicured part and examined it.

"Dinner!" called my mother from the front porch. "Now!"

"What are you having?" asked Tony.

"Hot dogs, hamburgers, stuff like that."

"What are we waiting for?"

Too nervous to eat, I sat outside at one of the picnic tables swirling ice around in a cup while everyone went through the food line in the kitchen. Chuck came out carrying his plate and sat down next to me. I stiffened. Mom drifted by and sat a basket of pretzels down on the table. We made eye contact for a second and she found an excuse to stay within earshot by futzing with the tables and chairs.

"Look," he said without making eye contact. "I guess I owe you an apology. I'm sorry I teased you about that. It won't happen again."

I was so shocked that at first, I was speechless.

"Um, sure. Thanks," I finally managed.

He turned towards me and stuck out his hand. "Friends again?"

Finding the gesture disarming, I smiled. "Sure. Friends again." I shook his hand.

After dinner, we all set up our telescopes in the orchard, which was the least forested part of the yard. Tony and Chris brought the club telescope.

Darkness had fallen and Chris was trying to look at the gibbous moon, which hung like a giant half eaten vanilla wafer above the neighbor's house. The base of the instrument was not sturdy, and each time he had it in view, the telescope body slipped and he had to start all over again.

"I think I could get this to work if I had something to stuff in between the stand and the body - like some old newspaper or something. Do you have any?"

"Gee, I don't know," I answered. "Maybe there's some up in my laboratory. Let's go see." Just to be safe from any of my mother's character assassinations and accusations of ill doing, I took Kris along with me. The four of us, Tony, Chris, Kris, and I, were digging around hunting for newspaper when the conversation turned to the woods.

"So you two have been hanging around in here since you were pretty little," observed Chris as he peered out the solitary window at the dark and gloomy woods. "It's kind of spooky out there. I can't imagine little kids staying up here after dark."

"Why, you've never heard about the Indians?" I began, shining the flashlight on my face to further enhance the tale. They grinned widely and leaned into the circle. "Hundreds of years ago, when William Penn acquired this land, on it was an ancient Indian battleground. This was no ordinary battleground, no sir. For unbeknownst to the settlers, a fierce war had been waged in the very same valley you look down upon from this window, a battle with the dreaded Norse invaders. These Norseman, or Vikings, had come to the New World centuries before, while Europe was in the iron grip of the Dark Ages, and feared sea travel because they believed that horrible sea monsters roamed the deep. But the Vikings were not afraid, and they came here and called it Vineland. At first they lived along the East Coast, but after several hundred years moved inland, and founded a settlement in the valley below here."

"The Iroquois were also living here at that time, and began to resent the Vikings for hunting on their sacred burial grounds. A great war between the two sides was fought directly down over that hill, which resulted in the massacre of hundreds of Indians. As a result, their restless spirts wander the woods, protecting their sacred lands and burial grounds from desecration. The Viking settlement was eventually destroyed by plague brought over from Europe by marauding warriors."

"Is any of that true?" asked Tony.

"I have no idea. We made up the story as kids. There are some archeologists who believe the Vikings did travel to North America. Nobody really knows where Vineland was. This place is as good as anywhere, and it's certainly full enough of wild grapes. But the ghosts, I assure you, are real."

"Has anybody ever seen them?"

"Yeah! My sister has. I've heard them. If you go down to a certain spot in the valley you hear bees, swarms of them. It starts out quiet and gets louder and louder. You can hear it no matter when you go down there, even in the dead of winter. We never knew what it was, until one day my cousin, who studied Indians, told me that one of the Iroquois tribes was the bee keepers." Just then, off in the distance, a dog howled.

"Woah! A chill just went up my spine!" said Chris.

"That's a really cool story!" added Tony.

"Another time," I continued, "when my siblings were little, they heard them. The room that Linda and Bob slept in directly faced the woods, and one night they heard someone walking out of the woods and up towards the house. The footsteps stopped on the driveway, and Bob ran and woke up my dad, who went outside with a flashlight and checked. He found nothing. But, as soon as everyone was settled back into bed, the footsteps started again from the exact same place they stopped. The specter walked up to the house, rattled the door, and walked back down into the woods."

We were all startled by the sound of the door opening. "Hey! What are you guys doin' up there?"

I pressed my hand to my chest and peered down the trap door. "Chuck!"

"Well, who'd you think it was?" He put his hands on his hips and gazed up at us, while Jeff and Keith piled in after him.

"Is that your chrome paint?" called Jeff, waving the can above his head from me to see.

"Yes, that's it." Tony and Chris climbed down the ladder to get a better look at the can of paint. "Let's see." He proceeded to spray the aluminum ladder, which was already silver. The paint, however, was much shinier.

"Hey! It looks pretty decent! Now you have a chrome ladder!"

"Yeah, and you've trapped us up here," I observed.

"Oh don't worry! It'll dry in a few minutes."

Kris and I lay on our stomachs and watched from the trap door, fumes from the paint hanging thickly in the air, watching the boys carry on. They laughed and chattered, picking up objects and making funny remarks. We didn't realize at the time that the paint fumes were much more concentrated downstairs where the boys were. So we lay upon our stomachs, peering down at them, beaming at each other with the satisfaction that we were providing such stellar entertainment for an obviously cool group of people.

"Is this can empty?" asked Chris holding a can of blue spray paint.

"I think so. That's the stuff I used on the Galaxie."

He sprayed it several times onto a piece of paper until he was convinced. Then he began to dance around, spraying the empty can under his arms like deodorant. The others howled and pointed, and it took him several minutes to realize that they saw something he didn't.

"Oh no!" he laughed, "and on my new shirt, too!"

"If I live to be 100," sniggered Chuck, "I'll never forget the star party where Chris painted his armpits blue! You'll never sweat again!" They were all laughing so hard that they forgot all about us.

"Let's lock them in!" suggested Kris.

"Ok!"

We sprinted down the ladder and out the door, Kris holding it shut while I searched for a stick to jam it. We sat there all smug, listening to their muffled laughter, when my mother materialized. She glared at us and pointed abruptly towards the door.

"You open that door right now!"

Reluctantly we complied, doing our best to hide our smiles. As we opened the door the boys spilled on onto the lawn in one large heap, laughing spasmodically. My mother shook her head in disgust.

"You should have better manners! While all of you were goofing off in the shed, I was out here entertaining the rest of your guests!" she scolded before storming off.

"I guess that's the end of that," observed Chuck as he lay sprawled out on the lawn, his eyes following my mother.

And he was right. Heavy clouds were rolling in and everybody but us kids had already called it a night. The adults were packing gear into the trunks of their cars, my mother flitting from one car to another bidding them goodbye. I wished they could stay forever and I prattled on to delay their departure. Reluctantly, they also began to pack their cars. The final moments of my party had arrived.

"This was a pretty good star party," said Chuck, nodding with approval as he opened the door to his car. "One of the best ones I can remember. See you in a few weeks at the business meeting." With that he slid into the driver's seat, started the car with a roar, and peeled out in the driveway. Tony and Chris followed him. They waved as they drove by the two of us, standing alone at the end of the concrete walk. Neither Kris nor I said anything as we watched the red tail lights disappear behind the thick pine trees, and the sound of engines and crunching gravel die away. All that was left was the chorus of katydids and the flickering of lightening bugs. There was a dim flash and some seconds later the rumble of distant thunder.

All evening, I had been excited and happy, but now as I watched those red lights fade away, I began to experience the emotional fallout that always arrived on the heels of those happy evenings with my friends.

Like a fiend lurking in the shadows, a gripping sensation clamped across my chest. Another sleepless night was rapidly approaching. I wished the fun and carefree distraction provided by my friends didn't always come to this same end. A lump rose in my throat.

"Wow! What a great party! I sure am glad you invited me!" bubbled Kris, unaware of my condition.

"How could I not invite you? We've been planning this for ages."

"I'll bet your Mom wishes you hadn't," she laughed.

I started towards the porch to sit down. Kris followed. "I don't think we've ever really had fun without making my mother mad," I observed.

"No, I suppose not." She dropped into a chair beside me. "But you're right! They really are cute guys. You're lucky to hang around with them."

"I still never get asked out," I pointed out.

"That's only because you're thirteen. When you're older, things will be different."

My anger flared. I had to hear this over and over again from the adults, and now her, too? I walked out into the yard and lay down on the grass. Stars played hide and seek behind the clouds that were still rolling in.

I felt her sympathetic presence behind me. "Are you mad about something?"

"Just life in general. It isn't fair. It's not my fault I'm thirteen. It was an accident at birth."

"You were a wild success tonight! Don't sell yourself short. Don't give up. It might happen tomorrow, or the day after that! You just have to keep trying."

I struggled for a way to explain. "Do you ever feel like the best is behind us now? That somehow, the best part of our lives is over?"

"No, not really. Why?"

"I don't know, it just seems like, things were better the way the used to be. There is something wrong about the way things are now. Like life is broken and there's no way to go back."

"I don't know what you mean. We had a great party tonight. School will start soon. Maybe that's it? Although you'll be in ninth grade this year. You'll rule the school."

"It's not that, it's just, never mind. I can't explain it."

There was no way I could explain, no way I could make her understand, mostly because I wouldn't admit the truth to myself. What had happened that summer was affecting me now, every day, whether I was willing to admit it or not, which in this case was not. I had lost something significant. I now saw the world differently and was painfully aware of our vulnerability and how fragile life really is. I'd begun to look back upon my earlier childhood through the rose colored glasses of nostalgia.

Those were the days, back then, I thought with a stab of pain.

When mothers stood in kitchen doors called us from red wagons to pot roast suppers. Saturdays and summers seemed to last forever. The smell of freshly cut grass and Campbell's chicken soup mingled with that of play dough. Fathers drank coffee on the porch in the evening while lightening bugs winked in the gloaming. We never seemed to grow tired of the games we played and there was something about the light, something that was gone now. Oh the golden warmth and security of those days!

"Hey you two! It's late and I'm going to bed," called my mother from the porch. Kris and I exchanged looks.

"See you later, alligator," sang Kris on her way out of the yard.

"After 'while, crocodile," I called in return. We'd been doing this little ritual for years. There were no street lights back then. Walking home at night felt like being dipped in ink and let loose in a coal mine. To keep from being scared we called these phrases back and forth until one or the other of us arrived home and blinked the porch light on and off. "See you later, alligator," I called into the void.

"After 'while crocodile," she replied, nearly home. When her porch light blinked, I blinked our porch light in reply and went into the house.

The light in the kitchen blinded me at first, being used to the darkness outside. My mother stood by the sink in her pink nightgown, holding a glass of water.

"I hope you had a nice time at your party. I think it went well."

So, she was over being angry with us for playing in the shed. "I think it turned out well too," I agreed.

"I heard you got an apology from Chuck."

I nodded.

"You aren't the only one with growing up to do. You taught him a good lesson about limits. Now you're both better off."

I stared at her. "I guess I never thought of it that way. I always assume I'm the one with the problem."

She laughed. "Hardly! It's late. I'm going to bed." She turned and looked at me like she expected me to follow.

"I'll be up in a little while."

"Alright. Turn out the lights when you come up. And don't stay up too late."

As I didn't eat earlier, I was then ravenously hungry. I dug through the refrigerator and sat down at the table with some leftover French onion dip and a bag of chips, then mentally reviewed the evening. Chuck said it was the best star party he could remember! And apologized!

I pushed the dip away and leaned back in my chair with a sigh. I wondered what he would think if he knew the truth about me. Nobody else besides Martin knew about that. I wondered if they ever sensed that something was wrong. Would they be nicer to me if they knew? Or would they blame me like most other people?

CHAPTER 15

I was more aware than usual of the arrival of cold fall weather that year. I tried out successfully for color guard in junior high band so I had much less clothing between me and the cold at parades and football games. That winter as I sat shivering in the bleachers, my grandmother - as my parents put it - started downhill. Dad was late picking me up one night and I remember standing outside the football field in Vandergrift watching the snow flurries whirl about in the halo of a street lamp. Then Mom pulled up.

"I'm sorry we're a little late," she apologized. "Your father had to rush Grandma to the hospital. She called in a panic right after we got home from dropping you off. Dad went to get her. He had to have her admitted to the hospital. She's at Citizen's."

Guilt pressed in from all sides. How long had it been since I had attended a *Lawrence Welk/Hee Haw* Saturday night bonanza at Grandma's? My Grandmother was dying. The only one I had! And where was I? In a skimpy outfit she was sure to hate, parading around with the band in subzero weather.

The next evening, we went to see her in the hospital. It was the same hospital where I was born, Citizens General Hospital in New Kensington. Built in 1916, the imposing brick structure was also where my mother and Aunt Gerk graduated from nursing school. Back then, they didn't allow children to visit people in the hospital; there were signs up everywhere demanding NO CHILDREN UNDER 12. Nurses in white uniforms and funky caps enforced this ruling with an iron fist (the funky caps were presented at their graduation, and the design of it indicated which nursing school they were from). It was a relief I was finally old enough not to have to worry about that anymore. It always seemed so insulting.

Grandma lay listlessly in an ICU bed under a cold white light. She didn't even know who I was.

"Billy has the measles", she told one of the nurses. That's what she always called my dad. Then she looked at me, standing there with my arms crossed in a puffy coat. "Who's that with the baby?" I stared in horror while my parents patted her hand and told her everything was OK. It was doubly creepy due to the arguments and unpleasant discoveries going on about social mores surrounding sex and reproduction.

On the way out my mother whispered, "When your father was little, he had the measles and was in the hospital. She associates hospitals with that. She's confused. She thought you had a baby because of the way you were standing in that coat."

From the hospital, she went to a nursing home which to hear the old generation of my family talk was pretty much a synonym for hell. Christmas that year was rather low key for the first time in my life. It was cold, really cold. I rode up to see Grandma on Christmas Day, seated between my two brothers in John's diesel truck. It still smelled vaguely of puke because he'd gotten drunk a few nights before and thrown up on the side of the door. The barf froze solid. Due to the continued cold weather, he had a terrible time getting it off. Our dad shook his head and rolled his eyes.

It was a couple days after Christmas, in the no man's land between Christmas and New Year's, when it happened. I was lying in bed late one morning, as there was no school due to Christmas Vacation. I was in that liminal state of being neither awake nor asleep. Unlike my previous experiences of long lucid dreams full of traceable clues, this dream was a flash and was over in an instant, before I even had a chance to note many of the details. I saw a man die of a heart attack. A man that looked like my father.

I sprang up in bed with ice water racing through my veins. An icy sleet fell outside in the gray morning light. I inhaled – no rose water. So this apparently hadn't come from Grammy. I jumped out of bed and ran downstairs in a panic. The scene I found was the opposite of the fear raging in me or even the cold death of the short disastrous dream. I found both my parents snug as a bug in a rug reading their newspaper in the living room. Warm pools of light from the eagle themed 1976 bicentennial living room lamps surrounded them and steam rose from their nice cups of hot coffee.

"Is everything OK?" I asked, trying to sound calm and not upset them.

"Sure, why? Is something wrong?" Mom asked.

Should I say anything? I decided no. If I was wrong, I'd just upset everyone over nothing and they would think I was imagining things. If I was right? I'd just have to be vigilant. "No. I'm fine," I lied.

"Good, then take your clothes upstairs," said Mom. "I'd like to clean up the living room and start putting the Christmas decorations away, so I need your stuff out of here."

My brothers and sister bought me fashionable clothes that year. I got two pairs of designer jeans, a long wool sweater, and three pairs of leg warmers in colors that coordinated with the sweater. Mom thought this fashion absurd until she realized how warm they were. Then she bought herself a couple pairs of teenage leg warmers and wore them back and forth from work over her white panty hose with her nurse's uniform and clunky white orthopedic nurse shoes. This, of course, looked absolutely ridiculous, but she didn't care one bit.

I put on my new clothes and got ready to go down to Kris's house. I wondered, was this all just paranoia over my dad's upcoming open heart surgery? He had a heart attack in 1972. I remembered that. It happened at work so I didn't remember it happening, but I remembered being taken to the hospital to see him, and a nurse bringing him in a wheelchair to a waiting room because kids weren't allowed to visit hospitals back then. Recently, he'd started having bouts of angina. The previous summer while we were on vacation, he and I went on the cog railway up Pike's Peak in Colorado, and his lips started turning blue. He took some pills and the episode went away, but incidents like this had brought him to decide to have elective open heart surgery. It was planned for a few weeks later in January.

I thought about telling Kris, but once I got down there, I started to doubt myself. Everything was peachy keen down there too, with opened presents everywhere and her black cat, Midnight sucking down strands of silvery Christmas tree "snow" like spaghetti. I wondered if I'd seen my dad dead, or if it was somebody else? Her dad looked kind of like my dad and he'd had heart problems, too. I didn't want to upset her, so I said nothing.

The mystery was solved a few days later, on New Year's Day. I was hiding upstairs in my bedroom with a towel stuffed under the door. Every year, my mother made pork and sauerkraut for New Year's Day and I found the smell of the sauerkraut to be the worst thing imaginable. I'd spent part of the day at Kris's house and part of the day hiking around outside as it wasn't unbearably terribly cold. Once the early winter darkness came, I was not keen on being outside any longer. It was late in the evening when the phone rang. For a while after that, I heard them downstairs having a quiet conversation that I couldn't make out. Then, my mother came and knocked on my door. I opened it to a face full of hot humid sauerkraut stench and my mother daubing her eyes with a Kleenex.

"Someone from the church just called. Reverend Fisher had a heart attack. He's dead."

I crumpled backwards and sank down on my bed. "What?"

She came in the room and sat down next to me. We both sat there dumbly and stared into the mirror above my dresser. "Reverend Fisher had a heart attack. They took him to Citizen's Hospital, but he didn't make it."

I gulped. "This is my fault."

Her head whipped towards me. "How is that possible?"

"I had a dream! A couple days ago. If I would've figured it out, none of this would've happened. But I thought it was Dad! They look alike!"

She let out a long breath. "Well, that explains a few things, like why you've been acting so strangely the last couple of days. What exactly did you dream?"

"It was short, just a picture, really. I saw him lying there dead and knew it was a heart attack. It was over so fast I didn't see the room or if anyone else was there. And I woke up with horrible feeling of impending doom."

She sighed. "There's nothing you could've done. Even if you had realized it was Reverend Fisher – and why would you because nobody suspected he was in bad health – what could you have done? Warned him? He probably would have laughed it off. Or nobody would have believed you. Or it would have happened in spite of anything you did to try and stop it."

"Then why have the dream at all?" I yelled.

"I can't answer that. I think it's just that happens, when you're psychic. Both your grandmothers were psychic so it doesn't surprise me that you are. Grandma Mason dreamed about what happened to you, before it happened. She tried to warn us. It didn't work."

"But wait," I said. "When you told me about that before, you said she dreamed that we died."

Mom shrugged. "That's what she said. It was all the other accuracies I realized afterwards, the bridge, the bicycles, the man ..."

"But we didn't die! How do we know that something she did, didn't change it?"

She blew her nose. "I guess I never thought of it that way before. But still, there's no way to know that for sure. And back to this business about Harry Fisher? With a dream that vague, there is no way you could've prevented this. So you need to just put that right out of your mind."

I really wanted to ask Grandma about all this, but she was in a nursing home and didn't even know who I was half the time.

The pastor's death upended life at Puckety UP entirely. Being in ninth grade, my Sunday school class was right in the middle of confirmation curriculum; we were due to be confirmed that spring. Reverend Fisher had been teaching the class, so it was weeks before things resumed and his widow graciously agreed to take over and finish it.

The biggest fallout that I witnessed was my dad. Harry, as the adults called him, was my dad's BFF. For years after that he played the cassette recording of my niece Sherise's baptism while he puttered way in his workshop, just so he could hear Harry's voice. I also realized he'd very likely told him what happened to me. Dad had to be getting support from somewhere.

Shortly after that Dad underwent his open heart surgery with great success. He lived for almost thirty more years and died at a ripe old age from respiratory failure, caused by all the asbestos he was exposed to during his early years at ALCOA.

***

I was wandering around in a big red brick hospital I'd never seen before when I realized I was dreaming. The hallways were full of patients in wheelchairs, nurses, and various other hospital personnel, hurrying along to unknown destinations, unknown fates. They could not see me. That was what made me realize I was dreaming. But it was not a dreamscape I'd seen before. As I wandered through the hallways I noticed the bulletin boards. They all seemed to be covered with decorations made from paper lace doilies and pink or red construction paper hearts. Occasionally, one had a little paper Cupid pasted in the center. This struck me as odd as I was in the grips of the post-Christmas blahs.

An increased sense of urgency drove me to search for something. Eventually, I turned down a darkened hallway in the oldest section of the building which led to a small waiting room. In one of the nasty naugahyde chairs, all alone, sat Grandma Mason. She was wearing a very old wedding dress and was holding a bouquet of flowers that were brown, shriveled, and dead. I went over and sat down beside her.

"What are you doing here?" I asked.

"I'm waiting. I have to go soon."

"What do you mean? Go where?"

"I'm bleeding. My time has come."

My eyes watered as I realized what she meant. "You can't go!" I insisted. "I'm not ready for this!"

She patted my leg. "Please don't be upset. I stayed as long as I could, mostly for you, but I just can't do it anymore. My body has had it."

Then a door opened up and an extremely bright light shone through it. It was so bright I couldn't see anything in the room, just the bright white light.

"I have to go now. But don't worry! You're going to be fine. I'll be fine. This is the natural order of things. I'm actually looking forward to this. I miss my husband, my parents, my daughter ... it's been a really long time since I've seen them. I know that's difficult to understand for someone your age."

"But if you go, won't you miss us?"

"Of course I will. But I'm not really leaving you. I'll still be there; you just won't be able to see me in the same way."

She stood up and walked into this light. I didn't think I could even stand to watch. At the last minute though, my curiosity got the best of me and I looked up. She was in the white light now and was completely transformed. She was young! The dress looked brand new and the flowers were white and fresh. She smiled at me, waved, and tossed the bouquet. I caught it. I looked down and saw that the bouquet was made from three white Easter lilies. They were so real I could smell them! The pollen from the stamens in the center came off on my fingers, powdery yellow.

I woke up with Great Expectations jabbing me in the back and the evening sun glittering through the icicles hanging from the gutter outside my bedroom window. Too much Miss Haversham! I should stop binge reading this English assignment! Unlike other kids who hated these classics, I always got hooked on them and read them the whole way through in one or two days. I'd fallen asleep after school reading in bed.

The morning it happened, I knew. It was about two weeks after I had the dream. I heard the phone ring late at night. The phone ringing in the middle of the night was always bad. I procrastinated going downstairs for breakfast because I knew what was coming. When I could avoid it no longer, I went down and sat at the table. A pile of well done, finely sliced bacon sat on my plate. Nobody made better bacon than my dad. He sat down across from me.

"Grandma died last night," he said.

I ate my bacon in silence.

"She started bleeding and they flew her in one of those life flight helicopters to West Penn Hospital, but she died right after they got there."

I looked up at the clock. "What time was it?"

"About half past midnight."

I got it now. I remembered the clues in the dream: Valentine hearts and paper doilies.

"Do you know what today is?" I asked him. "It's Valentine's Day. She died on Valentine's Day."

He smiled. "Oh, you're right. I forgot all about it. She always did say that everyone in her family died on a holiday."

I remembered the dream and I understood her message. I put on a brave face and went to school that day, for once not worried about the fact that I didn't have a date or a card or anything for Valentine's

Day. My dad usually gave me a heart shaped box of candy, but that year he forgot, and I didn't bring it up because even at that age, I could understand why.

The day of her funeral, we had unseasonably warm weather. It was almost 70 degrees outside. It reminded me of a Christmas Eve a year or so before when it was warm like that, and Bob and I went down to the creek and built a dam in it, playing like kids, even though I was twelve and he was thirty-two.

After the big funeral and lunch in the church social hall, we began the process of breaking up Grandma's little rented house. This quaint ritual was really the end of her personal identity. It transformed her from a family member into possessions that sit in each of our homes and remind us of her. My parents were old pros when it came to dead grandparents. After all, they'd been through it three other times. Despite their business- like demeanor, we all knew it was the end of an era. She was the last member of that generation.

"How did she ever get so much stuff in this closet?" lamented my mother as she pulled yet another suitcase from its dark depths. Boxes, bags, and old hats littered the bedroom floor. Dad was packing clothes in the car to be delivered to the Salvation Army. Aunt Mary was out in the living room making arrangements to have an antique table crated and shipped to Arizona. I sat on the bed, trying on the hats.

"You can have those if you want', offered Aunt Mary from the doorway. She went over and began folding linens from Grandma's big blanket chest. My father returned with a cardboard box, which he sat on the bed in front of me.

"Grandma's will says that everyone gets back the things they gave her as gifts. These things are yours."

Inside the box was a little red rose in a clear vase that I gave her one year for Mother's Day, and a ceramic bear I made for her in Girl Scouts. He was designed to hold a box of baking soda and was still cold from the refrigerator. He had been a Christmas present. Here was all that remained of the days when I had a Grandma. Something glittered from the bottom. I reached in and drew out a pin.

"Oh look. Here's the pin I gave her for Mother's Day. Remember? That year they were selling these family pins? That they set with the birthstones of all your children? I think you got one, too."

"Yeah. I did get one that year, too", reminisced my mother.

"You should go through the jewelry box and make sure we didn't miss anything," suggested Aunt Mary. She opened it and pawed through the contents. "All that's left is costume jewelry. Do you want it? In fact, you can have the jewelry box if you like. Your Dad gave her that and I'm sure he doesn't want it." I went over and opened the top of the box. Inside were a variety of pins and necklaces, many of which I could remember her wearing. But there was also a box. A box that I remembered, and now realized had been hoping was still there.

"I remember this. She showed it to me a long time ago." I opened the box and there it was, exactly as I remembered it. It was a little necklace made of pink porcelain roses. "I can't believe no one else took this."

I sat for a while, holding the box with the necklace and earrings, gulping down a lump in my throat. I was a five-year-old with my hair up in pink ribbons. Grandma bent over and showed me the necklace, which somehow looked much larger and more impressive back them. I could smell Juicy Fruit gum. I remembered the candy stash in her dresser drawer. I turned and saw the dresser drawer was open and empty.

I forced the memories back, packing the jewelry box and the rose necklace with the rest of my things I left for the car. It was the first of many occasions where I would ride away in a car holding part of my life in a cardboard box. I breathed in the earthly air and realized the last clue. The air smelled just like Easter.

✳✳✳

It was a warm spring day as I walked through the Covenanter cemetery. Only this time, the stones were not in their usual neat rows. They were in concentric circles like Stonehenge. Because of this, I knew I was dreaming.

I'd been in this place many times before, long before I knew what Stonehenge was. It was another dreamscape, one that belonged to my great grandmother, Susan Grant Black. I'd never actually seen her in it, but her presence and authority permeated the entire dreamscape like a diffuse sort of light.

The tombstones in this cemetery had an unusual quality where if you touched them, you sort of just knew the person associated with it. It occurred to me that I could use this to conduct research. If I could find a stone corresponding to some of the people in my mother's past that I needed to know about, I could find out about them this way. In particular, I wanted to find the little girl who died in the woods, and the other one who had been with me that day. Problem was, I didn't know either of their names.

Well, there weren't that many stones so I decided to just start trying them. The one next to me was rather memorable and I was near the center, so I decided to start there and go inwards, hoping that neither of my parents would wake me up anytime soon. It was still summer, so there was a good chance they'd let me sleep until I woke up on my own.

I put my hands on the first stone. Images of a young woman in a bustle dress filled my mind. I was still vaguely aware of standing in the cemetery but the images were all around me in 3D. In addition to the visuals, I felt her personality very clearly. I saw courting and barn dances and buggy rides, then a wedding and a death in childbirth. The baby was there too, smiling and cooing. Not the right person. I removed my hands before I became too enthralled with that person's life and forced myself to move onto the next one.

This one was a man. I saw battles I thought were in the Civil War era, a family, the death of his wife, his own death many years later while living with his son and daughter-in-law. Not the right one either!

I kept moving around the circle testing stones and realized that as I went in, the time periods were farther back. I was going the wrong direction. But before I could turn around and go the other way, I noticed a really interesting tomb in the very center. It was an elaborate chest tomb, out of place here. It looked like it belonged in some cathedral. Unable to resist, I went to check it out.

There were no names or dates on the magnificent tomb. Did I dare? I did! I touched it.

Poof! I found myself standing inside of a very large room – far too large to be inside the tomb, I thought. Piled everywhere were things – all sorts of things – clocks, furniture, dishes, every imaginable thing that people could have owned. Did all this stuff belong to the people in the cemetery?

Then I noticed something – something of mine! Not long after I was born Mom made me a large stuffed Snoopy dog out of an old coat of Grandma's. I loved that dog! He got played with a lot, and washed a lot, and not long ago he had finally disintegrated. I had to allow him to be thrown in the garbage. It was heart wrenching. How could I feel that way about a stuffed dog? He wasn't alive, he was a thing. It shouldn't hurt him to go to the dump any more than it would have hurt Grandma's coat. Yet, I cried like a baby and felt horribly guilty for weeks.

And here he was! I picked him up and hugged him, my tears soaking into his restored fur. I tried to get ahold of myself, I was gonna wake up if I kept on crying like that. I took a deep breath and looked up. I noticed a very large elaborate antique doll. I marveled at the detail and complexity of her dress, her hair, how perfect she was.

And then I woke up.

Damn! I thought. I let myself get distracted from my goal *again*! Still, something about the doll seemed significant. I remembered it so vividly.

Later that day, I cornered my mother in her bedroom, folding laundry. I told her the dream in as much detail as possible, even describing the color and trim on the doll's dress, her hair, and anything else I could remember.

She lit up with recognition. "I know that doll! When I was about six years old, Mammy – Susan Grant Black, that is – had this little girl around the same age as me. She wasn't their natural daughter - they adopted her. It's written in the old Bible they had where they recorded all the births, marriages, and deaths. This little girl got an ear infection that turned septic and she died. Her name was Mildred. They buried her with that doll! Ugh I was so upset! A beautiful doll like that, in the middle of the Depression! I would've loved to have had a doll like that! And they *buried* her with it!"

She balled up a pair of socks and threw them into the basket.

"Humm," I said. "Mildred, Millicent. Kind of close don't you think? Maybe that was the girl in my dream?"

"It's possible," she agreed.

"But Mildred didn't die in the woods, I take it?"

"No, she died at home in her bed."

Mom picked up a stack of Dad's underwear and crossed the room to his dresser. "Why do you put Dad's clothes away? I mean, he's an adult, right? I'm not even an adult and I put my own clothes away."

"Because it's something I agreed to do when we got married," she said.

"Why?"

"Because that's the way things were done," she said in frustration. "Why are you bugging me about this?"

"I dunno, I guess because it seems to me that women get a bum deal in life."

"Well I'll grant you that," she conceded. "But there are more important battles to fight than who puts away the underwear."

To be honest, she'd fought more than a few and won. Like when she went back to work in 1980, Dad learned to cook! We choked down a few really bad meals until he got the hang of it, too. Still, I always felt like my mother was not really cut out to be a 1950's housewife, even if she was good at it. The house was always clean and she could materialize a meal out of thin air if people showed up unexpectedly.

Mom was most like herself, I thought, when she was painting with her oil paints. She tried to teach me once and I was hopelessly awful at it, but she would sit up in the spare bedroom with her old wooden easel, her metal tubes of paint and glass jars full of stinky turpentine and paint ocean scenes and trees and all sorts of things. There was a song on the radio back then called "Starry, Starry, Night" by Don McLean that is about Vincent Van Gogh but parts of it always reminded me of her.

> *Starry, starry night*
> *Paint your palette blue and gray*
> *Look out on a summer's day*
> *With eyes that know the darkness in my soul*
> *Shadows on the hills*
> *Sketch the trees and the daffodils*
> *Catch the breeze and the winter chills*
> *In colors on the snowy linen land*

Other parts of it reminded me of her mother, Grammy:

> *A silver thorn, a bloody rose*
> *Lie crushed and broken on the virgin snow*
> *Now I understand what you tried to say to me*
> *And how you suffered for your sanity*
> *How you tried to set them free*
> *They would not listen, they did not know how*
> *Perhaps they'll listen now*

Because no matter how much my mother and The Aunts placated me, I still felt like Grammy had a message, a major message, and I really wanted to someday be able to figure it out and boldly proclaim, *"Now I understand what you tried to say to me."*

CHAPTER 16

April 1984

K ris and I were in her bedroom after school one day, lounging around. Her bedroom was in the back of their house and faced south. It was already starting to get dark and the clouds above the woods were stained purple. It was not a large room. Her house had five bedrooms, but the only one of any great size was the master occupied by her parents. The walls were painted a cheery peach and she had two dressers, a small desk, her bed, and a nice big closet.

"You're not gonna like this," she said. "I saw Martin putting the moves on some chick a few lockers down from mine."

I shrugged and looked out the window.

"I can hardly expect him to skip his senior prom just because his mom won't let him take me. Leave him alone."

His mother never did relent and over time, the phone calls grew less frequent. It just sort of cooled itself off into a nice friendship that lasted many years.

"He's obviously not letting any grass grow under his feet," she commented with annoyance. "Why should you?"

She had a point. She also had dates! That year, she turned the magical age of sixteen and started to get asked out while we were out trawling for boyfriends. It was awkward and I ended up bawling more than once. She offered to turn them down but I told her not to worry and to go for it. I didn't want to become a millstone around her neck. So far, none of these nibbles had yielded anything worthwhile but at least her streetcars were stopping to ask if she wanted a ride. Meanwhile, mine were still hitting the accelerator when they saw me waiting, to borrow my mother's favorite analogy.

Kris said, "I heard about this under twenty-one dance thing called Fantasy Rock. It goes on every Sunday night at the Holiday Inn down by the Tarentum Bridge. It's like a night club, only there's no alcohol. I don't think there would be many kids from Kiski there. It's probably all Burrell, Valley, or Highlands. This would be great for you! I think we should go and check it out." She had a good point. Kids from other school districts would be unaware of the gossip and elementary school baggage swirling around me. It seemed like an excellent strategy.

We both knew a fair number of kids from Burrell, as both of our churches were in Lower Burrell. Valley was in New Kensington and Highlands across the river in Natrona Heights. The Holiday Inn was near where all three of these school districts intersected.

So we went! We went every Sunday for what seemed like many weeks, and listened to very loud music and drank overly sweet and under carbonated pop. We dressed up, made ourselves up, danced, and tried to look alluring.

"Wear this," Kris insisted, pulling a cream and burgundy striped blouse from my closet. "And wear it with THOSE jeans. Trust me! I promise this will make you look older."

"All right," I conceded and got dressed. My dad was waiting to drive us to another night of Fantasy Rock. We'd been going every Sunday all winter and still nothing much had happened. I could hear my father shift his weight and jangle his keys in the hall downstairs, both of which indicated that he was tired of waiting.

"Let's not bother with boys tonight," I suggested. Kris agreed. We were sick of boyfriend hunting. Tonight, we would just enjoy ourselves like the good old days before there were any boys to be concerned about. A few years later, Kris would wisely observe that when you gussied yourself up and went out nothing ever happened. But woe to the girl who would presume to run down to the corner drugstore in sweat pants, un-showered and wearing no makeup. She will inevitably come face to face with Prince Charming in the checkout line.

We squirmed our way onto the dance floor where we met up with several other girls we knew from our churches. After several songs, we were tired and got in line for drinks, then stood along the side of the room catching our breath. "Jump" by Van Halen blared on the sound system and the lights from the dance floor flashed everywhere. It was too loud and crazy for any meaningful conversation. The song ended and a slow song came on. I felt a tug on my sleeve.

"That guy over there is looking at you," Kris said in my ear. "I think he's going to ask you to dance!"

I gawked around in surprise. "Where?"

"Right over there," she nodded off towards the opposite dark corner of the room. "Don't stare!"

"Which one?" There were several boys standing together, all of whom were now looking at us.

"The one in the gray parachute pants!"

I flushed. "What should I do?"

"Get ready! He's coming over right now. Don't say anything stupid and good luck!" Then, she was gone! I barely had time to shut my mouth before he was standing right there in front of me. All of our other friends had done the same disappearing act but I knew they were watching from somewhere. I smiled nervously and waited.

"Do you want to dance?" he asked. In the gravity of the moment I had forgotten to breathe, and it took me a second to answer. He stood there waiting to see if I was going to pop his ego like a soap bubble.

"Sure," I said. He looked relieved.

So we headed out for the dance floor and began exchanging pertinent pieces of information like names, ages, and schools. His name was Ron and he was only one year older than me. He went to Highlands, a different school district on the other side of the river. As we danced and talked, Kris would periodically emerge from the throng and give me the "OK" sign. No doubt his friends were doing the exact same thing behind my back. When the lights came on and it was time to find our friends and rides home, he asked for my phone number. That was the next move, and in my elation, I had forgotten to be anxious about it.

So then began one of those brief periods in life where everything is perfect. I had achieved my goal! I had a steady boyfriend! There were nightly phone calls with the expected mild parental confrontations about phone bills, movies followed by ice cream sundaes at Isaly's, weekend afternoons spent at picnics in his parents' back yard, and walks around Natrona Heights. And new friends! Ron was in an entirely different social caste than I was. He was one of the "in" people. He was the star pitcher for the baseball team and in the student government. So I became somewhat of an instant celebrity at this other high school. I was living somebody else's life, the very life I'd always envied.

The Aunt Farm Aunts, wisecracking dispensers of babushka wisdom that they were, warned me to be careful what I wished for. They were, of course, right. I discovered that popularity is a lot like a job. Every weekend, there were parties we were expected to attend, along with many, many baseball games and basketball games. I took him to my Astronomy Club events and he managed to fit in even with us geeks. For an introvert like me – not that I even knew what an introvert was let alone that I was one – this soon got to be way too much.

The first inkling of trouble ahead was a creeping resentment of the nightly phone calls. At first, it was exciting! No more waiting around for phone calls that never came! Yet, as the weeks went by, I started to feel like every night was a little bit too often. It was hard trying to think of enough things to talk about. I missed my favorite TV shows and lying in bed listening to the stereo all evening. I missed Kris, who faded into the background without any discussion. It was as if all the girls had some sort of unspoken agreement to disappear from each other's lives once we had boyfriends. I wondered what was wrong with me. I had what everyone wants! So why was I not happy?

All this commitment greatly increased my need to be driven about in the car. My mother hated this! She insisted that being chauffeured around by one or the other set of parents was not a date. I didn't care what she called it as long as she did her share of the driving. My brother, Bob was living at home temporarily after the loss of his non-tenured teaching position at Bowling Green University. With the tail end of the baby boomers graduating college, there were too many college professors and not enough college students causing a recession of sorts to hit the secondary education establishment. He never did have another job teaching after that one. He moved to California that fall and got into desktop publishing. During that summer he stayed with us, and took over chauffeur duty as an act of gratitude towards my parents.

Mom was waiting for the bottom to drop out. To me, it came as a complete surprise. As I recall it, the particular night began like any other. Ron babysat for a young couple who lived a few houses down on his street. They had a preschool aged boy. I was excited when he asked me to baby-sit with him. My father, however, was not amused.

"What's the big deal?" I asked, an hour or so before I was due to be dropped off. My mother, Bob, and I were standing in the kitchen. Condensation clouded the windows and the spaghetti was almost done.

My mother exchanged a sly glance with Bob. "Your father doesn't like you baby sitting alone with Ron because he remembers what he would have done at that age."

I was scandalized. "We've never done anything!" They looked at each other and smirked. "I mean it! How could you think something like that about me!"

They started laughing. Martin's prediction had come back to haunt me in spades. Having passed beyond the period of doubt and speculation, the relationship settled into something of a routine. We went to each other's family picnics and our parents were used to having both of us around. It seemed to me that, given the way people acted and the comments they made, they all had the types of thoughts Martin had warned me about. Because of that, I was starting to get a little embarrassed and uncomfortable around our friends and family sometimes, even if I wasn't consciously unaware of the reason I felt that way.

The evening of babysitting began like an episode of *Ozzie and Harriet*. The house was only a few doors down from Ron's house on his tree lined street in Natrona Heights. Several other neighborhood kids were in the backyard with our charge playing kickball. They thought I was cool and both sides wanted me on their team. When it came time for dinner, neither one of us could cook so we ordered pizza and made a salad. Break out the Pepsi! The kids loved it. When 8:00 PM rolled around, Ron put the little fellow in bed as instructed. For about a half an hour, he kept sneaking back downstairs to spy on us. After a few stern warnings, he returned to bed and fell asleep.

The remainder of the evening we spent in the immaculate living room. They had one of those sectional sofas when they were a relatively new thing. Ron brought a camera so we amused ourselves taking silly pictures of each other. Then he tried to take one of us together by holding the camera at arm's length, what would today be called a selfie. 10:00 PM found us necking on the couch.

"Do you think we'll ever go the whole way?" he asked out of the blue. I stared at him. I was not expecting this to come up. Not that we'd ever talked about it, but everyone knows that nice kids didn't do that sort of stuff and I just assumed he knew that.

"Not anytime soon," he back pedaled. "Like maybe when we're seniors?"

"Maybe," I said in order to end the awkward conversation. Although what I was actually thinking was more along the lines of when pigs fly. The comment killed the mood. To break the uncomfortable silence, he switched on the TV. Over the rest of the evening my feeling of unease increased.

At 11:00 PM, my brother arrived to take me home in his frightening looking old blue Plymouth Volare. I hopped into the front passenger seat, and as soon as we were safely started on the road home, I came apart at the seams.

"What's wrong?" he asked. "Did something happen?" Bob never treated my problems like they were stupid, even when I was a year old.

"Not really," I sobbed. "I just feel awful and I don't know why! I've never felt this way at the end of a date with Ron before. I can't think of any reason. We didn't have a fight. It just came on me all of a sudden. I started feeling funny later in the evening. Then, when I got in the car, it got really bad."

"Can you think of any way to describe it?"

I thought for a moment and took a deep breath of cool air from the open window. "It feels like imminent doom. Like I'm afraid I'll stop liking him."

"Why would you stop liking him?"

"I dunno! Could I just wake up some day and not like him anymore? Could he suddenly stop liking me? That would be the end, wouldn't it?"

"If you stopped liking him, then wouldn't you want out of the relationship?"

"No! I want it to work! It HAS to work! Is it normal to feel like this? Is it a stage? Will it go away? Or does it mean the relationship is a failure already?"

Bob sighed in compassionate frustration. "I'm sorry, but I don't really know. I wish I knew what to tell you. I don't know that much about relationships, either."

I wondered how that could possibly be for a guy in his thirties with a PhD. I didn't feel like he was holding out on me or anything like that. What I didn't know was that he was gay. My mother didn't tell me that until a couple of years later when I was in high school. Then it all made perfect sense. They'd all known for several years because he came out of the closet at our brother John's wedding in 1979, a drama that somehow went entirely over my head.

"What happened right before you noticed this feeling?" he asked.

I thought back. Uh, we were making out on the sofa. Don't think I want to tell him that! I wasn't 100% sure he wouldn't rat me out to Mom. And the comment about sex? No freaking way! "Well, he said something about when we're seniors," I hedged.

"So it was talking about something in the future? Like he thought you wouldn't be a couple then? Something that made you afraid he wants to break up?"

"No, he was talking about us still being a couple then. I guess ... I just never thought ... about that far ahead."

"So you're afraid of something in the future?"

"Yes. But I'm not sure exactly what."

Despite my withholding information, that was the truth. Was I afraid of sex? I wasn't sure, but I definitely wasn't interested in trying it. I still didn't understand why anyone would want to do that but I didn't think I'd have to worry about it for a long time. I was fine with the making out and that's all kids our age were supposed to do. Like most kids, I lived in the moment, concerned only with not getting my ass kicked now. I'd never thought about what it would mean if we were still together when we were seniors. If we weren't, that would mean a failed relationship, to go with my failed childhood and my failed life. If I lost this guy, would my improved status with my peers vanish like fog? Would they laugh at me and think it failed because I wasn't good enough? I wiped my nose on my sleeve and looked out at the river as we drove across the Freeport Bridge. There was a river gravel harvesting barge with a big crane at one end working and its bright lights danced on the dark water. The shapes of the hills were inky against the night sky.

"Are you sure you aren't overthinking this?" Bob asked. "Why not just take things one day at a time. Get a good night's sleep, and see if you feel better in the morning?"

***

It was dark when I found myself standing before the Aunt Farm. The wind gusted through the trees and stars chased each other among fast moving clouds. The air smelled of fresh clay. I turned and looked down the hill and saw Grammy's moonlight garden. I was dreaming! I'd seen this garden before but I'd never been inside it. It always felt like somehow it would be dangerous to go in. Everything in the garden was an iridescent silvery white, almost glittering against the dark background of the woods. Exotic roses spread their petals, so delicate that they appeared as if made entirely of dewdrops suspended in the moonlight. Ferns had feathery leaves so ethereal that they seemed barely there. I stood at the edge and peered in. I needed to talk to her! Was she in there somewhere? In spite of my doubts, I opened the gate and went in.

Once I crossed the threshold of the gate, I was not in a garden or even outside! I was inside the house, in the master bedroom. The windows were open and the lace curtains floated on the breeze like the ghost I was trying to find. Well, this is really messed up, I thought. Now what do I do?

Then I noticed a door that was never there before. I opened it and went into an entirely new room, with several other rooms off of it. Wow, I thought!

In the middle of the room was a table with a black rotary telephone sitting on it, like the one in the Aunt Biggie's bedroom. It rang, startling me. I picked it up.

"Hello?"

"It's Grammy."

"Oh my God! It's you! Why didn't you do this before? It's so much easier," I said.

She laughed. "It takes a great deal of skill on both sides for this to happen. We're both still learning. So it will not last long. I need to tell you: don't let other people tell you what you want. Back in my day, everyone told you exactly what you wanted and when you wanted it. We didn't even know to question it. SO QUESTION IT! Figure out what you actually want."

I deflated. "I don't know what I want anymore."

"Figure it out," she said.

And then I woke up.

***

I kept my problem to myself for the next week or so, although from the squirrelly way my mother gave me the side eye, I knew she suspected that something was going on. I lay awake at night trying to in vain to reason it out. Everything was perfect. Yet, I felt terrible.

"You worry too much," Kris advised as we paused on our bikes at Shearsburg Crossroads. It was a warm, sunny Saturday at the end of May and the surrounding hills were striped with rows of newly planted corn. We were on our way to the senior high to watch Ron's baseball game against Kiski, the last one of the season. She took a drink of water from her canteen and passed it over to me. "Why would you stop liking him for no reason?"

"I don't know!"

"Everything happens for a reason, right? So if there is no reason, you won't stop liking him. Unless he gave you a reason?"

I shook my head and handed the canteen back. "No."

"Then I don't know what to tell you other than, like, take a chill pill."

We turned down Shearsburg Road and picked up speed going down the long hill past Morrison's sheep farm. We'd been riding down this road since we were at Weinel's elementary school which was near the end of Shearsburg Road. It was almost entirely downhill. In years past I could ride the entire way from Shearsburg Crossroads to Weinel's Crossroads without even touching the handlebars, arms outstretched, steering the bicycle by leaning from side to side. But after that, a fairly long hill up Route 356 stood between Weinel's Crossroads and the high school. We would be huffing it up that one.

We hadn't gone on a bike hike, as we called these longer excursions, since what happened three summers before. I don't remember what made us decide it was safe this time, other than the passage of time and the fear of missing the last baseball game of the year due to not being able to bum a ride from either set of parents or Kris's older sisters.

It seemed like old times as we buzzed down the road past Mannarino's pond. The owner of the property, Kelly Mannarino, was the boss of the New Ken Mafia. You could see the pond from the road but the house was far back behind it, hidden by trees most of the year. The compound was surrounded by a wooden fence and had a long governor's driveway with a gate at each end. People in the neighborhood liked the guy, but most were also a little afraid of him, and there were always rumors about dead bodies being hidden in the pond. Kelly Mannarino had died a couple years prior and the property sat quietly with both gates locked.

After we arrived at the high school, I sat on the warm metal bleachers with the popular kids at Highlands and basked in the reflected glory of Ron pitching a no hitter. A few kids from Kris's grade came over and sat with us, and for once I was not intimidated. I felt like an equal.

"So you're going with *him*?" one of them asked. He was obviously impressed.

"Yes. For three months in a row," I said.

Kris smiled with satisfaction. I hardly seemed like the same kid who used to embarrass her by entertaining her friends with ridiculous stories while hanging upside down on the monkey bars during recess.

"Oh my god," he said. "Is that a sucker bite I see on his neck?" They all laughed. He lifted up my hair. "Do you have one to match?"

"Cut it out!" I scolded. They all assumed it was just false modesty, and continued teasing.

"I wonder where else he has one? Nudge nudge, wink wink!" They broke out into peals of rowdy laughter. I wanted to slip through the hole between the bleachers.

So now the whole are-you-or-aren't-you sex thing was up for public speculation at both schools? Was there no sense of privacy or decency? I was terribly afraid the happy increase in social status I was enjoying was about to take a sharp downward turn into being branded a slut. And if the dots got connected between that and what happened to me? I was afraid to even speculate about that. I'd internalized my mother's fears. I felt the beginnings of a panic attack. Why was this happening now? I hadn't had one of these in over a year!

Just then something happened on the baseball field. I was so wrapped up in my ballooning panic that I didn't see it. One of the boys had just been injured. Coaches and parents mobbed the field and all attention was focused on the ensuing drama, so nobody but Kris noticed me slip out and disappear behind a thick stand of pine trees lining the school driveway.

Kris ran after me. "Hey, whatsamatter?"

"I don't feel good," I gasped, crouching down to avoid passing out.

"Can you ride home?" I shook my head no. "I'll go the pay phone and call for a ride. Just wait here. I'll be right back."

It seemed like forever until she returned. I tossed my cookies in a trash can back behind the baseball field. As I waited, I saw an ambulance roar up the driveway. Whatever happened must have been bad!

Finally, Kris reappeared. "Your dad is on his way."

"What's going on?"

"One of the guys on Kiski's team broke his arm. They're taking him to the ER."

"Oh my God, that's awful," I said. "Was it anyone we know?"

"I don't think so. He's a grade ahead of you and from Vandergrift. Your friends were starting to wonder what happened to you, so I told them you started feeling nauseated and your parents were picking you up. So, no problems there. They said they hope you feel better and Ron will call you later.

My dad creaked into the circular drive in his beat up old pickup truck. He got out and put both of our bicycles in the back while we scrambled into the cab.

"So what happened?" asked Dad when he got back in the truck.

"I don't know," I said. "I had a panic attack."

"What caused it?"

"I don't know!" I screamed. "We were just talking and ... and it happened!"

"All right, all right! Settle down. We'll be home in a few minutes. Your mother's waiting. I'll drop you off with her and then take Kris home."

Mom had it all in hand. She asked me no questions when I got home, just had me lay down in bed with a cool washcloth on my face and an ice bag on my head.

"I hate to have to remind you of this," she said sitting next to my bed, "but you have church confirmation tonight."

I looked at her like she was nuts. "You've got to be kidding me! How can I go like this? I have a splitting headache!"

"I know you don't feel like it, and I don't blame you. I don't know how else to say it, but I just have this gut feeling that you should go. You have plenty of time to get dressed. I ran you a nice hot bath, and I'll make you a cup of tea so you can take some assburn for the headache."

I smiled involuntarily about the assburn.

Just then, Tam the Siamese cat jumped up on the bed, and she stroked him until he began to purr.

"Look. Tam came to see what the matter is." She cast her eyes back down at the floor. "Do you remember when you went out for the swim team earlier this year? You were really nervous and afraid, and the coach was picking on you?" The cat pranced up and down the bed, rubbing both of us with the side of his face. Then he lay down next to me and began to groom himself.

"Yeah. So?"

"Do you remember that I told you to pray about it, and after that you were able to get into the pool and everything was fine?"

"What's your point?"

"The point is that I think you should give the whole thing, all of it, over to God."

"What? That's not the kind of gift you give to God! You give God things like a beautiful voice or the ability to speak a dozen languages! Not bad things!"

She stood up and put her hands on her hips. "It's God's job to make silk purses out of sows' ears!" I looked at her in disbelief. "I'm not kidding you, it is!"

"What's a pig's ear have to do with any of this?" I shot back.

"Just get ready for church. Trust me for once!"

"Oh, all right."

Later that evening, I was sitting in the church social hall, grimacing to stretch the dry skin on my face. I breathed into my cup of coffee hoping the steam would help. Why couldn't I have remembered to at least put some face cream on?

"Hey, you made it!" said Tim dropping into the chair next to me.

"Where else would I be?"

He held his hands in front of his face to block an imaginary blow. "Whoa. Nice mood you're in."

"Sorry. I shouldn't take it out on you."

"What's up?"

"I had kind of a bad afternoon. It's over and I'd rather not think about it."

The rest of the class sat down at the table and through their combined antics, I soon forgot my misery. We sat at our table and joked, while people drifted by and wished us well on our confirmation. The sun shone through the small windows, illuminating the construction paper crosses and coloring book pages of Jesus and his sheep tacked to the bulletin board by the Sunday school teachers.

Soon ladies in flowered aprons began to set steaming dishes of chicken and noodles, biscuits, mashed potatoes, and succotash out on the buffet table. Dishes of Jell-O salad, fruit, and cake followed. Since this feast was in our honor, we went first.

"First table served! Put this on the calendar!" I joked to my mother as I walked past. There was a standing joke in our family that whatever table we sat at would be called last. If we sat at the first table, they started with the last table. If we sat at the last table, they started with the first. Once we tried sitting in the middle, and they started alternating from both ends. It was the family curse.

When the dinner was over, we all walked across the parking lot to the church building. The rhododendrons flushed pink against the red brick building with its white trim, and white steeple standing out against a clear blue sky. We joined this church when I was in early elementary school. Before that, when Linda, Bob, and John were growing up and when I was very little, we went to a Presbyterian church in Leechburg. We left that church because of a scandal. Mom told me about it some years later. Apparently the minister had been sexually harassing one of the staff and this resulted in one of the last church trials that ever happened in our neck of the woods.

They used to have church trials a lot. In the 18th and 19th

centuries, they'd haul each other before the session for all sorts of disputes and "bad" behaviors. When things got really out of hand, it got pushed up to the next level (the Presbytery) and then they had a church trial, which was a lot like a US court trial. By the 20th century, they could no longer hang you or put you in the stocks. They could just kick you out of the church which didn't mean much when you could just go to another denomination down the street. I suspect this is why they stopped bothering with them as often.

Long story short, my father was an elder and he stood up for the victim, so got hit with some pretty severe backlash. It was bad enough that he moved his membership to another church in a different town.

I sat in a sea of friendly faces with Tim and the rest of our class, the last class taught by Reverend Harry Fisher. Many of them were older than my parents, and I'm sure most of them are long gone by now. I still dream about them sometimes, back in that time and place. They were down to earth and friendly; nobody ever told anybody they were going to hell. They fed hundreds of elderly people through the Meals on Wheels program. They always had a smile and a handshake for you. During that time when my parents were often socially ostracized by people in the community because of what happened to me, that must have been a lifesaver.

Before collection was taken, they introduced a group of actors invited to perform. Two clowns ambled in from the side entrance, while a third emerged from the rear of the sanctuary dragging a large sack down the aisle. All heads turned to see this clown and his exaggerated gestures of hauling this heavy sack towards the front of the church, smiles slowly creeping across the faces of young and old alike.

Finally, he reached the front, where the other two clowns had commandeered the offering plates while everyone's attention was diverted. They opened the sack, reached in, and drew out a red brick painted with the word ANXIETY.

They lobbed it into the offering plate with a loud clang.

The next brick, FEAR, went in. Beside me, Tim's eyes had grown round and large. Then came SHAME. I noticed the girl next to me digging furiously in her purse for a tissue. I didn't understand then, but a few years later she confided in me that she'd been molested by her grandfather.

WORRY and DEPRESSION finished it off. After placing the plate full of bricks on the altar, the clown picked up his sack, tossed it over his shoulder, and left.

***

After school let out, Ron came over one day to go swimming in the creek. It seemed only natural that I would introduce him to my world, having spent the spring in his town stomping grounds of Natrona Heights.

The woods back in those days was our playground. We spend entire days roaming around it in all sorts of weather. In the winter, we went sledding down the super steep hills along the gas pipeline. In the spring, we went to see the daffodils that came up around the ruined foundations of what was once a log cabin, picked and ate wild ramps, and smelled the skunk cabbage that, along with the ramps, was one of the first things to come up in the spring. All summer long we swam in the creek, built and maintained our system of creek dams, caught crayfish, snakes, lizards and toads, mined clay from the banks, hiked, and swung on the huge wild grape vines. Unfortunately, the wild grapes were not good to eat; they had huge seeds and were a lot like marbles covered with grape skin. In the late summer and fall, there were tons of wild black raspberries. There was enough sassafras growing back there all spring, summer, and fall to feed an army. Because of that, we rarely bothered to pack lunches.

Our neighborhood was built on top of a hill that used to be a farm like Morrison's. A road ran through the valley between our hill and Morrison's, but in the valley on the other side were the woods. At the very bottom of that valley ran both a small creek and a gas pipeline. Because of the pipeline, there was always a cleared trail along there. Most of our days in the woods started off with us walking down over the hill from my backyard, through a patch of May apples where little box turtles hung out, past a huge patch of poison oak and an exceedingly large old oak tree with a trunk too thick to put your arms the whole way around. Just below the giant oak was a trail maintained by the next door neighbor that cut across half way down the hill and came to a T at another trail that went straight down to the pipeline. Once there, you could turn right and go up into the haunted Indian grounds or left towards the swimming hole, the sled riding hills, the old cabin foundation, and the long pipeline trail that went farther than you could walk in a day.

We only occasionally ventured into the haunted Indian grounds. It was a strange place! Everywhere else in the woods you could always hear birds and animals, but in that one place it was eerily silent. When the housing plan was first built in the 1950's my sister said the Indian spirits were not happy and would come out of the woods to rattle doorknobs and other poltergeist like things to show their displeasure. She said she even saw the reflection of one in her bedroom mirror once. However, by my time they had apparently given up on trying to scare us all away and kept to themselves in the creek bottom. They would scare you away if you ventured into their territory. Sometimes you would hear footsteps behind you. Other times you would hear bees, as if a swarm were all around your head, but you couldn't see anything. I've had that happened to me in the middle of winter with a foot of snow on the ground.

So that day I took him on a tour of all that and then we stopped and spread out our beach blankets on a sunny grassy bank next to the largest swimming hole in the creek. We waded around for a while and skipped stones across the surface of the stream. Then we rubbed coconut smelling suntan oil on ourselves and lay down to work on our tans. I was almost asleep when he dropped the bomb.

"I have something I've been meaning to tell you."

I opened my eyes in alarm. "What?" I was expecting him to break up with me after an opening like that.

"It's something I did in eighth grade."

"Is that all? Go on."

"Well, you know Ryan?" he began. Of course, I knew Ryan. That was Ron's best friend who lived down the street from him. He had a rock band and a girlfriend he had been going steady with for 2 years. They did it. Everyone but their parents knew about it.

"Ryan used to have this tree house in his back yard. We were up there one day with two girls. Ryan was with Ann, and I was left talking to this other girl. When Ryan and Ann went in the house, she wanted to do it with me."

I gaped at him in absolute astonishment and horror. "You told me you never did it before!" I said.

"I know, I know," he admitted. "I meant to tell you, but I was afraid you'd be mad at me. It turned out all right though. She didn't know what to do, so I kind of took over. We're still friends."

I glared at him. "FRIENDS? You don't do that with your FRIENDS! And you still SEE this girl?"

He cringed. "It's kind of hard not to. She's in some of my classes. You won't tell anyone, will you? It's not something I'd like to have go public."

"If you're so ashamed of it, then why did you do it?"

He winced. "I couldn't really refuse. It's s guy thing. She brought it up, and I would have looked like a total wuss if I'd said no. I didn't have a girlfriend at the time so I couldn't use that as an excuse."

Just then we heard a tractor. It was Mr. Copeland – the nice elderly man who gave me the Galaxie – mowing his fields. He drove down to where we were sitting and we talked to him for a while.

After Mr. Copeland left, we went back to my house. I told Ron I was tired and asked my mother to drive him home.

"You're not mad at me?" he begged repeatedly.

"No," I said. "I'm just tired and I need time to think."

After we dropped him off, I had a dilemma on my hands. I desperately wanted to unburden myself. But I'd promised Ron I wouldn't tell.

"Something happened today, didn't it? You look miserable," my mother observed.

"It was something Ron told me. It's so awful, I can't repeat it."

"Believe me, whatever it is I've heard it before. So you might as well go ahead."

I stared at the dashboard.

"You'll feel better if you just get it out."

I sighed. "Ron told me he did it with this girl at school, and he's still friends with her."

"When did this happen?"

When he was in eighth grade."

My mother relaxed. Apparently she didn't find this as upsetting as I did. "Well, you're not married to him, for Pete's sake! And this happened long before he met you. It's not really that surprising."

"He told me he'd never done it before!" I wailed. "He lied about it!"

"In that case, I don't blame you for being a little upset. But aside from the lying, it isn't that big of a deal. Kids sometimes experiment like that. They think it's safe because there's no emotional involvement. I wouldn't bother worrying about it if I were you. It's over and you can't do anything about it. Are you afraid he still likes this girl?"

"No. I'm just disappointed in him. I wish he'd never told me. I don't know why he did."

"Well, I can tell you why he did. He's pressuring you."

I stared at her in horror. This suggestion was unbelievable and a million times worse than finding out he wasn't a virgin.

"He most certainly is not!"

"Oh, yes he is. He's a normal guy, isn't he? Granted, he's being nice about it, and he's probably unsure of himself. He may not even be totally aware of his own motives. Why do you think he told you he's still friends with that girl? He wants you to see that he did that before and nothing bad happened. He's pressuring you. That's bringing out sexual feelings in you, and you don't feel ready to deal with them."

"Ugh! Stop!" I pressed my hands over my ears. This was NOT a conversation to have with your mother! " I won't listen to another word!"

She laughed.

Then I felt guilty. "I promised him I wouldn't tell anyone. You won't tell anyone, will you? I feel like I betrayed him somehow."

"Of course I won't tell anyone. Don't feel bad about it. It's an entirely different thing telling me than telling your friends. I'm your mother. I won't tell anyone, not your dad, not the aunts, no one. I promise."

"You won't think less of him or treat him differently?"

"No. He'll never know you said anything to me about it."

The relationship never was quite the same after that. There was always a little bit of awkwardness. He went to Florida with his family on vacation, and when he came back we both spent less time with each other and more time with our own friends.

I continued to wrestle with my questions and anxieties and eventually, after a lot of thinking and considering, I decided maybe it had something to do with the relationship and I broke up with him.

For a while after that, life was fun again. Kris got her driver's license that spring and for the first time, we had some real independence. Providing cars for four girls to drive was a tall order for Kris's family, given that they all had jobs at the Ponderosa Steak House in Lower Burrell.

Her father's solution was to buy several AMC Gremlins, a type of hatchback compact car made in the 1970's. They were cheap, they were easy for him to maintain, and by having several the parts were interchangeable. He also had a couple Gremlin cocoons outside of his workshop that he scavenged for spare parts. This scheme allowed him to keep all these kids getting to work and school on time with a minimum of expense. However, at any given time we might be driving around in a Gremlin with a yellow body, a blue hood, and green doors but hey, it was transportation!

Kris also started working at Ponderosa shortly after getting her license, which meant that I couldn't spend as much time with her that summer as we had in the past. Meanwhile, Lisa was going into junior high which got us over that puberty divide, and we started spending a lot of time that summer going on bike hikes, eating ice cream, and flirting with boys.

CHAPTER 17

April 1984

Since I was spending a lot of time riding bicycles with Lisa, my parents called me into the kitchen one Saturday morning and told me Grandma Mason had left me some money in her will.

"We thought since you are riding bicycles a lot more these days, you might like to spend it on a new bike," Dad suggested, as he flipped a cake of shredded wheat in the cast iron frying pan.

My jaw dropped. "You mean like a 12 speed?" I'd had fantasies about 12 speeds for a couple of years, but was still riding the old 1960's 3 speed I'd been given by a cousin after I outgrew my 1970's kid bicycle with a banana seat and high raised handlebars with plastic streamers.

"Sure, if that's what you want. She left you $300. That should be plenty to get a really nice one. We can go shopping for one today if you like."

"Can we go to Gatto's?" I asked. "Lisa wants to get a bike there. They have way nicer bikes than Kmart."

"I remember them," said Mom over a cup of coffee. "They've got a couple of those antique penny farthing bicycles like my grandfather had. The ones with the giant front wheels. I've seen them ride them in parades."

Gatto's Cycle Shop is probably the most well-known business in Tarentum. They opened in the 1960's selling motorcycles, and by my time they had opened an entire bicycle department.

"Sure I don't see why not," Dad agreed. "It's your bike and your money. You should get the one you want."

So we went to Gatto's. I was surprised at the size of the place, and they had a great selection of bicycles – really nice ones. They had exactly what I wanted – a Schwinn Traveler 12 speed with drop handlebars. The particular one I bought was from the year prior and on sale so I got a better bicycle than I would have been able to afford, otherwise. I was waited on by a really nice looking young blonde guy named Jay. The entire bicycle department was serviced by good looking young guys and they were all so nice I had to come up with a reason to go back!

Lisa turned out to be the reason. I went back with her when she bought a bike, and the ploy worked. Jay, asked me out. He had a very pleasant, charismatic personality and quick sense of humor. He was a flatterer. My friends were extremely impressed, especially Lisa, who insisted he was so unbelievably good looking. She scored one for herself when he introduced her to his thirteen-year-old cousin and they had a passionate telephone relationship that lasted part of the summer.

Common interests: that's a concept my mother explained about relationships. Yeah, it's nice to have something to talk about during all those phone calls and dates. Turns out, it takes more than just a Y chromosome. One of the issues I struggled with going with Ron was his intense involvement in organized sports, when I did not like sports. So I thought, surely it will work better this time! Jay was also into antique cars and science. We had common interests!

I spent many happy days that summer at Jay's house. We puttered around in the garage with his car for hours. He was restoring a 1940 Ford. By this point I'd discovered that the Galaxie had a rusted frame, making it un-restorable since it is illegal to weld the frame. So I was more than happy to funnel my enthusiasm into his car.

I remember one night we took it out for a spin, unregistered and missing most of its body, in the warm night. Giggling in the night air, we rode past lonely houses with pale lights in their windows. The doors and fenders were back in garage drying under a coat of primer. Hell, the car ran! That itself was a huge accomplishment.

It was rare for us to be alone as there was always a party brewing at his house. It was a lot like Kris's house only with boys! He had three brothers. Down in the basement was a TV with a VCR - not a common toy then. Crowds of kids hung around in the basement when not upstairs raiding the refrigerator. Like with Ron, these were the popular kids at Valley and I was a secret impostor – a geek disguised with makeup. Yet, it was incredibly fun just the same.

That first magical weekend I was invited to go boating on the Allegheny River with Jay and his brothers. We drove to the boat dock under the Tarentum Bridge and launched the craft. It was an older boat that they bought and fixed up together as a project; they told me all about how they replaced the engine with a huge V8 for more power. As they launched the boat, the water lapped against the concrete boat ramp and the breeze blew in from the water with a curious petroleum component. The water was far less clean in those days before all the heavy industry along the river disappeared.

I'd never been out on the river before and I had no idea all the wild things you can only see from there. They knew all of the interesting things to go see. The Allegheny River has a system of locks and dams that keep the water at a navigable level. Before the dams were built in the 1920's, you could wade across the river, my parents said, during the dry season in summer. In Grammy and Pap's day, it froze solid every winter and they used to ice skate down it to The Point in Pittsburgh.

The locks, which are basically water elevators, are not always open to recreational traffic so we were limited to the area between Lock and Dam number 4 at Natrona and the C.W. Bill Young Lock and Dam in Acmetonia. I remember once sitting with my mother, while waiting for fireworks to start, watching boats go through the lock. The doors open on one side and a bunch of boats go in, and then the doors close and the water level is raised or lowered, depending on which direction they are going. Then the doors open on the other side of the dam and the boats drive out.

We saw monstrous concrete slabs that now served as diving towers for local kids. This shocked me as my mother did a great job of scaring us away from the river by telling us stories about how the bottom went out a few inches and then dropped to twenty feet deep, and how it was full of dangerous currents and scary holes with whirlpools that sucked you under. Yet, these kids didn't seem to care as they waved to us from the tops of these industrial ruins and swung out on huge bull ropes doing aerial summersaults before cannonballing into the water.

There were big round drums sitting in the river like giant building blocks – these were for mooring barges, they told me. Some of them still had old barges floating beside them, so rusty that you wondered how they stayed afloat. Some had been there so long they were covered with grass and trees! The barges often marked places where old industries used to be, like factories or coal mines. On the shore behind them, you could often see derelict concrete and metal structures or pieces of old blast furnaces standing like sentinels in the encroaching woods. There were still a few active mills in those days, but they were closing at a very rapid pace and taking the local economy down with them. After only a few years, they started to look abandoned, empty but for the wind howling through them as they bled rust into the ground.

We cruised around all day until the shadows were long, and I honestly think it was the most fun I had in years. I sat on Jay's lap, shivering in the cool wind. Sunlight glinted off the water which sloshed against the boat in protest if we slowed down. He kissed me, laughing, my hair blowing across our faces, and his brothers exchanged glances of mock disgust.

The day of reckoning with my past started like any other that summer. Jay invited me to go to Learnerville Speedway. The air was warm and humid, but cooler under the tree cover of Jay's yard, the sun gilding everything with its evening light. He was finishing up at work, so I got a ride from my Dad. I beat him there because when I arrived I found no one home but his younger brother, Mike. Mike was the same age as I was but being a guy, seemed younger. He nearly always grinned and seemed as if he was up to some sort of mischief, and when he opened the front door and saw me, he beamed a friendly welcome. Once inside, however, he began to look a little embarrassed.

"Does Jay know you're coming over?"

"Yeah. He called me about an hour ago. Where is he?"

"I'm not quite sure. I just got back myself and there's no one else here."

"Oh well, I'm sure he'll be along."

Mike seemed to take my reassurance to heart and began to raid the refrigerator. "Do you want a Coke or something?"

"Sure." The icy Coke crackled and hissed its refreshing coolness. I followed him as he bounded down the stairs to the basement entertainment room.

"Lookie what I got", he sang, waving an electronic toy above his head. "It's baseball. Wanna play?"

"OK", I answered as I enthusiastically removed my cultured veneer to join him in a rowdy, giggling game of electronic baseball. After several games, the crunching gravel of the circular drive announced someone's arrival. Mike and I must have shared the same thought as we hurried upstairs to see if it was Jay. Mike opened the front door, much to the surprise of a boy of about twenty who stood on the front walk.

"Oh, it's only you," he said.

He frowned. "Who were you expecting?"

"Have you seen Jay anywhere?"

He turned and pointed toward the road. "Yeah. I just passed him going down Freeport road."

Mike picked up a baseball and glove that were lying with the shoes by the door. "What an asshole! His girlfriend is here."

The older boy straightened. "You're Jay's girlfriend?"

"Yes."

He looked like he was about to ask me something but a loud thumping sound began behind us as Mike started bouncing the baseball off of a wall and catching it with the glove. Then the door from the garage opened.

"If Mom catches you doing that in her living room, she's gonna kick your ass!" scolded Dan, the eldest brother. Mike just shrugged. Then he turned to me.

"Let's go outside and wait."

The older kid left with Dan for the garage. Just then, Jay pulled in, followed closely by his mother's silver Corvette.

"Sorry I'm so late", Jay apologized.

We sat outside on the lawn waiting for friends to pick us up. I was expecting the same group of his friends I already knew. What showed up that day caught me completely off guard: a black primer coated 1970's muscle car full of long haired motor heads smoking cigarettes. One of them could have been the younger twin of the man who had abducted me three summers before.

Shocked speechless, I found myself in the car driving away with these guys, way out into the middle of nowhere, until I had no idea where we were. I didn't think I could find a phone to call my Dad even if I did know. I kept reminding myself that these guys were no more than a few years older than me, that they were not the same ones I saw with my attacker in the black primer 1970's Nova that tried to run us off Route 56. And Larry, the look alike, was not the same guy. Yet every time I looked at him I saw That Guy. They were all having a great time, joking and horsing around and completely oblivious to the fact that I was on the verge of a nervous breakdown.

My rational mind knew that I should not be having a problem with this. These guys were Jay's friends. What right did I have to pass that kind of judgement, and on nothing but a superficial resemblance? Why couldn't I just go to the racetrack and have a nice time like everyone else? I tried to focus on deep breathing so I didn't cry and ruin my cool kid façade.

At the speedway we met up with a few more kids including another guy who had a girlfriend. She was older than me and smoked – not the type of kid I usually hung around with – but I hung out with her anyway, as she seemed safe.

At some point Jay realized something was wrong. "What's the matter?" he asked.

"I just want to go home."

"Why? Don't you like the races?"

"The races are fine. Maybe another time. Can we just go?"

"OK. I'll talk to those guys. I think I can talk them into leaving." Luckily he did and before long we were being dropped off at Jay's house, dark and quiet. The other guys seemed kind of peeved that the evening ended so early, but I didn't care. As soon as they were gone, I began to sob with relief.

Jay piloted me quietly downstairs to the TV room where we sat on a brown leather couch. It was almost dark outside and we didn't bother to turn on any lights.

"Come on, you've got to tell me what's going on."

I hesitated. I'd never told Ron. This was new territory, telling a guy I was dating.

"If I tell you this, you might not like me anymore," I cautioned.

"Why? What is it? I can't imagine anything that bad."

"Well, I um, something happened to me a few summers ago. Something bad. I was abducted by this guy and ..."

"And what? Raped?"

I nodded. I was shocked. How did he guess that? Was Mom right about guys being able to tell?

"It was a guy like Larry?"

I nodded again.

"You don't ever have to be around him again." He put his arms around me and let my cry.

"What exactly happened?" he asked. "Can you tell me?"

"I went for a bicycle ride with my niece Noelle, who was eight at the time. I was eleven," I began. I wasn't sure why I trusted him with this. I'd never actually told anyone before, just hinted at it with Lisa and Kris. "We rode up to that overhead bridge by The Bonfire."

The Bonfire was a small restaurant with a golf driving range down the road a few hundred feet from the bridge. We didn't go there often, but years later I found out it was originally built by Sam Mannarino – the brother of the mafia guy who lived down on Shearsburg Road – as an illegal gambling parlor. That part of it was long gone, along with Sam Mannarino himself who died in 1967, but it still had its rustic hunting lodge feel. The heads of Sam's non-human victims were stuffed and mounted on the wood paneled walls. The Aunts sold them Pap's stuffed moose head to round out the collection. The last time I ate there, the moose head was still there, a quiet symbol of my family's presence in the community.

"Go on," he said as I stared off into space on my mental tangent.

"We were sitting on the bridge when a guy drove under it. He noticed us and made some sort of a face. But we didn't think anything of it. He must have driven around the bend and parked his truck, then got out and walked up through the woods. We'd forgotten about him by then. Cuz he came out of the woods behind us and told us some story about his brother falling and breaking his ankle in the woods. He asked us for help so we went with him into the woods. He pulled a knife on us. He threatened to kill us. I think he meant to. But after he did that, he let us go. Noelle was upset and crying and I think he just wanted away from us as fast as possible. So we rode our bikes home, and then they took me to the ER. And that's pretty much it."

"Holy shit, that's crazy. Who all knows about this?"

"I'm not really sure. A couple of my friends know. My parents, obviously. I think there was some rumor about it that went around because people started treating us different, afterwards. Please don't tell anyone!" I begged. "It's bad enough as it is!"

"No, I won't. Don't worry. I'm glad you told me. It explains a lot. We won't go anywhere with Larry again, I promise."

"Your friend had nothing to do with this, really!" I sniffled. "The guy who did it was a whole lot older. I'm sure your friend is a nice guy. I don't mean to act like this."

"Don't worry about it. Come on. You don't look well. Let's go upstairs and I'll make something to eat."

Jay was a toaster oven master chef. We sat at the kitchen island while he piled cheese and toppings on pita bread. Trying to break the tension, he kept up a running commentary on light topics.

I sat at the kitchen island looking across the darkened dining room. Behind the table were large patio doors with an amazing view of the Tarentum Bridge. It was completely dark now but the bridge had lights on it, and the lights of Tarentum sparkled behind it.

"Look at the bridge," I said. "It looks like it's just floating there."

"Yeah," he said. "When the leaves are off the trees you can see it even better. I used to sit and look at it when I was little. One day I was sitting in the living room playing and I saw a guy do a perfect swan dive off of it."

"What? You're kidding! A suicide?"

"Yep. I ran and told my Mom and she called the police. They

eventually found the guy plastered to one of the bridge piers." He shuddered. "I probably shouldn't be telling stories like that at a time like this."

"No, it's all right. What time is it?"

"It's ten. Dan is closing up at work and he'll be home in enough time to get you home by eleven," he reassured me. Jay had just gotten his license and was forbidden by his parents to drive alone with passengers, so his older brothers or friends rode us around.

I heard a ping as the timer went off on the toaster oven. "That's the pita! I'll be right back," he said.

And then, somehow, I was back in 1981. I could hear the cars on the highway, like sighs. It would soon be dark. Noelle is screaming hysterically. I have to get her out of here before that guy comes back, before it gets dark. I take her by the arm and drag her towards the sound of the highway. I feel something trickle down my legs. I think it's sweat. Thorns tear at my legs but I don't even feel them. Finally, we climb through a bush and are back on the side of the road.

"What are we gonna do?" she cries.

"Go home and tell Grandma." I always call my own mother 'grandma' when she's around.

"We can't actually tell her that!" Tears stream down her dirty face.

I grab her by the shoulders and shake her. "Listen! What choice do we have? You get on that bike and you follow me. Don't stop and don't look back! You understand? You just keep on following me no matter what happens!"

I get on my bike and ride fast, my teeth chattering in the wind. Thankfully, it's all downhill going home. We speed into the yard and I drop the bike on the front lawn, and then run into the house.

Noelle bolts past me though the screen door, up the stairs and out of sight.

"What did you do to Noelle!" scolds my mother. "She's terrorized!"

"I was raped," I said. No point beating around the bush.

She starts down the stairs. "Where did you learn that language?" When she rounds the corner and sees me, she gasps.

Silence.

I hear something dripping on the linoleum and realize its blood. My blood. Everything goes fuzzy. My mother hauls me upstairs and puts me on my bed. I push her hands away.

"I need to examine you! Stop fighting me! What did this man do?"

"I already told you!"

"Tell me in your own words!"

"What do you want me from me? I don't have any other way to explain it!"

"We're taking you to the Emergency Room."

"NO!"

"You don't want some pita?" Jay asked, bewildered.

I blinked and looked around. I was back at the kitchen island. What the heck just happened? I swallowed a huge upsurge of nausea.

"I feel kind of sick," I explained.

"Are you sure? You haven't eaten anything all evening. You ate nothing at the speedway and that was hours ago. You're sure you're not hungry? At all?"

I shook my head.

He put his arm around me. "Are you on drugs or something?"

I shook his hand off. "No!"

"Dan is here; he has to take you home now or you'll be late." He put his hands on my shoulders and pressed his forehead against mine. "I'll call you tomorrow, OK?"

***

A sound awakened me. It was daylight, sunny and bright. More than that – evening! How did I sleep that long? I sat up in bed and listened. Something wasn't right. It was quiet, too quiet. Usually I would hear lawn mowers humming outside, dishes clanking in the kitchen, and the TV. Where were my parents? I got out of bed and went downstairs. Nobody. I went back upstairs and checked my parents' bedroom, the bathrooms, the basement, the cellar. Nobody! I looked in the garage – the car was there but no parents. The truck was in the driveway. I went outside onto the side porch. No neighbors out, no cars coming down the road, no birds singing, no clouds in the sky, no wind. It was like the whole world was just holding its breath.

I heard a stick crack behind me and spun around. There was that man, the one who attacked me, standing there pointing a gun at me.

"I warned you I'd kill you if you told anyone." He began to squeeze the trigger.

I screamed and turned to run back into the house.

BANG.

Time seemed to be in slow motion as I felt the bullet penetrate my back and abdomen. The stone sidewalk moved up to meet me as I fell. I lowered my hands and felt the blood run between my fingers as I lay on the ground. I closed my eyes.

When I opened my eyes again I was lying in bed! The blood on my hands faded away, leaving me sprawled and staring at my clock which blared 11:11. It was the next day! It had all been a dream! The night before I'd been at Jay's house, I told him about what happened to me. My memories of the evening were like stale leftovers. I knew I was awake this time, as I could hear my parents talking, as the neighbors mowed the grass. Yet, the pain in my stomach was still there. I went in the bathroom and threw up blood.

Things were not going too ducky that summer for Kris, either. She had been dating a guy who turned out to be an asshole. Of course, this was obvious to all of us observers and we all breathed a sigh of relief once he was out of the picture, but she was really grieving the loss. So, I set her up on a double date with Jay and me and his friend, Gabriel. Gabriel was one of those punk rockers, with dark, almost black hair cut short on the sides and long on the top. He must have put a good bit of mousse in it as it was fairly full with one long strand drooped over his forehead and almost covering one eye. He always wore his collar standing up with a bandanna tied around his neck.

Gabriel was a really nice kid and she needed to get out and meet some nice people, I thought. Unfortunately, it was obvious that they were both uncomfortable and none of us were having fun. We began driving around aimlessly, Kris looking out the window.

"Looking for a red Camaro?" asked Gabriel, who by now was fully aware of the ex-boyfriend. Both Jay and Gabriel knew him from school, and they thought he was a pompous, arrogant jerk. "Orange," she corrected. The temperature in that car must have dropped twenty degrees.

Gabriel was the eldest of seven, and his family had little money left over. The fact that Gabriel bought his classic Mercury Comet and maintained it was a testimony to his own abilities, as he did not come from the kind of family which bestowed Camaros on its offspring. These subtleties were not lost on Jay, who came to Gabriel's defense.

"Camaros are like assholes," he said. "Everybody has one."

"Hey, you guys, why don't we go to a movie?" I suggested, trying to prevent an argument. I leaned forward between the two front seats. Jay put his arms around me from behind and started kissing me on the neck. "Knock it off," I scolded, half angry and half playfully, giving him a shove.

"What's playing?" asked Gabriel.

"I don't know, let's drive past the Cheswick Theater and see. *Purple Rain*, maybe?"

"I've already seen it," said Kris. So had I, but I was willing to see it again to keep things upbeat.

On the way to the movie theater, Kris and Gabriel began to talk a little. Jay, seeing that they no longer needed his undivided attention, began a campaign to persuade me to make out with him. Now I knew that, among kids in those days, this was considered normal. I had to admit I liked kissing him, but he never seemed content with that and was always testing boundaries.

When we got to the theater, there were no movies that interested us. We decided to give it up and go home. Gabriel dropped Jay and me off at my house while he took Kris home. My parents were in bed, but the kitchen light was left on. He kissed me good-bye, then turned around on the porch to smile and wave good-bye again from behind the screen door. My feelings must have been showing on my face.

"What's wrong?" he asked.

The tears I'd been holding in started to escape. He came back in and grasped me by the shoulders. "What's the matter?"

Gabriel was back from dropping off Kris and was idling along the road in front of my house. He honked the horn.

"It's, it's you!" I finally blurted.

"Me? What did I do?"

I pulled away and turned around. "In the car earlier. You're pressuring me! Can't you take a hint? I hate it when you do that."

"I wasn't pressuring you! I was just kidding around!"

Another impatient honk.

"I wish he would quit that honking!" He reached out for me again, and I recoiled. "Look, I'm sorry! I didn't mean anything by it." He sighed in frustration. "I have to go. Gabriel's waiting. If he doesn't get home by midnight, he'll get in trouble. That's why he won't shut up. Look, I'll call you tomorrow, OK? I'm so sorry!" He turned and ran to the waiting car.

I felt kind of stupid, standing there in the kitchen. I had no idea what to do with all the intense feelings swirling around inside me. Then I noticed, out of the kitchen window, that Lisa and her mother were still up, sitting on their porch. I could go talk to them. Anything but stand here. So I walked over. It wasn't until I saw their shocked expressions that it dawned on me what I looked like: disheveled, face streaked with tears and mascara.

"What the hell happened to you?"

"Jay happened", I said, somewhat embarrassed and relieved at the same time. I sank limply into a lawn chair. The air was humid and full of a chorus of bugs. Heat lightening glimmered in the distance behind the trees of the woods.

Lisa sighed. "What did he do?"

"All night, he wouldn't leave me alone! Pawing at me, kissing me, trying to get me to ... you know."

"Typical guy," Lisa's mother pointed out. "This is why we try to dissuade you girls from dating the older ones. They're even worse than the ones your own age."

"It was a double date! It was awkward! Kris is probably pissed at me." I scoffed. "She set me up on a horrible double date last year. I guess we're even now."

"Maybe you should take a vacation from boyfriends," said Lisa. "Whenever you have one, you're miserable all the time."

"Why can't they just date and have fun? Why are they always maneuvering for sex?"

"Because they're guys and they're full of hormones."

"That doesn't make it right!"

"No, but its biology. You can't reason with biology. Some girls will, so they try until they find a girl who gives them what they want."

"That isn't fair."

"Nope. It isn't! But it's reality."

I must have talked to her for about an hour. During that time Lisa's mother called my mother, who came over clad in her old blue bathrobe to retrieve me.

"Let's go home. I'll make you a cup of tea and then maybe you can get some sleep," she said. I drank my tea slowly for fear that I would throw it up, then washed my face and went to bed.

✳✳✳

I woke up the next day to birdsongs. Wrens peeped, doves cooed. My window was open and a nice cool breeze stirred my lace curtains. That's odd, I thought. Last night, it was hotter than hell. It must have rained. Still, awful cool for July. July, but very little freedom left. Band camp was due to start soon. Band camp: school before school. Kris said it was fun. I wasn't so sure of my decision to give up a month of my summer going to band camp so when school started, the band would be ready to take the field during half time at football games.

I got up and rubbed my eyes, went in the bathroom and splashed water on my face.

When I got downstairs, I got the shock of my life.

Mom. Lying on the kitchen floor in a pool of blood. Shot. I found Dad on the living room floor along with Tam the Siamese cat.

Nausea rising, I ran outside. That's when I realized I was dreaming again. I was in a beautiful dreamscape of my home. Gorgeous flowers bloomed everywhere. The sky was half day, half night, with brilliant constellations showing. The moon was as bright as a new penny. I'd had so many happy dreams in this place! And now it had been invaded!

On cue, my attacker stepped out from behind the lilac bush. My lucidity was no match for the surge of abject terror. Again, he pointed the gun at me and I just stood there like a deer in the headlights. He pulled the trigger. I felt the bullet rip through my stomach again, where the pain was. I felt myself falling, falling .... Until I opened my eyes and found myself sprawled in bed in a hot sweat.

It was still hot outside, but very early morning. I got up and went downstairs – no bodies lying on the floor. It was one of those few times when you were awake but not sure if you are dreaming or not. I turned on the TV low so I didn't wake up my parents, took a Benadryl, and lay down on the couch. Eventually, I fell asleep.

My parents left me there when they got up, and didn't wake me until later when Jay called, as promised. He said he would be over that evening to talk, after work.

Later that evening he arrived. "What do you wanna do?"

"Let's go for a walk. We can walk up to the township garage."

We started up the dark road, the moon gleaming brightly above. It was a quiet evening, nothing audible but the fiddling of cicadas and the sigh of an occasional car on the main road. For a while, we walked in silence, the gravel crunching beneath our feet. We passed neighbors' houses, their porch lights spreading soft halos of light across neatly manicured lawns. Behind them, the woods loomed deep and dark as its trees whispered in the faint breeze. The gravel piles grew like shadows as we drew nearer to them.

"I never worked so hard to have a girl in my life, as I have you," he said, daring to address the elephant.

"Just what the hell do you mean by that?" I laughed. I felt like a cat with his fur rubbed all the wrong way.

He rolled his eyes. "You know what I mean."

"Oh, enlighten me, please."

"Why do you always push me away? I'm trying to be gentle, I'm trying to make it enjoyable for you. Meanwhile you're like a porcupine."

"All right, I'll make this easy for you. Cut it out!"

He rolled his eyes again.

"I don't get it. You know about what happened to me. So why would you try to get me to sleep with you? Especially after you doing this is obviously upsetting me? I'm having nightmares about it again, Jay, nightmares! That hasn't happened for a couple years."

"I wasn't expecting that. I knew it would take time. I just didn't think it would take this much time."

"This much time? Are you kidding me? We haven't even gone together for a full two months yet!"

"True," he conceded. "Maybe I have been a little impatient, but I was only trying to help."

"Wait. Let me get this straight. You think, that by pressuring me to sleep with you, you're somehow helping me?"

"Well, yes."

"That sounds a bit self-serving to me!"

He stopped and faced me. "What do you mean?"

"Come on! I'll grant you it's more creative than prove-you-love-me or some of the other bullshit guys use, but all boils down to the same thing, doesn't it? You trying to get me to do something I don't want to, because you DO want to."

He shook his head. "You won't get over it, until you do it."

"Get over what?"

"Get over what happened to you."

I scrambled up a gravel pile and eyed him suspiciously from the top. "Just what the hell makes you an authority on the subject?"

"He scampered up the gravel pile after me. "I do know! I know another girl who was raped."

I glared at him. "Who?"

"Someone from school. Nobody you've met. When she was fourteen, some guy took her out to the middle of the river in a boat and raped her. She was messed up for a while, but eventually she got through it."

"And you, helped with this?" I put the word helped in air quotes.

"No! Not me. Somebody else. A boyfriend. Although she turned out a little bit sleazy."

Now I was thinking about some of the things Mrs. Fine and the other psychologists she had consulted on me had said about this.

"You know, I've been to like, psychologists and talked about this? Like people with advanced degrees on the subject, who actually KNOW what they're talking about? They said that some victims become sleazy (air quotes) to try and make what happened to them mean less. So, if you're willing to do the act with just about anybody, then that make the assault less meaningful, less painful. It's really not a good long term solution because it IS meaningful, and it IS painful, and all that doesn't just go away because you do something to try and make it seem like it's no big deal."

He looked shocked. "They really told you that?"

"Yes! Your one experience does not make you an expert! More importantly, how your friend did or didn't turn out has nothing to do with me."

"But it does. You're afraid of it, right? Who wouldn't be? You have to face the fear eventually."

"It ain't that simple. You're comparing apples and oranges. Rape isn't sex. It's not the same thing. Believe me if it was, nobody would ever do that and the human race would die out in one generation."

He just shrugged. "Sooner or later, you'll have to grow up and deal with it."

"Is that the best you can do? Well, I vote for later."

"Why?"

"Because there are like a million good reasons to avoid it that have nothing to do with fear! Or at least, fear of rape. How about fear of being branded a slut? Fear of the whole subset of problems that would come from opening this particular Pandora's box? Don't try to tell me there wouldn't be any problems because I know better having already had it happen just with dating in general! How about fear of getting pregnant? I'm going to college! No to mention that my parents would friggin' kill me, and never trust me again! How could anyone as smart as you be so stupid? Haven't you ever thought of any of this? If anyone around here needs to grow up, it's you."

He held his hands up in defeat. "Whoa. OK. Fine. I promise I will never pressure you again. Cross my heart, hope to die. Nothing but chaste kisses unless YOU make the first move."

"Deal."

For a while, things went back to being all hunky dory again.

***

The following Sunday I wandered around Fantasy Rock looking for Jay. But I couldn't find him. We came together with Gabriel but shortly after arriving, we all got separated. There didn't seem to be anyone else there I knew that night.

Eventually I found Gabriel. "Where is Jay?" I yelled over the din.

"Huh?"

He couldn't hear me. He gestured for me to follow him out into the hallway. He knew the guy running Fantasy Rock and he nodded to him as we left, to ensure we could get back in without paying a second time. My ears rang in the sudden absence of noise. The carpeted hallway sucked up all the sound, so even the people arguing with someone at the front desk seemed faint.

"What's wrong?" he asked.

"Have you seen Jay anywhere? He said he had to talk to someone for a minute and then he vanished. I've been looking all over for him."

Gabriel shook his head. "Oh shit! He hasn't done anything like this in a long time. I thought he was over it."

"Done what?"

He fidgeted nervously. "We'd better go outside."

I followed him out to the parking lot. We sat down on one of the benches.

Gabriel sighed and looked embarrassed. "I've known Jay for a long time. He's a good friend. But sometimes he can be a real jerk. I am really sorry about tonight."

"You don't have to apologize for him. Just come out with it. What's going on?"

"It's this Cindy girl." I stared at him with growing fury. "You probably know her. She goes to the same school as you. She's older than you but in a lower grade. I think she might have flunked a year. I thought I saw her when we came in and I worried there would be trouble."

I did know who he was talking about. Cindy had been in my grade, my class even, in elementary school. Sometime before junior high she had flunked a year, maybe even two years. I hadn't seen her at school for a long time. I didn't think her family had much money and she may have been having trouble at school because of a bad home life. At least that was what I heard. Which made her at least sixteen, maybe even seventeen, as I was a year younger than most of the other kids in my class.

He sighed again. "To make a long story short, and I am sorry to have to be so blunt, but since you won't sleep with him he thinks can sleep with her and keep you as his...", he swallowed. "His respectable girlfriend."

"That's twisted!" I snapped.

"I agree."

"So has she actually consented to this arrangement, or has he fed her some line of bullshit?"

"I honestly don't know. I thought he'd finally grown out of this kind of crap."

I shook with rage. He's obviously done things like this before. I could have asked Gabriel for more history but at that point, I didn't even want to know.

"I'm gonna kill him! Or dump him! Or … I don't know. Why does everything have to turn to shit? It's like, God forgot about me, so for a little while I had it all. And then he remembered."

Other kids outside were giving us weird looks. "Why don't we go for a short walk until you calm down? Jay can't go anywhere since I drove. There's a great view of the river right above the parking lot."

We went across the edge of the parking lot and climbed up a weed covered hill behind the hotel. From that vantage point, you could see practically the whole valley. The lights from the town of Tarentum cast shiny streaks across the dark surface of the river. Cars streamed across the Tarentum bridge. A barge full of coal came from around the bend, dragging a wake behind it that set the streaks of light gyrating. The mournful cry of a Conrail diesel locomotive pierced the night as traffic halted at the railroad crossing directly across the river.

"Hey, look! There's a train!" I said. The whistle I heard was because it was approaching a level crossing just past the Tarentum bridge. The long string of boxcars stretched back under the bridge and as far downriver as I could see. Soon the locomotive vanished behind the buildings of downtown Tarentum.

"Yeah, I see it. You like trains?"

"I love trains. I always have."

We stood there for a while, taking in the view. I suppose I'd known on some level that this would never work out. I looked over at Gabriel. He was a nice person. Why did I always end up with the wrong guy? I felt a tear escape from my eye, and wiped it away discretely.

"I'm really sorry about all this," he said.

"It's not your fault. I'm probably better off without him. I'm probably better off without anybody. I can't do this. I think I 'm going crazy," I admitted.

Gabriel looked alarmed. "Just because of Jay? Really, he isn't worth it."

I sighed. "No, it's more than that. It's the thought that being with him would make things better. It seemed to at the beginning. Turns out, it just made me worse. I really wish I hadn't told him things!"

"Why?"

"He could use it against me."

"He can be a jerk, but I don't think he'd do something like that. What did you tell him?"

"All of this mess may have happened because I told him. But it wasn't like I could avoid it! Something happened and I had to explain."

"What is it?"

"You wouldn't believe me if I told you."

For some reason he looked as if he honestly cared. I ran over a mental checklist of everyone I'd ever told. It was a short list. I really wanted to know what he thought. How much trouble was I really in?

I looked out at the river. "I was abducted when I was eleven."

"You were what?" He eyed me with a curious mixture of wonder and horror.

I crossed my arms and turned to face him. "You know those kids whose pictures show up on the back of milk cartons? I was almost one of them."

"What exactly happened?"

I turned away. He knew the answer.

"You didn't know this guy?"

"No. I did see him a few time afterwards, though."

"Where?"

"Down in Leechburg. Along Route 56. "

"What about the police?"

"They don't believe me."

"How do you know?"

"I just know! I remember the things they said, back when it first happened."

"That's insane! That was how many years ago?"

"Three."

"The whole department's probably turned over since then. You should go back and try again."

"I can't do that!" Well there was an idea that would never have occurred to me in a million years! Go back? Wasn't that door shut and bolted years ago? Or was it?

He grabbed my forearms and shook me gently. "Why not?" he said. "What do you have to lose? How will there ever be any justice, for anybody, if no one will come forward? You may not want to tell me exactly what happened to you, but I can hazard a pretty good guess. And I think that's serious enough for a second look. You have enough spunk and determination to take this man off the street."

I shook myself loose. "Why should I be bothered? Don't I have enough trouble already?"

"Look, making a life for yourself and having a relationship – that's all great stuff. Do you really think you are ever going to be happy until you deal with it somehow?"

In the silence that followed, things began to look different. What did I have to lose, really? This was the first time anyone gave me any real, practical advice about it. He seemed so adamant. Was he right?

"Do you really think the police would listen to me?"

"You'll never know unless you try. If they don't, then you're no worse off than you are now." He paused. "What did this guy look like?"

"He had long, stringy dark hair, full beard, he was one of those hot rod junkies. His hands smelled like a car engine."

"Jay and I could go under cover and try to find him."

"I think I've had enough help from Jay, thank you."

"Well, think about it. We better be going now. Let's go find Jay and make him come home."

"We can't go back inside without paying."

"Don't worry about it. I know Geno, they guy who runs the dance. He'll understand."

We returned to the hotel and Gabriel found Geno, a hefty, muscular Italian man with a thick mustache. They talked for a moment, then Gabriel returned.

"He said it's OK. Stick close so that we don't get separated." I nodded a thanks to Geno on my way past.

We wandered about in the dance, lights flashing all around us. We found Jay standing in a dark corner talking to Cindy.

"You go get him, I'll wait outside." I screamed in his ear. He nodded. It was more embarrassment than I could take. I sat impatiently on the vinyl seats in the motel lobby until Gabriel came out pulling Jay by the arm.

"Let go!" He looked really peeved.

"It's time to go home, Jay," said Gabriel as Jay scowled at both of us.

I raised my fist. "I otta..."

"Hold it, you two! That's enough!" intervened Gabriel.

Not much was said on the way home; I sat with my back turned. When we got to my house I told Gabriel good night, thanked him for everything, and got out. To my surprise, Jay also got out.

"Look," he said. "Can we just talk?"

I spun around. "No! I'm done talking. This is obviously not going to work out. I'm sorry, but I can't deal with this."

I went into the house and left him standing there, shocked. I don't even know how long they sat there before they left. All I knew was defeat. I'd walked away from something I really wanted. I loved the way he talked to me. I loved the way he looked. I loved the activities we did together. I loved his family. But the sex problem would not go away. I could not think of any way to compromise or solve it, and the whole Cindy thing made me doubt his integrity. It made me remember something Kris said about not being able to put the toothpaste back in the tube. That if a guy had already had sex, he could not go back to not having sex. So I needed to stick with virgins.

At that time though, I was done. I'd had it. My theory about getting a boyfriend and creating a life that was the envy of other kids my age? It failed. More than that – I made me worse! For the first time since that star party in the summer of 1982, when I first realized a guy could like me, I was out of ideas. I didn't know of anything else that I could do to try and fix my broken life.

CHAPTER 18

A Lucid Dream

When I opened my eyes, I was sitting with my back against one of the ancient tombstones. I stood up in warm, fresh air. The sky was a brilliant blue and the landscape bright and sunny; the grass was as green as green could be. I knew where I was, and I knew I was dreaming. I was in the dreamscape of the old Covenanter Cemetery. I stood up. The circles of stones spread out around me. I touched one and the warm stone filled me with images of someone else's life, someone else's essence. I remembered the previous dreams and thought I should resume my search for the girl who died in the woods, and not let myself get distracted again by rooms full of lost items or other tangents.

The cemetery stood on top of a hill. I heard the sigh of a car driving down the highway partway down the hill on one side. I remembered from other dreams that the highway lead to a small town with twin churches. On the back side of the hill, the tombstones continued to spread out in nested circles until a dense forest met them at the bottom of the hill. A cluster of broken headstones sat neglected at the lowest part of the cemetery, the vines of the forest threatening to engulf them.

I thought, maybe the girl who died in the woods is down there, near the woods. As I walked down towards the lowest corner, I noticed that these broken stones were not the only ones down there. Damaged and overturned markers littered the forest floor as far as I could see. I placed my hand on one of them and got nothing. They were cold, lifeless, forgotten. Curious, I began following them, deeper into the woods, lower into the valley. Who were these lost souls, neglected and forgotten in the entangled underbrush?

The ground began to rise again as I ascended the next hill, which was much higher. The forest ended not far from the top. Behind me, I could now see the Covenanter cemetery with its Stonehenge like center and its rings of headstones, the highway, and off in the distance the stone towers of the twin churches.

In front of me, rising out of the vines covering the ground, were the strangest looking grave markers I've ever seen. They were obelisks made of black wrought iron, their sides like lace. Incredibly detailed leaves and Celtic motifs wound their way towards the darkening sky. Others were Celtic crosses also made of intricate ironwork. They were obviously very ancient. Some of them had toppled over and now lay on their sides in tall grass and vines. I reached out my hand to touch them.

"Don't."

I turned around and there stood Susan Grant Black. She looked as she must have as a middle aged woman. Her auburn hair was pulled neatly into a bun at the back of her head. She wore a high necked black 1890's style gown with a full trumpet skirt that stirred in the breeze. With one hand she held a white shawl across her shoulders.

"Do not touch the markers or go beyond here, lest there be no way for you to come back again."

"What is this place?"

"It's between the worlds."

I squinted beyond the iron memorials, where a faint mist obscured what lay beyond like a veil. There was a path going from the edge of the ancient cemetery into the woods beyond, through the mist.

"Who are the markers in the woods? The ones that don't work?"

"They belong to those who are forgotten."

"That's so sad! Everyone deserves to be remembered. "

"It's not what you think. They no longer have a connection to this world. They're happy and well in another world. This one isn't the only one there is. I think you've realized that by now."

"Well I'm looking for someone and I think you know who," I said. "Can you show me which stone is hers? Or is she one of the forgotten ones?"

I felt my great grandmother's ice cold grip on my shoulders. "Listen! In this world you choose your own master. That which we give our power to, it becomes our master." The cold of her hands became like pain, cutting into my skin and causing me to gasp.

My eyes stared out into the darkness. I felt the warmth of the bed and turned to see the clock said 5:55. Was this it? Was I going to die? Had Susan Grant Black come to take me across the veil?

It was that eerie silence that made me realize I was dreaming again. I was in my bed, it was morning. The nightmare again! This time I decided to find a way to fight back. I got out of bed and went downstairs, peeking around the corner of the kitchen to see if my mother's body was still lying there, it was. Same with Dad and Tam in the living room. I was less afraid of them now, knowing they were not real. I still didn't want to look at them, so I went out the front door.

The dreamscape was even more beautiful than before! There were flowers everywhere. Even the trees were blooming. The air was heavy with their scent. The sky was half day, half night again. The moon was full and radiant, and the sun gilded everything in the yard – the grass, the flowers, the plants. Even the house seemed to glow.

As expected, the rapist appeared in front of me. But this time I was ready. I conjured the biggest gun I could imagine from behind my back and shot him at point blank range, blowing him into a hundred pieces. After the smoke cleared, I got an unexpected and unpleasant surprise. Each piece of him had grown back into a whole man and now instead of one of them being after me, there were a gazillion! I ran back into the house, locking the door behind me. I stood with my back against the hard wooden door. Why didn't that work?

"The back door!" one of them yelled. I saw them all run past the living room window towards the back of the house. I knew there was no way I could run through the house and lock all the doors fast enough. I'd also have to run through the kitchen and step over my dead mother to lock the kitchen door. I had to go find help. So I opened the door and ran across the road to Lisa's house.

Then I made the gruesome discovery: he'd already killed all the neighbors. Every house I went to was strewn with mutilated corpses. How many miles would I have to go to find someone else who's alive?

I went back to Lisa's yard and climbed the biggest, thickest fir tree I could find. Inside its branches I was completely concealed, although I could see the rapists systematically searching the whole area for me. Exhausted, I fell asleep hugging the tree.

I snapped awake to find myself lying in the front yard. I heard laughter. Over near the woods I saw the neighborhood kids gathered around a campfire like we always used to do. They were cooking something that smelled wonderful. Worried that the rapists were still around, I ran towards them. Then I saw a pair of red eyes in the woods. I looked around and everybody was gone but me. I heard a low growl. This was no rapist. Frozen to the spot with fear, I stood there as a large bear burst from the woods and ate me.

In the days following when I reflected back on this dream, this imagery was so bizarre I couldn't even attempt to explain it. Many years later I read that in Native American spirituality being dismembered and eaten by an animal was to take on its spiritual power. It is a type of shamanic initiation dream. A shaman is someone who has a childhood near death experience that enables them to see other realms. This certainly seemed to fit my circumstances. I also read about how the Appalachian Granny Magic that Susan Grant Black had practiced was a product of both Native American and the ancient Celtic shamanic practices. My ancestors had brought it over with them from Ireland in the early 18th century, and these two cultures came in contact in the United States. They had a lot of similarities and so they blended. I believe that Susan Grant Black sent the bear medicine to enable me to do what I had to do.

I woke up back in the fir tree, in the original nightmare, getting angry. Whose dream is this, anyhow? Susan Grant Black's words drifted through my mind: That which we give our power to, it becomes our master.

I climbed down from the tree and went back to my own front yard. Immediately, he was there in front of me.

Before he could do anything, I announced, with as much authority as I could muster, "I take back every last bit of power I gave you. You have no power over me!"

Then I turned around and started walking. I worried I'd fail again and feel the bullet. Instead, I found myself back at the cemetery, walking across the highway out onto a vast expanse of sand. I walked for a long time, until the anger had subsided and I began to feel very tired. I came to the ruins of what was once a great wall. Huge rocks lay haphazardly in the sand, as if some giant had thrown them there. I realized these were the ruins of the great temple in Jerusalem. Exhausted, I lay my head down on one of them. It was warm, the sand was warm. I fell asleep.

"Look", said a voice. When I lifted my head up, I was laying on Jesus' lap. He was pointing towards the horizon, where the sun was rising, filling the sky with gold. Then I sat straight up in bed, awake. The bathroom door was open and sun came streaming in the window and reflecting off the mirror in the bathroom and the mirror in my bedroom, filling my room with light, dazzling glorious light!

The world didn't look any different, but it felt totally different. When I went downstairs for breakfast and hogged down more food in one meal than I'd eaten all summer, my parents first stared a me, and then at each other. My stomach hurt no more.

Because of that dream, waking reality turned itself 180 degrees. I had become the bear. I was no longer the prey, hiding and worrying and looking for someone to save me. I was the predator now.

I was ready to go out and find my destiny. As Grammy had promised at the very beginning, everything (and everyone) I needed was given to me. The next part of the journey had begun.

Acknowledgments

I would like to thank my awesome editor, Leslie Fowler Doyle for her hard and patient work. Also my husband Bill for his support and putting up with the long hours it took to write and format this. And most of all for those who took this journey with me, although most of them have crossed over to the other side now, there is not a finer group of people I would have chosen to be my companions on this journey.

About the Author

Laura Mason Lockard writes entertaining and inspirational historical, paranormal, and young adult fiction. She loves to read ghost stories! Having designed and sewn period clothing for over 25 years, she guarantees that her characters ALWAYS wear period correct underwear. A business analyst for a major financial technology company, Laura currently lives with her husband in the North Hills of Pittsburgh, PA in a 200-year-old house full of antiques, harps, and cats. She reads all your awesome Amazon reviews and wants to know what you are looking for in your next historical adventure. Visit her on the web at:

www.lauramasonlockard.com

Did you enjoy this book?

I'd love to hear what you thought about it!
Please leave a review on Amazon.

Want to read more?

Sign up for my mailing list on my website and receive a free book!
You will also be notified when book two is ready for preorder.

Made in the USA
San Bernardino, CA
02 May 2020

70748651R00231